FLIGHT INTO EGYPT was originally written in 1980 to explore the profound impact of the historic Egyptian–Israeli peace accord. Now, due to the nature of world events, the author has added to the original text his probing interpretation of the Sadat assassination, with a stirring photographic supplement.

—The Publishers

Coming in March by Amos Elon:

TIMETABLE

FLIGHT INTO EGYPT

AMOS ELON

PINNACLE BOOKS   NEW YORK

For Danae

The author is indebted to Professor Shimon Shamir of the Shiloah Institute for African-Asian Studies at the University of Tel Aviv for his invaluable advice and for making available translations of some Egyptian texts quoted in this book.

Grateful acknowledgment is made to Faber and Faber Ltd and to Harcourt Brace Jovanovich, Inc., for their kind permission to reprint lines from "The Love Song of J. Alfred Prufrock" from *Collected Poems 1909–1962* by T. S. Eliot. Used by permission.

FLIGHT INTO EGYPT

Pinnacle Books edition, published by arrangement with Doubleday & Company, Inc.

First printing, October 1981

ISBN: 0-523-41623-7

Printed in the United States of America

PINNACLE BOOKS, INC.
1430 Broadway
New York, New York 10018

"These stories may be far from history, where one usually reads that such and such king sent such and such general to such and such war, and that on such and such day they made war or peace, and this one defeated that one, or that one this one, and then proceeded somewhere. But I write what is worthy to be recorded."

Abul Fazl Bayhaki, historian (A.D. 995–1077) in *Tarik i Bayhaki*

Considered one of the most outstanding Israeli writers, **Amos Elon** was a soldier in the 1948 war. Since then, as a columnist on the liberal Israeli daily *Haaretz,* he has covered the great events in Israeli life, and has been a foreign correspondent in Washington, Paris, and Bonn. His books include *Herzl* (a biography), *Between Enemies: A Compassionate Dialogue Between an Israeli and an Arab* (with Sana Hassan), *Journey Through a Haunted Land: The New Germany,* and the best-selling *The Israelis: Founders and Sons.* His first novel, *Timetable,* was published by Doubleday. Mr. Elon lives in Jerusalem with his American wife.

— *OCTOBER, 1981*

ON OCTOBER 6, 1981, I happened to be in my office in Jerusalem looking through a new anthology of Egyptian short stories translated by Sasson Somekh, which he had just sent me. A colleague came in and said, a bit tentatively, that President Sadat had been shot in Cairo. One of his own soldiers had fired on him during a military review in Cairo.

"Can you believe it?" he said. "It appears that the men on one of the tanks in the parade turned their guns around and fired at the grandstand."

In a flash, I thought that this was some sort of ghastly office joke; then I knew it could not be. We stood around a transistor radio.

Was this the beginning of the end of peace? The first shot of the next war? The news was confused and appalling. Sadat was said to have been flown by helicopter to a nearby hospital; but there was no announcement about whether he was dead or alive. He was certainly seriously, probably mortally, wounded. Radio Cairo was broadcasting the Egyptian National

Anthem while Jerusalem radio was recirculating every wild rumor and speculation voiced by politicians and commentators around the globe. The Libyans, Soviets, Palestinians, or Iraqis were said to be behind the attempt on Sadat's life. The army had been a mainstay of his power. Was the army rebelling against him? The reporter on Radio Amman, the government-controlled Jordanian station, announced solemnly, "This is the end of the Camp David agreements," and then, in more pressing tones, "the Israeli Ambassador in Cairo is packing his suitcases and preparing to return home.

Radio Damascus said, "The traitor is dead."

At 5 P.M. there was still no bulletin from the hospital. Radio Cairo was broadcasting patriotic songs. Other leading Egyptian personalities were said to be dead or wounded. No one knew yet if the attack was part of a concerted coup d'etat.

At 6 P.M. the announcement came that Sadat was dead. We stood around silently. I walked home alone through the quickly darkening streets. There is no dusk in this city, night falls abruptly after day. The park in the wooded valley adjoining my house was deserted, but for some reason the war memorial across the valley was brightly lit. Through the open window of a nearby house I heard another news broadcast. The announcer was quoting Colonel Qaddafi of Lybia and Yasir Arafat of the Palestinian Liberation Organization. They had congratulated the assassin. Arafat was quoted saying, "I shake his hand."

In the Middle East—cursed are the peacemakers.

I HAD ASKED nearly everyone I had met in Egypt whether or not this peace depended upon one man.

Almost everyone had replied firmly with the same answer: NO. Some had assured me that in breaking the seemingly endless cycle of violence and by making formal peace with Israel after thirty years of war, Sadat was following the Egyptian people rather than leading them. How important was this distinction, I often wondered aloud, in view of the fact that in Egypt, under Sadat's authoritarian rule, the press was muzzled and public opinion hardly mattered? I was told that even a dictator cannot govern alone.

Nearly everyone I met assured me that Egypt was tired of war, and was yearning to find itself again, rediscover its authentic identity, which in the days of Nasser had been watered down in a flood of Pan-Arabism. It was eager to work on its real problems, domestic problems—poverty, ignorance, hunger and disease, rural superstition and backwardness, over-population, corruption, industrial inefficiency, and misadministration. And yet the tragedy of Sadat's presidency was the failure of his policies at home. He never even began to answer the veritable explosion of expectations for a better life set off among Egyptians by his sudden peace with Israel. Perhaps the domestic problems were too great. They were certainly over-whelming.

Their overpowering scale was brought home to me dramatically by an Egyptian friend, Dr. Mohammed Mahfouz, a few months before Sadat's death. Dr. Mahfouz, a leading Egyptian physician and a former minister of health, was visiting Jerusalem with other members of the Egyptian Parliament. One afternoon we sat in a rooftop restaurant overlooking the Old City wall. To the south, some new residential quarters spread over the hills toward Bethlehem. Mahfouz gazed at the lovely view and asked how many people lived in that area. I said approximately a hundred thousand, perhaps a hundred and twenty thousand. He nodded sadly and then said, "Let's compare this view to the one visible from a similar rooftop in Cairo—say the Al Ahram Tower. There you would be looking at an area of similar size but populated by eight million people, more than the entire population of Israel, more than all the Palestinians, wherever they may be." Tewfik al-Hakim had said that with the money Egypt spent over the years on war, every single Egyptian village could have been rebuilt, or half of Cairo. I thought very fondly of Tewfik al-Hakim as I walked home that night. Only a few days before I had received word from him that he had read this book "not without pleasure." He wished it would soon be translated into Arabic, though he was not very hopeful that it would. He had gotten a copy while on a visit to Paris. He said that it was not available in Egypt. I thought of him and of other Egyptians I have met since, some in Israel and some on a recent return visit to Egypt. A leading politician and one of Sadat's closest aides told me when I last bid him *au revoir,* "Above all, don't worry. As long as President Sadat is around, everything will be all right. That is why we should all try to help him—Israel, too, should try to help him more."

"How?"

"By refraining from needless provocations, such as settlements in the occupied territories or indiscriminate air attacks on Lebanon."

"What if Sadat died?" I asked.

"There will still be peace," he said.

"Really?"

"Yes, but different peace."

"How different?"

"Sadat's flair will be gone. His sense of imagination. His unique sense of history. All this will be gone. But as Sadat did, his successor will also realize that it is in Egypt's best interest to live in peace in Israel."

I worry about this statement now. Everyone in his right mind always agreed that it was in Egypt's and Israel's best national interest to live in peace. And yet in the miserable tangle of the Arab-Israeli conflict, so repetitive, threadbare, infinitely sad, apparently insoluble, no Arab leader before Sadat had seen the "national interest" in this light. If generals and politicians never made mistakes, nobody would ever lose a war.

PRESIDENT SADAT was shot by Moslem Aborigines apparently not only because he made peace with the enemies of God, but, mainly it seems, because he refused to return to the pristine purity of Islam. He refused to halt industrialization, modern education, westernization in general, and take Egypt back to the dark ages, as Khomeini and the Ayatollahs have done in Iran. A demonstratively devout Moslem, Sadat had vehemently opposed all attempts to politicize Islam and had ridiculed the fundamentalists as a gang of fools, or as traitors masking their true (communist) faces behind pious beards. In this way he may have been overconfident. His murder did not precipitate a coup d'etat, yet Islamic Fundamentalism as a modern mass movement was born in Egypt in 1928, and from there its message radiated into the neighboring Arab countries. Religious fanaticism was the most dangerous legacy left by Sadat to his successor.

FEAR HAS MANY EYES and can see things underground.

Later that night, Israeli television vividly reflected once more the terrors that are always dormant in Israeli society, but on days like this come forward with particular force. Moving scenes of the past were shown—Sadat's arrival in 1977 at Ben Gurion Airport, his speech to the Knesset, the signing of the peace treaty in Washington, D.C., Sadat's voice, "No more war, no more war."

What went wrong for Anwar al-Sadat? I only met him once, but it suddenly occurred to me that he was more familiar than I realized. We are moved by and we remember losers because they touch our wounds. Spinoza defined peace not as the mere absence of war but as a great virtue that stemmed from courage. Sadat had such courage.

Anwar Sadat with the former Shah of Iran after Sadat offers the Shah political asylum and medical care in Egypt. (UPI, 1980)

A 1973 photograph of Sadat and Lybian leader Muammar El Qaddafi when the two statesmen were negotiating a possible merger between Egypt and Libya. (UPI)

President Jimmy Carter watches the historic signing of the Egyptian–Israeli peace treaty by Egyptian President Anwar Sadat and Israeli Prime Minister Menahem Begin on March 26, 1979. (UPI)

A happy moment on the north lawn of the White House after the signing of the Mideast Peace Treaty. (UPI, 1979)

Israeli Prime Minister Menahem Begin greets Sadat on his visit to Israel in 1979. (UPI)

Soviet President Leonid Brezhnev greets Qaddifi at Moscow airport on a recent official state visit by the Libyian leader. (UPI, 1981)

Sadat and U.S. President Ronald Reagan are in step as they leave the White House after recent talks concerning the American position on the Palestine Liberation Organization. (UPI, 1981)

October 6, 1981. An unidentified man in Egyptian army uniform fires a submachine gun at pointblank range into the Presidential reviewing stand, killing Egyptian President Anwar Sadat and at least five others. (Wide World Photos)

Man flees grenade and machine gun attack on Sadat. Over his left shoulder one of the gunmen can be seen firing at the reviewing stand where Sadat met his death. (UPI)

The assassination scene shortly after the shooting, as ambulances arrive to pick up the wounded and Egyptian troops surround the area. (Wide World Photos)

Egyptian security guard directs medics with stretcher on the presidential reviewing stand shortly after the attack on Sadat. (Wide World Photos)

The dying and the dead on the assassination scene moments after the attack on Sadat which left at least six fatalities. (Wide World Photos)

Former U.S. Presidents Carter, Ford and Nixon arrive with Henry Kissinger to represent the United States at the funeral of Anwar Sadat. (Wide World Photos)

Jihan Sadat, widow of assassinated President Sadat, shown momentarily overcome with grief at her home in Egypt during a meeting with representatives from the United States. The photograph next to her is of Sadat's son, Gamal. (Wide World Photos)

The funeral procession of assassinated President Anwar Sadat passes the Tomb of the Unknown Warrior outside Cairo. (Wide World Photos)

Egyptian Vice President (now President) Hosni Mubarak is shown with his hand bandaged due to injuries suffered during the attack on President Sadat. (Wide World Photos)

Egyptian soldiers carry Sadat's medals in the funeral procession at Nasr Stadium. (Wide World Photos)

Among the mourners at the funeral of Anwar Sadat are former American President Gerald Ford, Israeli Prime Minister Menahem Begin, former French President Valery Giscard d'Estaing and former U.S. President Jimmy Carter. (Wide World Photos)

Hosni Mubarak embraces Menahem Begin on Begin's arrival in Egypt to attend the funeral of Anwar Sadat. (AP)

President Ronald Reagan, Mrs. Reagan, Secretary of State Alexander Haig and Mrs. Haig attend memorial services for slain Egyptian President Sadat at the Washington National Cathedral. (Wide World Photos)

Egyptian Vice President Mubarak tells reporters that the assassination of President Sadat was a "criminal act by individuals, and not a coup attempt." (Wide World Photos)

Syrian Arab forces in Lebanon parade through the Moslem district of Beirut during a demonstration celebrating the death of Sadat. (Wide World Photos)

Secretary of State Alexander Haig warns of the threat to world peace after the assassination of Egyptian President Anwar Sadat. (Wide World Photos)

Palestine Liberation Organization chairman Yasir Arafat is shown during a 1978 anti-American demonstration in Beirut, Lebanon. (UPI)

The body of assassinated President Mohammed Anwar al-Sadat is lowered into its resting place at the Tomb of the Unknown Warrior while the world ponders the effect of the slaying on peace in the Middle East.

PROLOGUE

1980

SO NEAR A COUNTRY, and yet so far. As near to Israel, where I live, as Holland is to Belgium, or New Hampshire to Maine. Yet for thirty-one years, my entire adult life, it has been like the other side of the moon—unknown, a menace, distant and dark. Suddenly one morning, in the glare, the dust and rattle of a stifling hot workday, the moon turns on its axis. The dark side comes into view. A passenger plane departs from Tel Aviv airport and lands peacefully in Cairo seventy-five minutes later.

How I happen to be on this plane is another story. It was mainly as the result of outlandish exertions that may suggest in odd detail the stranger whole that has kept Arabs and Israelis light-years apart for as long as most of us can remember. Transatlantic telephone calls at all hours of the night, letters, telegrams, negotiations with an Egyptian ambassador in a Western capital. He was a friendly man who wanted very much to be helpful. For many months he came back with some such answer as "I suggested to Cairo that they allow you in. Cairo says the moment is not opportune"; perhaps next week will be more "appropriate." Or the one after. But it never was. Various well-wishers and middlemen intervened. This, too, led nowhere. In Egypt a decision on such a matter, which to some people may seem minor, appeared to be vested in the highest authorities of the state, some said in the President himself. And as the Egyptian-Israeli peace negotiations dragged on, from better to worse and back again to better, and the two parties litigated endlessly over euphemisms, commas, and semicolons, whenever President Sadat was angry with Prime Minister Begin it seemed as though he were taking it out on me. I was becoming rather paranoic in the process.

Finally, two nights ago, the ambassador telephoned. It may well have been the first time that an Egyptian ambassador placed a direct call to Jerusalem, Israel. He said that if I was able to get on this very special plane carrying security men and technicians to Cairo to prepare for the Israeli Prime Minister's two-day visit, as well as a number of newspapermen (who would, however, be required to leave after two days), he would make the arrangements for me to stay on.

Well, I am finally on my way, and that's what matters, I tell myself; although with a splitting headache, bleary eyes (we were told to be at the airport at 4 A.M.), and a sore throat from smoking too many cigarettes, going at long last into Egypt. The very phrase echoes Genesis.

Not that I haven't been there already, so to speak. A few years ago I traveled through some of the remoter parts, but in a rather inappropriate manner, or disguise, in a uniform. How different this is, I tell myself as I fasten my seat belt and mentally brace myself for shocks of recognition and discovery. In retrospect I think I was a bit smug. *Recognition* was certainly the wrong word. It implied the process of identifying something previously known and forgotten—or perhaps suppressed.

Even our departure is rather anxious. We almost do not get off the ground at Tel Aviv. Some of the airport personnel have suddenly walked off the job, demanding a 30 percent rise in pay. When we finally take off, after a considerable delay, the route we must take is long and circuitous. The peace treaty between Israel and Egypt is only three days old. It has not yet been ratified by the Egyptian and Israeli legislatures. The ratification will be merely a formality, but we are still, theoretically, at war. The passport control officer at the airport explained this to me very carefully as he read through my travel documents slowly, page by page; he was searching for the special stamp: *Valid for Egypt.* I had raced off to get that stamp yester-day afternoon from a reluctant, highly suspicious bureaucrat who officiates in a dingy little office in Tel Aviv. It was there that the headache that is plaguing me now began.

"Do you realize we have no embassy in Cairo?" he asked.

Yes, I do.

"Do you fully realize what that means?"

Of course.

"Don't dismiss it lightly."

I do not.

"If you encounter some trouble there is nowhere you can turn."

Yes, I know. But I don't expect to run into any.

"You might!"

Why?

"Because it is enemy territory."

Is it still?

"Technically, yes. If there is trouble, there is only one thing to do," he added.

What's that?

"Get yourself as fast as you can to the American embassy."

Okay. Can I have my stamp now?

"And don't flaunt your Israeli passport. Keep it wrapped away somewhere."

I must show it at the hotel, mustn't I?

"I suppose you must. But make sure it's really the concierge you are showing it to."

I will. May I have my stamp now? Please!

"Above all, don't talk to any strangers!"

How's that?

"You heard me. No strangers. It's the first rule! Do you under-stand?"

Yes, I do.

Plunk. Down went the stamp. I took my leave.

I

THE PLANE FLIES OUT FIRST over the Mediterranean, then
turns back south of Cyprus toward the Nile Delta. We are flying by
a circuitous route because there is as yet no recognized air corridor
between Israel and Egypt. The direct route over the old battlefields
would have taken us only forty-five minutes.

Still, as we come in through the haze toward the bleak coastline, I
reflect that thirty-one years in seventy-five minutes is not all that
bad. I peer out at the sand dunes and swamps below and my mouth
is suddenly dry with excitement and I grip my seat even though the
flight is smooth. It is hard to imagine a greater distance than that
which has separated Israelis from Egyptians until now. Proust, who
was an expert on the great voids that separate humans from one another, said in *Cities of the Plain* that distances are only the relation
of space to time and vary with that relation; yet both are outside of
human control. In thirty-one years of war the hostility was total,
the distance in human terms so vast it was almost metaphysical. "He
seems so near, and yet so far," Tennyson wrote in 1833, a calmer
time. Anyway, he was referring to a lover. In romantic literature,
lovers were always appealing to the gods to annihilate time and
space, and they usually failed. In the same poem, Tennyson wrote:

I have not seen, I will not see
Vienna; rather dream that there,
A treble darkness, Evil haunts
The birth, the bridal; friend from friend
Is oftener parted, fathers bend
Above more graves.

We are flying in fairly low. Here now, just over the coastline, is a large cemetery. It might be the outskirts of Port Said. A line of corrugated tin roofs alongside a desert road. There is the Suez Canal, a narrow strip of green embedded in the sand. And beyond it, the Sinai desert, under a film of mist. I remember some ten years ago lying in a ditch somewhere down there trying to discern faint and floating images on this side of the Canal through a pair of binoculars, while, all around, the vast lunar expanse exploded in shellfire. From the air the desert looks flat, with hardly an undulation; it stretches far out to the eastern horizon. Nothing but sand, or so it seems. Over these arid dunes two generations of Egyptians and Israelis have bled one another since 1948. In the far distance I notice a line of palm trees; other than that, nothing.

The stewards are now moving through the cabin, serving champagne. The three security men across the aisle refuse the proffered plastic cups. Ever since we boarded the plane they have been trying to look inconspicuous in their almost identical blue blazers. In the two seats next to me, an English television news star and his cameraman are sipping their drinks calmly. For them the unfolding process of Egyptian-Israeli reconciliation in the past year must have turned by now from drama to melodrama to the schmaltziest soap opera of the decade. I can understand that they are beginning to be bored.

In the seats behind us, the Israeli newspapermen seem tense and irritable. Sick jokes have been flying about the cabin for some time. "We should have taken the quick route—like the Phantom jets, ha, ha." More jokes in the same tone. They are indications less of bad taste, I tell myself, than of nervous tension and fear of the unknown. One of the Israelis—I have known him for years—lives in Jerusalem on a street called Conquerors of the Mitla Pass. Mitla Pass was the site of a famous battle in 1967 where the Egyptians suffered perhaps the worst loss of the war: the abandoned tanks and shoes and burned-out carcasses of steel have symbolized for Egyptians their most humiliating defeat in modern history. Such names were given to streets in many Israeli cities after the lightning victory of 1967. There is nothing uniquely Israeli in this custom. Many European cities are filled with similar manifestations of military glory. I had a friend in Athens who lived on Basil the Bulgar Slayer Street, and I once asked him what he gave as his home address whenever he landed at Sofia airport, where his business took him quite frequently. "Oh, they don't mind," he said. "It happened over a thousand years ago."

But here everything is still raw: on their side, the memory of a very recent humiliation; on this side, the pain and suspicion. I am grateful, suddenly, for the innocuous Jerusalem address I shall be able to present in a moment to the passport control officer at Cairo airport—I live on Diskin Street, named for nothing more incriminating than a nineteenth-century rabbi.

Someone asks, "You think this treaty is more than a scrap of paper?"

It's too early to tell.

"I'm certain it's only that."

Why are you so sure?

"Don't be naïve. What do you know about Arabs?"

Not much, I admit.

"You don't know a thing about their m-e-n-t-a-l-i-t-y! I don't trust them."

I find I must.

"Peace is the lies people tell one another between wars."

The steward is proffering his tray of champagne.

No, thank you.

"It's free!"

I'd rather have a glass of water.

"You don't want water. You want champagne."

No, thank you.

"Don't you like champagne?" El Al stewards are often a little overbearing.

Okay. Thank you.

"So why didn't you say so before!"

Through the window, still nothing but sand. The champagne is cool and fizzy. The plastic cup is cracked. The grayish dunes are the color of a dirty burlap sack. They shroud the debris of untold numbers of tanks and armored troop carriers, rusting in the sand, and the charred bones of those who burned in them. Ashes and scrap metal of politics. Eighty thousand Egyptians and Israelis are said to have perished on these dunes over the past thirty years. Some say a hundred thousand. No one knows the exact figure. If the dead could come back, would there have been peace sooner?

"Have a croissant with your drink."

Thank you.

The plane dips a little from side to side. The pilot assures us through the loudspeaker that we are not tipsy; he does this with the rudders, he says, on purpose, to celebrate the occasion. More drinks are served. The pilot's humor is also on the black side.

"The last time I saw this view," he announces, "was from the cockpit of a bomber. . . . We are approaching Cairo, where the temperature is . . . On behalf of El Al Israel Airlines and the crew . . . we hope you have enjoyed this flight . . . and to be able to serve you again . . . hmm, just as soon as they let us . . . on regular scheduled flights along this route."

We are crossing a line of deep green. The Nile Delta, dense as a beehive. Thirty-one years ago, almost to the day, the prominent Egyptian statesman Azzam Pasha predicted a bloodbath against the Jews more terrible, he promised, than that perpetrated by Tamerlane. In the Tel Aviv newspaper that I hold on my lap I read that President Sadat, who flew home to Cairo yesterday from the peace ceremony in Washington, once again has hailed the "power of love," which, he said, "overcometh everything, solveth every problem. . . . Where there was hatred we are sowing the seeds of love." Love, love. Nothing but love out of Cairo these days. Sadat has been talking like this for months. He is in love, he says, with God and mankind, and with all "Israeli mothers." He thinks of mothers as his main allies, in Israel and in Egypt. Statesmanship, he said the other day, was the "rule of love." I recoil a little at this endless talk of love. We are conditioned to resist such rhetoric, even from our own wives. Are we too cynical? Freud said, "In the final analysis we must begin to love, simply to avoid becoming sick."

The newspaper also reports that Egypt now has a new national anthem; it was played yesterday at the airport in honor of the President's return. It is their third anthem in the past twenty-six years. The first was the old royal anthem sung to the tune of the march from Verdi's *Aida*.

The text of the second was:

> O my weapon,
> I yearn for you
> For the battle, be on guard!
> Keen always to say,
> I am ready for war.

The latest anthem reads:

> My land! My land!
> To you I give
> My love and heart.
> Egypt, mother of the universe,
> You are my goal, my hope.
> On all mankind your Nile bestows its blessings.

The tune is also new. The rank of honorary general, I read, has been conferred upon Mohammed Abdul Wahhab, the composer. I decide to take this as a good omen, reminiscent of the recent news out of Melbourne that the Australians voted to make the old song "Waltzing Matilda" their national anthem instead of "God Save the Queen"—"send her victorious, happy and glorious." By all means let us have more waltzing Matildas everywhere, less victories and glory.

The pyramids are just coming into view. They seem rather flat from this height, dusty and yellow against the surrounding dusty yellow of the desert. Then Giza, and the islands in the Nile, a bit unreal, like mirages of Tahiti in the midst of so much sand and dust, with emerald-green lawns and palm trees, and polo fields and whitewashed hotels. Farther on, the skyscrapers protrude from under the haze. The rest of the city is buried in a cloud of pollution. The plane touches down and comes to a stop. We file out by the rear door, dazed by the light and heat, tense, smiling a little sheepishly, hesitant. And quite obviously wondering if this is real after so many years or just "a dreadful quiet worser far than arms, an interval of peace." Damn those phrases, I think. It is so hot, so goddamned hot. The pilot just said it was thirty-eight degrees Celsius in the shade. "They're putting the heat on, especially for us." We step out on the burning tarmac; the blaze seeps through the thin soles of my shoes. A hot wind blows and strikes me near-dumb.

There are no customs controls. No forms to fill out. As soon as we step down from the plane we are whisked away in tourist buses that have been waiting on the tarmac. The airport is still decorated with the flags and banners of yesterday's grand reception for President Sadat. Everything seems a bit worse for wear in the strong wind. Portraits of Sadat are hanging everywhere, on airplane hangars and fences and lampposts, and an especially huge one that drapes all the way down from the roof of the whitewashed VIP reception pavilion. HERO OF PEACE. SOLDIER OF PEACE. WELCOME HOME. We drive out by a side gate. There are few people about. A million Cairenes are said to have pressed against these fences yesterday, chanting, "Sadat, ya Sadat. We sacrifice ourselves for you."

The few people visible now, airport workers mostly, it would seem, in blue overalls or long peasant galabias, are waving with their hands and calling "Salaam," "Shalom." And yet to a bystander I imagine we might seem rather like prisoners of war being led off to an internment camp. We travel at breakneck speed through red lights and stop signs. Two roaring police motorcycles precede us. They wave aside the oncoming traffic and sound their sirens. We are followed by a truckload of armed soldiers. We race down the broad avenues of Heliopolis, the ancient City of the Sun where Plato and Herodotus went to school with the priests of pharaonic Egypt, now a suburb of Cairo. The avenues are lined with gaudy villas and barefoot children wallowing in the sand. We pass gingerbread towers and grotesque statues, and gateposts and remains of gardens that may once have been green but are now yellow and gray with neglect and buried in dust. There are surprisingly few trees. Though this is a built-up area, the overwhelming impression, as at the airport just now, is *sand*. Yellow sand everywhere, between the houses and, in broad patches, on broken-up sidewalks and roads, as though the desert were sneaking back through the asphalt to reclaim the works of man. In the glare of high noon the few people about turn and stare after us. We pass a wretched slum of mud houses and tin shacks huddled alongside the road behind billboards advertising American cigarettes and Kuwait Airlines. The man sitting next to me mutters under his breath, "Look at the wretched poverty. It reminds me of the drive into Delhi."

But for all the obvious wretchedness I see, I can't help feeling good to be here at last, to sense life on the other side. I feel a little guilty, however, and say, "Wearing galabias doesn't necessarily mean they are wretched. We also have our poor."

"Not such poverty," he says. I can't argue that. We turn into a side street and follow it for about a mile. There is nothing but empty desert on both sides of the road; and at some distance, the long monotonous façade of a public housing development. We arrive at an iron gate guarded by armed police. As we enter, the landscape changes abruptly. We drive through a green tunnel of trees, past well-tended lawns and tennis courts, and bridle paths for horses. A blue swimming pool. Rose beds. A sprawling four-story C-shaped building, a white and gold façade in mock English Regency. Wrought-iron tables, painted white, shaded by red-and-blue-striped parasols. And not a soul to be seen other than soldiers, hundreds of soldiers in steel helmets and heavy black winter uniforms, notwithstanding the great heat. All are carrying submachine guns mounted with bayonets. The blades flash in the sun. A banner is stretched across the road. It bids us "Welcome to Hotel al-Salaam. Cabaret.

Sports Club." The hotel is the finest, newest in Cairo, we hear. It has only just opened, and in the nick of time to be named in such an appropriate manner. The doorman is the first civilian we have seen since we entered the gates, although he too is resplendent in a red uniform with gold epaulets. We enter a spacious lobby. The floor, smooth and shiny, is of Italian marble. We stop under a huge crystal chandelier.

"Welcome, welcome to Egypt, dear gentlemen," calls out Mr. Sherif Akhmad as he comes forward to greet us. This may not be his real, or his full, name; it later turns out that he is a colonel in the Egyptian State Security Service, Mukhabarat. He is a thickset man, broad-faced, in a double-breasted blue suit, all smiles and handshakes and warm solicitations and good wishes. He tells us we may under *no* circumstances go by ourselves into Cairo proper. Not without an armed escort, that is, which he will be ready to supply at all times. We are the only guests in the hotel, he says. All others were cleared out this morning in honor of our arrival and in order to provide us real comfort. Good grief, I think with a sinking heart. This is going to be one hell of a trip. How far away are we from the downtown area?

"Ten miles or so."

Oh.

There are brand-new automatic telephones everywhere—as well as color television sets—but the telephone lines to Cairo appear to be out at this moment. It seems impossible to call anybody in the city, or elsewhere in the world.

What happened? For how long have the lines been out?

"Oh, for some months."

The contingent of newspapermen is on the verge of hysteria. I go up to my room to unpack my things. From the window I am able to observe the double line of armed sentries that surrounds the hotel, apparently on all sides. The sentries, spaced a few yards from one another, are standing motionless in the heat. From the window they look like black candles. I see only their felted backs. All are facing away from the hotel toward the encircling barbed-wire fence. What terrible dangers loom out there in the bare stretch of sand toward

Heliopolis, where the phoenix, I remember, is said to have come to die on a pyre of aromatic woods, only to be reborn? A certain feeling of claustrophobia is building up. We seem like prominent hostages, put up by a benevolent pharaoh in a luxury hotel.

THE OMINOUS PRESENCE of so many security forces was misleading, of course. A short while later I manage to sneak out of al-Salaam with little difficulty, although with some trepidation. I place myself in the hands of an old friend of mine who writes for the French newspaper *Le Matin*. He is a big, burly fellow who knows a trick or two, and he speaks Arabic fluently, with a distinct Egyptian accent. We simply walk up to the gate. He points at me and casually tells the sentry, "He's okay, too. Let him through." In retrospect, as I write, I am no longer sure we really tricked them. I rather think the sentry may have been too embarrassed to call our bluff and shame us by exposure.

But at the time, I remember, we marched quickly down the deserted road with a certain sense of achievement. A few hundred yards farther on we caught a bus to Cairo. The bus was nearly full. It rolled down the main artery toward the downtown area, leaving in its wake a long trail of diesel smoke. There were no free seats. We stood in the forward section.

"Where are you from?" the driver asked. "American? Ingliz?"

"Israel," we said in casual tones, and near-pandemonium erupted. The driver brought the bus to an abrupt stop.

"No!" he cried in Arabic. "You must be joking!"

We said we were not.

The driver turned around to the other passengers. "Did you hear that? They say they are from Israel!"

A few passengers pushed forward in the aisle, crying, "Welcome! Welcome!" The driver said, "Israel very good. Egypt very good. Peace very good."

Meanwhile a line of stalled cars had formed behind us, sounding their horns. The driver put his head out of the window. "There are people from Israel here! Real people!" The other drivers passed the message along, craning their necks to get a better view. I don't think

I have ever felt so conspicuous. All around us in the bus people were saying, *"Mabrouk, mabrouk.* Peace very good."

An elderly gentleman in a panama hat shook my hand and said, "Do you know Mr. Levi from Alexandria? He went to Israel twenty years ago."

I was sorry, I didn't. The driver finally shifted gears and started up again. We were slowly heading toward the main city square, Midan al-Tahrir (Tahrir Square), on the banks of the Nile. At first there was not too much traffic. But as we moved toward the center, gradually we became aware of the enormous size of the city, then—more stunning—the sheer mass that populates it. At one stop a great crowd was waiting for the bus. When we finally moved on, a cluster of people hung on to the door outside. A few climbed up the ladder in the back to sit on the luggage racks atop.

THE HUMAN MASS: The population of Cairo has increased fourfold over the past thirty-five years. In the early evening hours the streets of this enormous city, which are always packed, fill even more. The congestion, always great, increases to a point where one wonders if it can ever straighten out again. One thinks of Ezekiel: "Son of man, wail for the *multitude* of Egypt." I have never in my life seen such crowds. Almost everywhere I go, I find myself in a thick swarm, moving slowly in concert along the narrow sidewalks. A dark sun hangs in a foggy sky of dust and soot. The air is heavy and humid.

In the hazy light the city looks even more dense and congested. Two and one-half million people lived here in the 1940s. Today there are almost 10 million. The entire population of Israel could fit into a single district of Cairo.

But these are merely figures. Other cities have quadrupled their population during similar periods of time. What makes Cairo so overwhelming is the fact that the city's infrastructure has grown by only a fraction. The resulting chaos is evident everywhere: in the sad state of the public sewers, the overloaded telephone network, the water shortage, the periodic breakdowns in electricity, the public schools that operate on two, sometimes three, shifts a day. The high rate of illiteracy (70 percent) has remained virtually steady over the past thirty years despite an enormous growth in school facilities and in the number of trained teachers. Huge slum areas have crept into empty spaces, including cemeteries and mosques.

In 1948, before the outbreak of the first Arab-Israeli war, the average population density in Cairo was 11,704 people per square kilometer (about 27,000 per square mile). In 1966, just before the Six-Day War, that figure had risen to 20,549 (50,000 per square mile). The density today is said to be close to 40,000 per square kilometer (100,000 per square mile). In one particular slum area (Bab al-Sharia), the present population is 1.3 million—approximately 4 people on every 3 square yards—as high, I suspect, as anything in India.

Anis Mansur, the influential Egyptian editor said to be a close friend of President Sadat, wrote after the President's dramatic journey to Jerusalem: "Who is against the war? The soldiers themselves! The war has embittered everyone's life. The war has denied them home, street, and livelihood. Whoever reaches for the telephone and does not get a free line, or opens the faucet and the water does not run, or stands in the street for hours and waits for the bus which does not arrive, and when it does there is no space on it, not even on the steps; every young man who does not find work, and if he finds work finds no home, and if he finds a home cannot pay the rent, and so he cannot marry and contemplates emigration—all of these do not want war. None of them is in need of any philosophy to curse their fate. They curse those who took the riches of Egypt and all her resources and spent them on armaments and endless wars. They curse those [Arabs] for whom we fought and who are themselves getting richer and richer all the time. No, we must put a stop to the flow of gold and blood."

And yet I notice that the same Anis Mansur wrote in a recent issue of the mass-circulation magazine *October,* of which he is editor: "Give [the Jews] a chance and they will prove what beasts they can be. . . . What are they doing throughout the world? Smuggling drugs, running cabarets, and engaging in white slave traffic." I have been told that in the past Mansur frequently wrote in this vein. All the terrible deeds of the Jews, however, do not militate against peace. On the contrary, in this week's *October,* Mansur vigorously supports the peace treaty. "Egypt is doing nothing radical," he writes; "it merely follows in the footsteps of the Prophet Mohammed, who also made peace with the enemies of Islam. Peace will bring affluence. The crusade for prosperity is on its way!"

THROUGHOUT THE CITY, an overwhelming presence of police and militiamen. Not one policeman here and there, but groups of ten or twenty, heavily armed; and motorcycle patrols in fours and sixes. On Midan al-Tahrir, the great square built on the spot where the British army barracks once stood, some twenty or thirty thousand people are waiting for the suburban buses to take them home. Nearby, on the river esplanade, by the doors of the huge television building, a few soldiers are barricaded behind sandbags. The dense human stream flows around them as if they were stranded on an island: poor people in rags, peasants in wide robes, city people in fine double-breasted suits. I can imagine a similar congestion in Tokyo, or Bombay; many foreigners compare Cairo to Calcutta. But I wonder if one finds in any of these cities the same eerie quiet. Bismarck somewhere spoke of the "fanaticism of calm." My first reaction to it is a kind of fear. I know where that fear comes from. Then I tell myself that I must not succumb to generalizations. Westerners often see the East as either treacherously profound or touchingly simple.

There is a quality of grace and affability in daily life here that I have rarely seen elsewhere. Despite the terrible congestion, few seem to push, or kick, or raise their voice. The pace seems leisurely and slow. The encounter with the enormous human mass that surrounds me almost everywhere produces a first very powerful impression. It stuns me. And I cannot help remembering the scenes on television in 1967, of this very same crowd, running amok in these same streets on the eve of the Six-Day War, screaming for blood.

I DON'T THINK I HAVE ever experienced anything of the kind. It has partly to do, of course, with the thrill of being in a heretofore forbidden place. The origins of this thrill are obvious. They are partly sensuous. In the past thirty years none of us could come here, not for money or fine words, nor by the force of arms. And yet with not a single exception the Egyptians I meet are warm and hospitable and kind, and many of them say, "Welcome, welcome!" and "It's good that it is over." But unlike those Arabs in the occupied territories after the Six-Day War, they don't say "Welcome" to an Israeli because they are afraid and politic, but out of free will, or perhaps from fatigue.

Another thing strikes me, which I have never encountered before. I would call it the weight of time. It comes from the curious meeting here of the visible and the remembered. The past is more sensuous, more palpable in Cairo even than in Jerusalem, where I live. In Jerusalem the distant past also survives in stones, but they are mostly fragments and bits of pieces here and there of walls and foundations carefully dug up, cleaned, and marked to produce an illusion of the whole. I now realize that time is a less abstract notion than we think. In Israel we have the Book. It does not evoke a sense of time nearly so strikingly sensuous as does a perfectly preserved burial chamber five thousand years old with brilliantly colored frescoes on its walls.

The pyramids are more or less intact. Those of Giza are visible from the upper floors of many buildings in Cairo. The even more ancient step pyramid of Saqqara—one of the earliest known examples of human architecture—is less than half an hour away from the city's main square. It is not merely the constant talk one hears here of six or seven thousand years of uninterrupted history, but a syndrome produced by a combination of the tangible and the recollected. Unlike the stunning impact of the unending human mass, it comes upon one gradually, and then one is hopelessly caught up in it. I look over the rooftops at the pyramids, and down at the garbage on the street below. The dust rises in spirals. The sickle of a new moon hangs in the sky, still thin, and sharply pointed as a dagger. A great banner is spread across the wide avenue. It shows Sadat, dressed in the uniform of a field marshal, and with a golden scepter in his hand not unlike that of the boy-king in his sarcophagus in the Egyptian

Museum of Antiquities. The inscription under Sadat's picture reads: "Why peace? Well, what did we get from war?" I am told that this is the refrain of a current popular song.

THE SINGER IS Mr. Mohammed Nuch, one of the best known in Egypt. He specializes in folk music. Mr. Nuch is a broad-shouldered, heavily built man in his early fifties. His gray hair is combed back over a large forehead. The eyes are a raven black. He wears a wide, tailor-made galabia with delicate embroidery. His records, he says, are sold in tens of thousands of copies. During the Yom Kippur War—here they call it the October War—he entertained the soldiers in the dugouts. His winning smile comes quickly and spreads across the wide, olive-skinned face. "No, no. I didn't sing war songs. I sang patriotic songs," he says. "Songs of love. Love for this poor land I sang to them."

Mr. Nuch is standing in the lobby of an old Cairo art theater, where his new musical is being rehearsed. The name of the play is *Love in a Box*. It is an attack, says Mr. Nuch, on Nasser's Mukhabarat (State Security Service), which used to kidnap Egyptian opposition figures from Europe—an Israeli agent was once kidnapped in the same way—and ship them back to Egypt drugged and packed in a box. Why *LOVE in a Box?* Very simple, explains Mr. Nuch in his ringing tenor voice. Love is freedom. We are trying to say that freedom cannot be drugged or packed away in boxes.

"We have been singing only PEACE songs since 1976," says Mr. Nuch. I am not sure how to take him. There is an Arab proverb: When the calf is thrown, the knives begin to fall. Everyone gets in on the killing. Is the opposite true as well? If the calf were resurrected, would all get in on the feeding? Mr. Nuch is altogther too trendy for my taste.

But then he tells me that he has lost three brothers in three wars: one in 1956, another in 1967, a third in the 1973 war. The fourth now works as his drummer. We sip black tea with mint from small elongated glasses. Then he plays me one of his records. His voice is soft and comes with a slight, low growl.

I TAXI BACK TO THE HOTEL close to midnight, straining in the dim light to decipher the headlines in tomorrow's *Al Akhbar* and *Al Ahram,* wondering if ever two nations have made peace that knew so little of each other. The streets are bright with PEACE slogans and pictures of Sadat. They are still thronged with people. Words have formed the only bridge between us until now, a fragile, narrow bridge, which only the specialists bothered to traverse. I notice a back-page item in one of the newspapers, which reports that Professor Shimon Shamir's book *Egypt Under Sadat* has been translated into Arabic and will soon be published in Cairo by *Al Maaref.*

Shamir is a professor at the University of Tel Aviv. His book—an analysis of the great changes in Egypt after Nasser—was published in Hebrew more than a year ago. Shamir is one of the few area specialists in Israel who has been correctly gauging the mood of Egypt over the past seven years, saying that Egypt under Sadat was striving for peace with Israel, at least as one possible option, unlike Nasser's Egypt, which had been almost totally committed to war. How many of us have read that book, I reflect as we drive through the night? I myself read it only a week ago, in a bit of a hurry.

And what can Egyptians read about us? Almost nothing, I understand, except what is available in propagandistic tracts. For years we have lived apart from one another, or yet locked in a deadly embrace like two ferocious snakes. The peculiar nature of the relationship made any contact between us mutually destructive. The popular images on both sides were distorted. Behind every Israeli soldier, Egyptians saw a French foreign legionnaire or an English colonialist. Behind every Egyptian soldier, Israelis saw an SS man bent on genocide. We have lived for years in a world of demons and devils. As Nasser called Ben-Gurion "the worst war criminal of the century," so many Israelis called Nasser, and after him Sadat, a "Hitler on the Nile." Nasser announced that Israel's very existence was an act of aggression. Ben-Gurion claimed he sought nothing but peace, but in 1956 joined the British and French military expedition against Egypt. The hostility of Egyptians toward Israelis was not solely political. As the years went by, it was elevated to the rank of ideology and faith. Israelis—and Jews—became symbols of an abomination that must be destroyed, if need be, in a Holy War, as the Crusaders' kingdom had been. A school of anti-Semitic hate literature developed in Egypt as the years went by. It assumed such proportions that when I last saw a representative selection of anti-Semitic books published in Egypt by state-owned publishing houses, they occupied a long shelf in the library of a friend of mine in Jerusalem, the orientalist Yehoshafat Harkabi. I had seen Professor Harkabi over the years grow gray, then white-haired, in the painful process of collecting, reading, and annotating that filth. Harkabi's collection includes several Egyptian reprints, in Arabic, of the *Protocols of the Elders of Zion,* described in one translation as a "secret speech by Herzl at the Zionist congress." Nasser, on one occasion, himself recommended the *Protocols* to an Indian visitor. "It is important that you read it," Nasser said. "I will give you a copy. It proves beyond all doubt that three hundred Zionists, each knowing the others, control the fate of the European continent and elect their successors from among themselves." The remark can be found in the official collection of *Nasser's Speeches and Press Interviews** issued by a Cairo state-owned publishing house, as were the *Protocols.*

Other examples in Harkabi's collection: "The Jewish God is not content with animal sacrifices. To placate him, human sacrifices are necessary. Hence the Jewish custom of slaughtering infants and sucking their blood to mix it with unleavened bread at Passover."

"Jesus told us who they were. Mohammed warned us against them. God cursed them and destroyed their land."

The clear "aim" of the Zionists is to establish Jewish control over the entire world, "through the corruption of morals, financial speculation, the spreading of meanness everywhere, the destruction of religion, and finally through the use of murder as a means to achieve their goal." (Hassan Sabri al-Khuli, Nasser's "personal representative," in a lecture to the troops, published by Supreme Headquarters of the Egyptian Armed Forces [Cairo, 1965].)

Where is this al-Khuli now, I wonder? I have asked Mussa Sabry,

* (Cairo, 1958), page 402.

editor in chief of *Al Akhbar,* whom I visited earlier this evening in his office, if he knew. He said he did not know. Mr. Sabry is a witty, urbane, soft-spoken man, slightly bent over, with an easy and gracious manner. I liked him immediately. His office is lined with books in three languages. By his desk, on a side table, he keeps a pile of recent Jerusalem *Post*s. He reads the *Post* daily, he said, and with "considerable pleasure. I have for years." We must meet one another in a spirit of love and understanding, Mr. Sabry said. We had a very good talk. And yet I have been told by a man who visited Sabry here less than a year ago that on the walls of his office there still hung, in 1978, a few caricatures from Arab newspapers which, in style and in graphic detail, looked as though they had been inspired by the cartoons of Jews in Hitler's *Der Stürmer*.

As we sat chatting pleasantly in his office, I noticed that the cartoons were no longer there. Only pictures of Sadat, and one of Nasser in his familiar pose, the strong chin resolutely pushed out.

Yes, there was some anti-Semitic literature some years ago, said Mr. Sabry. He himself had never read any of those books. But yes, they existed. He urged me not to attach too great an importance to them, however. They had been the by-product of war, not its cause, he said, a form of "war racism." I asked him what he meant by this.

"Oh, similar to the propaganda directed against the Japanese in America after the attack on Pearl Harbor." Anti-Semitism was not indigenous to Egypt, he thought. Both images and slogans were imported from Europe. It was a form of foreign aid, like—here Mr. Sabry smiled, a bit mischievously, I thought—like nationalism, which was also brought in from the outside.

An interesting thought, I said, hoping to sound a bit ironic. Unfortunately, the fine distinction between genuine racism and "war racism" does not cut much ice with the survivors of the Nazi holocaust. Mr. Sabry readily granted this point. But anti-Semitic propaganda, he went on to say, never really made any headway here, not even in Nasser's day. And by now it was as good as forgotten.

Egypt and Israel will live in peace, Mr. Sabry said. He was sure of that. He spoke warmly about Israel, which he had visited together with Sadat in 1977. There would soon be cultural and economic exchanges between the two nations, as between Jews and Moslems in the Middle Ages. We could learn a great deal from each other. If both sides conducted themselves wisely, a new era would dawn, a golden age. He described it so ably, so convincingly, with such warmth, I simply could not bring myself to ask him what happened to the caricatures that had hung on his wall six months before.

BUT THEN I AM HERE in Cairo—not in Tel Aviv—tense and self-conscious, grateful for the hospitality I receive and engulfed in friendliness wherever I go, wanting desperately to believe that it really is all over; aware also of the stupidities and mistakes on the Israeli side over the years that helped whip up Egyptian hostility to a point where it began to feed on itself and become almost autistic. Is that self-perpetuating circle broken now? I have read somewhere that ultimate reality can be perceived only intuitively, by an act of the will and the affections. I am surrounded here in Cairo by a new reality, or so I hope. I sharpen my intuitions to it and pray that I am not misled. I sense that in Israel the intuition of most people is fed by different surroundings. Mussa Sabry said that in Egypt 99 percent of the population overwhelmingly supported the peace treaty; only some people in Sadat's government still wondered whether Egypt had made the right move. Within the government, Sabry said, there was still a strong suspicion of Israel's motives and a fear of being "betrayed" by Begin.

In Israel, when I left for Egypt, the opposite seemed true. The government appeared sure it had done the right thing at the right time. The public was still filled with suspicions that bordered on neurosis. This difference between Israel and Egypt is not difficult to understand. It comes from the contrast between a parliamentary democracy and an authoritarian state. Democracies do not easily go to war. When they do they tend to imbue the contest with a final, apocalyptic quality. When I left Israel there was little of the unrestrained enthusiasm for the peace treaty I notice almost everywhere since my arrival among the Egyptian masses. In Israel there was rather a strange, sour atmosphere of boundless suspicion and concern. When the moment finally arrived for which Israelis had been praying and waiting for decades—peace with the largest, most powerful Arab country—it came almost as an anticlimax. The peace negotiations had dragged on for too long, in the worst possible bazaar style, with frightful howls and grimaces all around and exquisite gestures of rejection and disdain. The negotiations had gone through too many downs, when everything had seemed lost, and ups that nobody believed in any longer. Until the last moment we were none of us certain whether we were about to cross the Rubicon, or whether we had just been fishing in it. The bargain was finally sealed in the ludicrous show-business atmosphere of a major Hollywood event.

What a strange sight it had been when Prime Minister Menahem Begin left Tel Aviv airport for the peace-signing ceremony in Washington! I remember watching the scene on television. It was gloomy. Only Begin smiled broadly, but with a bit of strain, I thought. The long line of well-wishers gathered at the airport treated him with restraint and consideration—as though they were sending him off to a funeral. "We build Jerusalem like men mounting the gallows," the poet Sh. Shalom once wrote, summing up in one memorable line the mixed moods of irony and enthusiasm that marked many a generation of Zionist pioneers.

The Israeli newspapers that morning—Friday, March 23—had been dark with misgivings. Aharon Megged, a fine novelist, wrote that his heart trembled "with sorrow" at the thought of Israel's losing Mount Sinai, sorrow also at the abandonment of "the desert—to the wind, the sun and the dead," an astonishing remark considering the fact that Sinai is inhabited by some fifty thousand Bedouin. The Egyptians had already announced plans to resettle an additional two hundred thousand Egyptians on reclaimed areas in the Sinai made fertile by piped-in Nile water.

"Where in the history of nations has such a thing been heard?" wrote Megged. "After victories, not defeats?" He criticized Foreign Minister Dayan for having declared the peace treaty "a very good thing." He, Megged, saw very little good in it; nor did he understand how people could toast the peace and say *"L'chayim."* "How can anyone be happy when the heart trembles with sorrow?"

Haim Gouri, another well-known author, published a similar paean to the lost desert, which he addressed in the imperative, as though bidding good-bye to a woman writhing at his feet, whom he caresses with tears in his eyes for the last time in his life. "Farewell, Sinai. Farewell, great expanse of land extending out to the horizon. Farewell, ancient memories." I wondered at that remark. Did Gouri mean to lose his memories now? Apparently, yes. "Farewell, ancient memories, memories of the Exodus from Egypt and receiving of the Torah [on Mount Sinai]." I gathered from this that Gouri had no further intention of celebrating Passover. "The Sinai wilderness," he continued wistfully, had been dear to us "from the earliest dawn of this nation." I am sure he checked that fact somewhere; I find no reference to it anywhere. "Farewell, magic, silent coral coasts [of the Red Sea]. Farewell." Gouri expressed a concern that the Egyptians would now think that wondrous land "is really theirs, not ours."

I mention such articles here as examples not only of a strident, militant nationalism—a minority mood—but of the general confusion and concern and weariness generated by decades of uncertainty and war. Many people simply could not bring themselves to believe that the kind of Egyptians whom, as it says in Exodus 14:13, "ye have seen . . . ye shall see them again no more for ever." Others were looking for bargains. "The Archie Bunkers of Israel," the novelist Amos Oz said, "would like to have peace without paying for it." The twelve years of occupation had accustomed people to its material gains. They had forgotten how it had come about in the first place.

Few in Israel before 1967 had made any claims to sovereignty over the Sinai Peninsula. When Israel conquered the desert on June 5, 1967, Moshe Dayan announced that we had "no territorial aims." The territory was held as a mortgage—to be released in exchange for peace. The appetite for it had come later. Too many people had grown used, for too long, to the state of permanent war. It was difficult to shake oneself loose.

An incident that took place in a Jerusalem high school, a few days before I left for Cairo, struck me as characteristic. The peace treaty was due to be signed in Washington on March 26, a Monday. The pupils of the two upper grades of that school serve as junior air raid wardens. They were told, in all seriousness, by the chief warden, that war was likely to break out on the following day, Tuesday. They were given coded signals, which, in the case of emergency, would be broadcast on the radio. When they heard these signals, they were told, they should rush to their posts and help people get to the shelters.

On the day the treaty was signed, prices on the Tel Aviv Stock Exchange fell sharply, as though life were imitating Brechtian fiction. "The Messiah," according to an old Jewish saying, "comes in rags."

The newspapers reported that on that Monday an old man had come to the Western Wall with a note to stick between the ancient stones. The note was inscribed: "Please, dear G-d, let this last for longer than one night." It reminded me of an exchange in Brecht's *Mother Courage:*

THE PRIEST: "Now we are in God's hand."

MOTHER COURAGE: "I do hope that things aren't as far gone as that!"

They were not, but many had difficulty in sleeping well that night.

II

SLEPT SOUNDLY LAST NIGHT and woke up feeling guilty. Am I simply callous to the concerns and excitements? It was mostly from fatigue, I tell myself. No dreams. Facts are better. Prime Minister Begin is arriving in Cairo today. It is an official visit, his first. The Cairo newspapers this morning make a point of saying that he has invited himself. They would have liked him to come at a later date. Ten Arab countries have just severed diplomatic relations with Egypt as punishment for signing this "separate" peace with the enemies of Islam. But Begin insisted. He wanted his legitimization. In *Al Goumuriah* there is a veiled reference to Jewish pushiness. He will be treated correctly, it is said, but as an exalted tourist, nothing more. I find myself, for once, applauding Begin's sense of theater, which I usually find obnoxious. Today it seems to be serving a useful purpose, adding a little moisture to the arid soil in which the seed of peace has just been planted. Perhaps it will help the seed to sprout.

Begin's plane, the *Israel Air Force Number One*—small countries ape the big these days—arrives in Cairo in a cloud of dust. The temperature is forty-two degrees Celsius. President Sadat is not at the airport to meet him, nor is Prime Minister Mustapha Khalil. Vice-President Hosni Mubarek, a former Air Force general, heads the reception committee. The officials in the Israeli advance party are furious at this slight and contrast it with the grand reception that Israel gave to Sadat in Jerusalem sixteen months earlier. Begin himself, as he steps down the mounted stairs, looks tense but composed.

Begin is a slight man of medium height. As he walks down the long crimson carpet I notice for the first time—I have watched him for years—that his pace matches his speech. At one moment it is slow and soft, and the next, strident and abrupt. He has the matted, dank face of one who seems to have spent a long uncomfortable night in a dark cave. It is as gray as his silk suit and glistens in the sun. His thinning hair is flying in the hot wind. The thick lenses of his glasses magnify the impression of grim determination in his eyes. The sun beats down on his bare head. He stands to attention stiffly. He looks a bit like an army recruit. The arms are pressed so tightly against the seams of his jacket they almost disappear in its folds. The Egyptian military band plays the Israeli anthem, "Hatikvah," with but a trace here and there of a mistaken note. The scene is broadcast live on Egyptian television. "Hatikvah" is one of the less cheerful national anthems—it begins with the words "Our hope is *not yet* lost." Its melancholy tune is adapted from Smetana's *Moldava*. Begin's eyes, in their large sockets, do not move. Nor does this survivor of the Nazi holocaust—his family was destroyed in wartime Poland—flinch as he faces the goose-stepping guard of honor which is fitted out in, of all possible accoutrements, World War II German steel helmets, long phased out in their land of origin. There are no speeches. Everything conceivable has already been said during the long-drawn-out process of negotiation.

"No twenty-one-gun salute?" a member of the Prime Minister's entourage asks with some irritation. No, according to Egyptian protocol it is not due. A strange silence envelops the airport, which has been closed for hours to all other traffic. The Prime Minister and his party walk down the short receiving line. The last to greet him is the Sheikh of Al Azhar, the main center of religious learning in the Islamic world. I am told by the only Egyptian reporter present (the others are Israeli or foreign) that the Sheikh is here by special request of the President to give an imprimatur of Islam to this act of peace. Soft drinks are served in the nearby Distinguished Visitors' hall. The conversation between Begin and Mubarek is broadcast over the television satellite:

"It is hot," says Begin.

"Yes, very hot," says Vice-President Mubarek.

"In Israel it is also very hot today."

"It is?"

"Yes, when it is hot in Egypt it usually is also very hot in Israel." It is not clear whether this is a political or a meteorological statement. "We have the same weather."

"I see."

"In Israel we call it *chamsin*."

"You mean it lasts fifty days?" In Arabic, *chamsin* means "fifty."

"No," explains Begin, *cham* in Hebrew means "hot." Very hot. A heat wave.

Silence.

"Have you had a good flight?"

"Yes, very good."

Silence.

"How long did it take?"

"Fifty minutes."

"I see."

Silence. The only real rapport one notices so far is between the secret service agents of the two countries. They hover about in clusters, whispering messages through their radio microphones to invisible but, one imagines, joint command posts. It is amazing how well they get on, who only a few weeks ago would have roasted one another at the stake.

A LOW TABLE IS COVERED with flowers in heavy vases. A large colored map is hanging on the wall above it. I have seen this map elsewhere—it seems a standard one—in Egyptian ministry waiting rooms and newspaper offices. The map covers a vast area from Morocco to the Persian Gulf (invariably called al-Khalij al-Arabi, Arabian Gulf), from the southern tip of Yemen to the Mediterranean in the north, with Israel identified as "occupied Palestine."

I can't help it: whenever I see one of these maps in Cairo, I am a bit nervous. Even now, with Begin and Mubarek in the same room exchanging pleasantries about the weather. It is not so much the nomenclature—I try not to give a damn about that—but the visual image of the geopolitical equation imprinted on the eye. When one looks at the tiny speck of red lost on the edge of what is called the Arab Middle East, one cannot help but reflect that if the present hostility continues, it may be only a matter of time before space and numbers settle the issue. I remember, years ago, walking into Ben-Gurion's office in Tel Aviv to discover that he kept a similar map over his desk. He was looking at it every day. When I asked him how he could stand it, he cited De Gaulle, who believed there were only two permanents in politics: history and geography. "That gives us a draw," said Ben-Gurion.

JOSEPH KRAFT, THE American columnist, is at the airport. He tells me, as we drive back into town, that M——, a political reporter for a large Cairo newspaper, was absolutely convinced until a short time ago that in the Israeli Knesset, above the Speaker's rostrum, there was a map of the Middle East that showed Israel's "historic domain" from the Euphrates to the Nile.

When M—— went to Jerusalem with President Sadat, he saw that the map wasn't there. His first thought was that it had been taken down for the occasion. He recently told Kraft that he was now finally convinced the map had never been there. Kraft says that M—— is normally the most skeptical of men. But for over twenty years he had been ready to take this canard for granted. So did many foreigners who lived among the Arabs. It had become truth by repetition.

THE TOMB OF THE Egyptian Unknown Soldier. A massive stone structure shaped vaguely like a pyramid. The Egyptians still build houses of mud, but their tombs are of everlasting granite. The tomb commemorates death in the abstract. In Israel we are accustomed, perhaps more than others, to mourn the anonymous dead. And yet we have as much difficulty in translating the abstract into personal terms.

The visit to this monument is Begin's first official stop in the Egyptian capital. He has been driven here by his hosts in an armored limousine. He steps out looking cool and smooth, much better than at the airport. The drums roll their dirge and the trumpets sound. The mounted cavalry is on hand; the men as well as their dark horses are done up in brilliant colors. Once again, the two anthems. The horses whip up the dust. The gray façade of the monument is inscribed with the ninety-nine "names of the existence," given in the Koran to God, "the all-knowing, the all-capable, the perfect, the *merciful*. . . ." In the center, a black slab of marble on which Begin places a wreath of red carnations.

His face is sealed. Behind Begin stands a somber-looking man whom he has brought along. His name is Chaim Weiler, he has lost two sons in the wars, and in one brief scene the mourning on both sides fuses: not only, one hopes, symbolically. The photographers eagerly focus their lenses upon it.

Later on, Begin says this was "the most moving moment," laying the wreath on the tomb of the Unknown Soldier. "The Egyptian soldier answered the call of his country and fought against us. He did his duty. For this I render him homage."

I argue over this with a man in the Prime Minister's party. I acknowledge that Begin wanted to be chivalrous. But couldn't he pay homage to the dead without invoking that carnivorous goddess Duty?

"You'd like to abolish duty?"

I'd like to reform it, yes.

"Everywhere?"

Sure. I find Sadat's vicarious heroism just as tasteless. The other day he said that during the last war he was proud "to order my sons to the supreme sacrifice." *His* sons, my foot.

"I don't understand. Do you want to strip the state of its authority?"

You mean its divinity.

"I said authority."

Its infallible laws?

"I mean that which makes people ready to fight."

What's that?

"Trust. Or anger."

Induced by the state, I say.

"You want to abolish the state?"

Improve it, maybe.

"A state no one trusts."

Not any more than it deserves, I think to myself.

I think of the cost of duty. Sadat's Minister of Finance is quoted in the morning's newspapers as saying that one hundred thousand Egyptian soldiers gave their lives over the past thirty years, doing their duty, as it were. With the $58 billion that the wars cost, Egypt could have rebuilt every single village in the Nile Valley, says the minister. A similar thought was expressed by Tewfik al-Hakim, the renowned Egyptian novelist, back in 1971. It took the politicians eight years and yet another war to arrive at the same conclusion.

THE PYRAMIDS OF GIZA and the Sphinx. More sepulchers of the dead, possibly the biggest, bulkiest ever devised by man. An industry of staggering proportions—how many human beings have dutifully given their lives here to institutionalize death? Prime Minister Begin and his official host, the Egyptian Minister of Justice, descend from the skies in a helicopter, like two Homeric gods mingling with mere humans. The entire area has been cleared of the tourists, camel drivers, and muleteers who normally crowd the site. Instead there are hundreds of soldiers in black winter uniforms. The temperature is forty-five degrees Celsius. When the engines are turned off, a great stillness pervades the site, until the photographers begin shouting and falling over one another in a rush to photograph the Israeli leader, with his profile superimposed upon the profile of the Sphinx. Begin's cheeks are pale. His forehead shines in the great heat. His chin is thrust slightly upward. His face is summed up in the sharply drawn lines of his mouth. This has always been, and continues to be, his main weapon, an indefatigable machine of rhetoric that has produced more sarcasm and patriotic pedantry than any other in Israel. He climbs in and out of the Great Pyramid. He has on occasion claimed the pyramids for the Jews, who, as he said, had built them with their own hands while in the Egyptian house of bondage. In one of his lighter moments, Begin even suggested that we might belatedly present Cairo with a bill for our labor.

"Mr. Prime Minister," an Egyptian reporter calls out, "do you still hold to the view that your ancestors built the Sphinx?"

No, he says, he does not. He is sorry, says Begin, he erred, by about one thousand five hundred years or so. There is no claim. He gives them back their pyramids; it is a gift that does not cost him too dear. The Egyptian reporters—more than twenty are here now—take the good news with something like satisfaction.

"Thank you, Mr. Prime Minister!" They are such polite people, the newspapermen of this semitotalitarian state. Begin says again how pleased and excited he is to be here. He delivers a lecture on pyramids in general and in particular, here, in Mexico, and in Peru. Then—he never seems to know when to stop—he adds, "When Napoleon was here in 1798, he said that four thousand years of history were looking down on him. Since then, 181 years have passed. Permit me to say, in all humility—I am a simple man—that 4,181 years are looking down on us."

He is that kind of man. Singularly pompous and egocentric, as, I imagine, most politicians must be. Without such toxic fuel they perhaps could not meet the rigors and demands of politics in a mass democracy. A man of considerable intellectual resources, by no means ignorant of the fact that with Napoleon he is invoking the name of a foreign conqueror—yet at the same time a compulsive rhetorician who derives a kind of sensual pleasure from the exercise of his vocal cords. An aggressive narcissist; too garrulous to be taught; too often tactless. I am told by an Egyptian acquaintance that Sadat philosophically remarked the other day, "What can we do, he is the best Begin we have."

No more controversial person ever held public office in Israel. A former terrorist in a society that holds terror an abomination: for many years he was the outcast, the despised pariah in Israeli politics. He was so marginal a figure in Israeli life that in most books written before 1975 he is mentioned only in passing, if at all. An opposition leader defeated in eight consecutive Israeli elections; in the ninth, in the wake of financial scandals that rocked the ruling Labor party elite, he won a stunning victory, to everybody's surprise, including, no doubt, his own.

Golda Meir called him a "rabble-rousing crypto-fascist." Ben-Gurion wrote that, given a free hand, Begin would "bring unmitigated disaster over Israel." At the very least he would make Israel's name "an abomination throughout the civilized world."

He is a conservative on most issues, from economics to foreign affairs. Not content with Israel as constituted within its internationally recognized borders, he has in the past claimed not only the entire area of Palestine but that of Transjordan as well. Had the Old Testament made mention of the moon as part of God's promise to the Hebrews in the Bronze Age, he would have annexed that if he could. Begin had in the past argued for many an adventurous action against the neighboring Arab states. In the late 1950s the Army reserves were, by mistake, called up over the radio. The orders were rescinded as soon as the error was discovered. But Begin had already mounted the rostrum of the Knesset to bless the soldiers marching; he had not paused to ask how, why, or even where to. In his memoirs, he rephrased Descartes to define his own motto: "I do battle, therefore I am." Moshe Sharett, a former Foreign Minister, once called Begin's mind "one of the most underdeveloped areas in the Near East."

And yet, by a supreme irony, this man of the strident, ultranationalist Right became—only a few months after his rise to power in 1977—the *peacemaker,* ready to make the very concession that the ostensibly moderate Labor government could never bring itself to do. Or was it, as his opponents later said, because he did not have a Begin to oppose him? The French, experienced in such matters, have a saying: *"C'est toujours la droite qui fait la paix"* ("It's always the Right that makes peace"). The corollary is, of course, that in most cases the Right also makes the wars.

THE RHETORIC. Why is there so little that is even remotely memorable in the public utterances of either Sadat or Begin? There is little difference between the prepared remarks and those made extemporaneously by the two leaders at any given moment. It was the same a few days ago, in Washington, during the peace-signing ceremony on the White House lawn. The strained speeches give weight to a general impression of anticlimactic distress. They are sonorous, perhaps readable, but leave little pressure on the memory.

To think that these two men lead two of the most ancient peoples in the world today. Chaldea and Sumer are gone; Europe was forests and swamps populated by barbarians when Israel and Egypt first met. And this is all they now have to say?

The only consolation that comes to mind is that the rhetoric is merely the libretto, which, as in most great operas, is of inferior quality. Posterity will forget the words and remember the music.

Is television a cause? It is an embarrassment to witness any of these events in person or see them on the television screen. One is frustrated because the actors are said to represent us, to carry on their shoulders the load of our ancient and more recent past, our problems and concerns. More than anything, one misses a certain dignity. The gold thread of Tilsit. This is not how things were on the raft in the river Neman. Not in Versailles, nor in Yalta or Évian. Villains were plotting at Yalta, but none picked their nose in front of a camera.

BEFORE SADAT TRAVELED to Jerusalem, the last Egyptian-Judean summit conference took place two thousand and thirteen years ago. In 34 B.C. Cleopatra visited Herod the Great in Jerusalem. Her main purpose was to press the Judean King into ceding to her further large tracts of his domain. The visit was not an apparent success. Its immediate result was a fury of charges and countercharges. Cleopatra claimed that Herod had tried to assassinate her. Herod said she had tried to seduce him.

Professor Michael Grant, the biographer of the two Eastern potentates, surmises that both allegations may have been correct; both were designed, for opposite reasons, to influence Antony, the superpower of his day. Grant says that Cleopatra was forever nagging her lover to dismantle the Judean state and turn its rich provinces over to her. To achieve this end, she would use all her famous wiles, vituperation, diplomacy, and sex. It was a kind of obsession with her, says Grant. Antony finally succumbed and gave her Herod's bitumen mines on the Dead Sea, Jericho, and the Gaza Strip. As for the rest he remained adamant; we do not know at what cost to him, emotionally or otherwise.

A STATE BANQUET AT Koubeh Palace. The former royal residence is plush, full of gilt and velvet and crystal chandeliers, slightly frayed. It was constructed over a century ago by a figurehead Khedive of Egypt. A few minutes before Begin's arrival, the flags are hoisted. The cavalry guard of honor has been in position for hours, flanking the main entrance. The security men have been waiting, too. They are becoming friendlier all the time.

"They are good," says an Israeli agent, admiringly. "Their methods are different from ours. But they are good." This afternoon an American reporter tried to interview a peasant in a flowing galabia who was reading a newspaper outside Koubeh Palace. Behind the newspaper, he says, he noticed an Israeli-made machine gun.

Because of the heat—few rooms in Cairo are air-conditioned—the round tables have been set up on the great lawn. The air is heavy with the scent of flowers and perfume. The ladies of the Egyptian political and military elite are elegant in long brocade and silk dresses. The fare, as so often on such occasions, is no more memorable than the speeches. Sadat speaks very briefly, three sentences in all.

"Let us raise our cups of precious Nile water," he concludes, lifting a glass of French Évian, "to Mr. and Mrs. Menahem Begin."

Begin gives a longer speech. This is the first time since his arrival in Cairo that he is meeting Sadat. Very little love seems to be lost between them. Undoubtedly both still suspect each other's veracity, and both are probably right. Begin does no wonders before Pharaoh in his speech—this much is clear—God has put none in his hands. But Sadat again says, "There will be no more wars, only efforts to achieve prosperity . . . and peace." And Begin recounts how, a few days ago, "I saw from afar a young Egyptian man in a wheelchair. I will never forget him. In our land, too, many young men sit in wheelchairs. I can never forget them." The man who once said, "I do battle, therefore I am" suddenly looks very tired and vulnerable. He is almost transparently pale.

Later, the Egyptian ministers and generals and their Israeli guests linger under the strings of colored lights in friendly, even animated, conversation. They compare anecdotes from this or that war—there have been so many—and comment on this or that fine point in the remarks of Begin or Sadat. An orchestra is playing behind the rose bushes. For a moment the brilliantly illuminated lawns of Koubeh Palace resemble Anna Pavlova Scherer's drawing room in Tolstoy's *War and Peace,* where, to the sound of clinking glasses, the guests encapsule the human tragedy in smiles and civilized bon mots.

"*Eh bien, mon prince* . . . tell me how you are . . . *chère amie,* set my mind at rest."

III

THE SHERATON HOTEL, where I am now staying, is in the heart of Cairo. It faces the Nile island of Gezira with its palm trees and lawns. I moved here a few days ago from the prison-camp atmosphere of al-Salaam, on the far outskirts of the city. Begin and his official party of attendant lords, journalists, and security men have gone home. I seem to be the only former enemy left in Cairo. This is not entirely true—another man, a television reporter, has been allowed to remain behind. He is staying in another hotel on the other side of the river. Still, it is an odd feeling.

Early each morning I wake to the sound of car horns and screeching tires. The glass doors in my room cannot keep out the heavy traffic noise below. It begins soon after five. I get up and open the thick curtain. I am wide awake and do not feel tired. Bliss is it in this dawn to be alive? My friend Yoram Kaniuk, the Israeli novelist, always says that only the very young or the very old are optimistic. He and I are at the awkward age of fifty. I have been in Cairo for about a week. The tension of being here and the constant stimulation of mind and nerves are still great. After four or five hours of sleep each night, I awaken with a start. The tension expresses itself in other ways, too. I find myself all too often twisting my hands, and have become a chain smoker.

I open the glass door and step outside to a little terrace. Even at an early hour long lines of traffic are jamming the roads below. The wide bridges over the Nile, a little farther on, swarm with cars and pedestrians in dark masses. The view up and down the river is stupendous, with its motorboats and feluccas and colored sails, and wide vistas that many have called "majestic" and even a little like islands in the South Seas, with their tall palm trees and mountain ranges of ice-cream-colored hotels and luxury apartment houses. Below the hotel, up the river on the right, is the sleek former river palace of a pasha. It is now the home of the Soviet ambassador to Egypt. Next door is President Sadat's official residence. He has a dozen more, in all the major cities and resorts of Lower and Upper Egypt. Sadat's Cairo residence is a three-storied villa, whitewashed, with dark wooden shutters, elegant in a subdued way, a Provence country house transplanted to the Nile a long time ago by a rich businessman and taken over by the state.

I look down on the President's roof from my terrace. The house once had a private embankment, at the foot of a large veranda facing the river. This has been cut away to make a public promenade. Yet the promenade is blocked by guards who urge the gazing bypasser to move along. In the other direction I see the great edifice of the former Arab Socialist Union, the party of Nasser, which had been the only political party in Egypt until it was dismantled by Sadat. When Sadat "liberalized" the economy and permitted the reemergence of a private sector, the Arab Socialist Union building was turned over to German, American, and Egyptian finance and investment companies. The Gezira Sports Club is immediately on the left. Once the exclusive playground of the British—"wogs" had a hard time entering, except as barmen—it is now one of the pleasure haunts of the New Class.

Next to the club I see the so-called Cairo Tower of Gezira, with the inevitable revolving restaurant on its top. There the diner is able to observe the pyramids on his right during the hors d'oeuvre, and on his left during the goulash with noodles. (The noodles resemble the tower's frilled façade.) The tower is said to have been built with CIA funds. Mohammed Heykal, in his book on Nasser, *The Cairo Documents,* says that Nasser deliberately insisted on this frivolous design as "an insult to the CIA," which had meant the money as a personal bribe to Nasser.

Immediately below my terrace flows the Nile. Down at a little promontory in the river they show you the place where they say Moses mewled in the bullrushes and Pharaoh's daughter pulled the crying baby up to the bank—the tourist guides know the phrases by heart. The poor still come to wash themselves and their babies and their linen in the river. The river at this point is wide and gray. Mussa Sabry, the editor of *Al Akhbar,* says Nile water is of a special quality. It feeds the mind, he says, and soothes the heart. Whoever has tasted of it will sooner or later return to Cairo. At the hotel we are served only *aqua minerale* in large plastic bottles imported from Italy. The butter on my breakfast tray is French; the grapefruit juice comes from an American can. The croissants are Egyptian, fresh and delicious.

Across the river, behind the Potemkin façade of bright hotels, the city is blanketed in a mist of soot and dust. It is as though a modern Moses, or Aaron, had taken "handfuls of ashes of the furnace" and sprinkled them toward the heaven and it became "small dust in all the land of Egypt . . . breaking forth with blains upon man, and upon beast." It is not the houses or rooftops that I see in that short distance, though they are visible in the soot, but rather the dark outline of another planet. It is so different from the immediate lush surroundings of my hotel. When one ventures close, to view it in detail, it leaves one confused, startled, outraged, desperate, furious, and alarmed. The terrible features of this vast area of Cairo have already been described by so many writers that it is by no means unknown territory to an informed visitor.

In these wretched hovels, without sewers or water, in dark warrens below and above ground, live an estimated three million people. Looking upon it with one's own eyes is different from reading about it in other people's books. A little upstream, at the foot of the hills of Al Muqattam, where the long, dead fingers of the desert extend into a populated area of shacks and hives and open refuse, an additional hundred thousand human beings huddle together in the cavities of the old Mameluke cemetery, within and between the tombs, in the remains of mosques, tin huts, barracks, and tents. Who can satisfy the explosion of expectation for a better life set off, there and elsewhere, by this sudden peace? And how? The ubiquitous glow is evident in many conversations. "Now there will be new housing, new jobs, better pay." Mussa Sabry insists that this is not so serious a problem as might appear. At the base, he says, Egypt is a very stable society, pyramid-shaped throughout millennia. The Egyptian is simple, warmhearted, well-mannered, disciplined, kind to his fellows, loyal to the government. One Egyptian pound ($1.45) daily provides a fair amount to an Egyptian family in the villages, he says. Food is heavily subsidized by the government. Beans are a staple and relatively cheap; potatoes are eight cents a kilo, rice fifteen. A small pita bread costs less than a penny. The last time the government tried to reduce subsidies—it will have little choice but to try again in the future—riots broke out. Almost a hundred lay dead in the streets at the end of the day.

Yussef Hattam, whom I met at a dinner party the other day, is a young doctoral candidate and social worker in a Cairo suburb. He says that Sadat's liberalization of the economy has only made the rich richer. The poor are as poor as before, perhaps worse off. The ulemas—Moslem priests—are the only social group that has not lost its credibility, that is not considered corrupt, says Hattam. I told Sabry what Hattam had said. Sabry shook his head. Yes, the ulemas enjoy great moral standing. Fortunately, says Sabry, they are paid by the government and are loyal to the state. It's always been like that in Egypt. The priests have always been the clerks of the Pharaohs. They do not compare to the mullahs in Iran, who are anarchists at heart and opposed to all government, says Sabry.

THE TELEPHONE RINGS in my room. I come in from the terrace and go to answer it.

"Good morning," says a cheerful voice. "I am Colonel Nabil. Egyptian State Security."

What?

"I am waiting for you down in the lobby."

Is there something in particular?

"No, just whenever you'd care to come down."

The truth is that I have been expecting this visit for some time. I consider how to handle it as I ride down in the elevator. The Colonel's full name is Nabil Abdel Salaam Yussef. He is a tall, exceptionally good-looking young man. He wears a smart Italian-type leather jacket. We settle at a little table in the coffee shop. Rather awkwardly he breaks the news. He is assigned to me as a companion. He does not say bodyguard. He will accompany me wherever I care to go, in Cairo, in the Delta, anywhere in Egypt.

Must you?

"I am sorry," he says with an embarrassed smile, "it is for your own security."

But I feel perfectly secure.

"I know, but I am afraid it is necessary."

Why? Everyone I meet is so friendly.

"Of course they are," he says; "we are an unjustly maligned people. It's not the Egyptians I should worry about, although there could always be some lunatic. I worry about the Libyans and the Palestinians. There are many thousands in Egypt. We would not wish anything unfortunate to happen to you. So you see . . ."

He reassures me by adding that he knows the best restaurants in town. "This here"—he swings his arm—"is just tourist trash." In a holster, under his jacket, I notice he is carrying a gun.

TAHSIN BASHIR OF THE Foreign Ministry comes for lunch. A refined man of the old school, considerable charm and intellect —diplomat, scholar, litterateur. His keen mind ranges with equal facility over problems of politics and of art on three continents. He is at home in Egypt and in the United States, where he went to school and served in a diplomatic post.

We shake hands in the hotel entrance and size up each other with our eyes. A first meeting of this kind in Cairo, I find, often begins like this, in a mutual, rather hesitant probing with the nervous ancility over problems of politics and of art on three continents. He is a gentle-looking man of small stature, in his mid-fifties, boyish, graceful, with a free and easy manner. The eyes are bright, with a diffident and at the same time observant and natural expression. He smiles, a bit wistfully, I think. Peace with Israel is a cause, I know, that has been close to his heart for years. I have read interviews with him in which he spoke very impressively of the need for a "historical compromise." His association with this theme, as well as his outspokenness, have brought him into occasional difficulties.

He is the former husband of Sana Hassan, a young Egyptian woman with whom I collaborated on a book* a few years ago. Ms. Hassan and I happened to be in America during the 1973 war and began that book before the guns had fallen silent. It was written in the form of a dialogue, and was, I think, the first time such a collaboration between an Egyptian and an Israeli had taken place. It took no great daring on my part but was an act of great personal courage for Sana, an Egyptian citizen, still Bashir's wife at that time. Bashir was no less than President Sadat's official spokesman. In the book, Sana firmly, unequivocally advocated peace—on moral grounds, not merely for pragmatic reasons of mutual survival. She was, I believe, the first Arab intellectual who publicly recognized the Jews' moral right to a sovereign state in one part of old Palestine. For this she was terribly, and meanly, maligned in the Arab and Egyptian press. Her situation grew more perilous when she visited Israel a short time later—the first Egyptian to do so in many years.

With this in the background—not much, but more than I have in common with any other Egyptian—Bashir and I settle at a round table by the window in a hotel restaurant. The Nile flows by outside, green and gray. We study the large menu. The fresh oysters are flown in daily from Paris. An Egyptian family might support itself for two or three weeks on the price of six, I reflect; but this is not the moment to say anything of the sort. We order kebabs.

Bashir's association with Sana (they have since been divorced) did not enhance his career in the government service. He felt at the time that she had gone too far, too soon, too publicly, yet he understood and sympathized with the purity of her motive and respected her right to act upon her beliefs. This, coupled with his own unabashed frankness vis-à-vis his superiors—people in Cairo call it his "Americanized straightforwardness"—led to his removal from his

* *Between Enemies: A Compassionate Dialogue Between an Israeli and an Arab* (New York: Random House, 1974).

post as spokesman for the President. He is currently ambassador to the defunct Arab League; a more thankless job for an Egyptian diplomat right now cannot easily be imagined.

And yet I detect no bitterness in him, no regret. I am immensely relieved, for, as Sana's collaborator, I admit I could not help feeling a little guilty in his presence.

"Finally, we have peace," he says. "Thank God. This peace is like a little baby that has just been born. It still cannot walk. It's still ugly. It cannot talk. It causes lots of problems all the time. But like a good Jewish mother, we all ought to say, 'It's the only baby we have, our very own.'

"But make no mistake," he continues. "You must not misinterpret the warm and friendly welcome you are no doubt receiving here." Egyptians are good-natured people. They are patient, tolerant, well-mannered. Tactful. Life-loving. And with an earthy sense of humor. But the man in the street still believes the establishment of the State of Israel was a moral injustice, since it came at the expense of the Palestinian people. And yet the man in the street wants peace. He wants it very much. If a decent solution can be found to the Palestinians' desire for self-determination, the average Egyptian is ready to forget the past. He will live with Israel and with the Israelis— perhaps even cooperate with them in many fields. "That is the historical compromise I have talked about. It cannot be between Egypt and Israel only. It must involve the Palestinians.

"Don't make a mistake," he repeats. "Many people here are undoubtedly telling you they are Egyptians, not Arabs. This means that they have made peace with themselves, not with you. They are sorting out their identity. This is important, but has little to do with what we are talking about. The peace treaty that was just signed does not depend on Egypt's finding itself."

On what does it depend, then?

"On curing the wounds. We all of us feel damaged, maligned, paranoic. We are all sick. It is very hard to make peace between sick peoples."

Even *peace* has become a sick word, I say; it has been run into the ground for too long by too many. In Israel we talk about peace as a way to feel, to behave. The Egyptians, I tell Bashir, speak of it mostly in terms of international law, as a cessation of war.

Bashir thinks that this is so because of the unresolved Palestinian tragedy. "You said you took the land—you took a piece of bread because you were hungry. That convinces me, yes. But what about the others—the Palestinians are also hungry." Bashir knows a great deal about us. He seems to have read everything he could about Israel and Zionism. His remarks are punctuated with quotes from Achad Ha-am, Chaim Weizmann, and of course Martin Buber, Kalwarisky, and the rest of the Zionist moderates who through the years had racked their brains to find a means of compromise—in vain. They never found any responsible Arabs or Palestinians ready to talk with them, and so Buber and Kalwarisky ended their lives talking mostly to each other. Bashir knows this very well. True, he says, in the past there had never been any Palestinians ready to share their compromises. But now there were, even among some of the leading activists of the PLO.

Bashir also knows that the Israelis will not suddenly say *mea culpa,* nor does he think they should. By the same token, they cannot expect the Palestinians suddenly to recognize the Israelis' moral right to Palestine. It is enough if each side only accepts the other with civility and respect. Even Egypt did not make peace because it granted Israel a moral case, but rather because Sadat understood that there was no solution to the conflict by force. Neither the Israeli Army—even if it has an atom bomb—nor the PLO revolutionaries are capable of resolving it. Peaceful coexistence is the only alternative. Let us therefore stop enumerating the rights and wrongs, says Bashir.

We must try a new experience, he says. Let us begin a process in which the common experience of peace will conquer past feelings of injustice. Bashir is an existentialist, not a moral preacher. He considers Israel's security concerns on the West Bank as legitimate. They must be met. But the Palestinians on the West Bank and in the Gaza Strip have a parallel right for self-determination. It is at least as inalienable as that of the Israelis. Palestinians mustn't be second-class citizens in a Jewish state. They should determine their own institutions and decide themselves for or against federation with Jordan, with Israel or Syria, or with Egypt or even the United States, "and live in peace with you. Yes, you have a right to insist on that.

"But the Palestinians also have certain rights which you must not continue to ignore." In the end the Palestinians will reconcile themselves to Israel's existence, Bashir thinks, if Israel doesn't insist on having the whole cake. The Palestinians will say, "Okay, the West Bank is not all of Palestine, but it is better than nothing." Some Israelis will bewail their historic Eretz Israel, but most, Bashir says, know that the ancient frontiers of Israel have always been abstract, indeterminate, divine promises of poetic, symbolic nature.

It all seems eminently reasonable to me, I say. But does it seem so to the Palestinians? Bashir thinks it eventually will. But since they are the aggrieved party, he says, so Israel must take the first step. They are the new Jews, he says, clamoring for a national home. . . . Bashir has a highly developed sense of irony. It has caused him some difficulty in his past career as a senior civil servant. Irony is an old-fashioned quality, mature, perhaps elitist. Revolutionaries detest it, children don't understand it; it is more commonly found among men than among women, perhaps because it runs counter to the creative process.

THE NILE IN LATE afternoon. I lean over the bridge that spans the river from the island of Gezira to the East Bank. The pyramids are on the West. The ancient Egyptians lived on the east side and buried their dead on the west, in the direction of the setting sun. The land of the living and the land of the dead were neatly separated by the water. At the *son et lumière* spectacle near the Sphinx last night, the BBC voice in my earphone solemnly intoned, "In the course of time, all human achievements crumble and fall, but the spirit that conceived these monuments cannot perish."

At this hour of the day a weird pink and green light is reflected in the water. Staring at it, I lose myself. Bashir says that some claim the Nile had a voice. What does it communicate? Bashir says, "Rhythm." I have heard similar remarks from other Egyptians, some in jest, some in all seriousness. I am intrigued by the great variety of comments about the river. The Nile is said to have a "bride." A miraculous drop of water is said to fall into the river from the sky each year, on the night of June 17, called Leylet en Nukta, Night of the Drop. Yussef Hattam, the social worker, says he has heard a farmer say that the river affects the moon and the stars in their courses. Everything in Egypt, of course, began with the Nile ("Egypt is the gift of, etc.") and many a discussion of modern Egypt and its culture begins and ends with the Nile.

The exact location of the source of the Nile exercised the imagination of past ages; it was said to spring forth from the stone of wisdom itself. Because of the Nile, Egypt was the promised land of all geopolitical theories, centuries before the German school of Karl Haushofer made a fetish of them. The Egyptians call the river Bahr el Nil, the Sea of the Nile. I find this appellation hauntingly beautiful. Its origin may be Herodotus: "When the Nile floods the land, all of Egypt turns into a kind of sea. Only the cities remain above water like the Aegean islands. At such times ships no longer keep the course of the riverbed but sail right across the plain."

The great floods—at once life-giving and destructive—are a thing of the past. The High Dam at Aswan, built by Nasser in the 1960s, has put an end to them. The dam permits the rational use of water, produces great amounts of electric power, and has been called a modern pyramid. It seems odd that so life-enriching an enterprise should be called a tomb.

Behind the dam is the new artificial Lake Nasser, 311 miles long, 6 to 37 miles wide. A single wall holds back a gigantic mass of water. Some 12 billion tons of liquid are poised, as it were, over the heads of 40 million people. Bashir spoke of bombs at lunch: neutron bombs in Israel, and relatively simple nuclear devices that might reach the hands of terrorists and guerrillas in the course of the next few years. The sun is low over the rooftops. Its disk is jaundiced yellow, as though it had rolled in the dust. I recently read a learned paper in which a Haifa professor is speculating about the vulnerability of the High Dam at Aswan. If it burst, he writes, the consequences would be apocalyptic. Lake Nasser would come crashing down on Egypt with such thrust and speed that nothing would remain. When it reached Cairo—hundreds of miles away—the tidal wave could be fifty feet high and move at a speed of over one hundred miles per hour.

MRS. AMINA ES-SAID lights one cigarette from another. Excessive smoking is a habit many Egyptians and Israelis share. Nowhere outside of Israel, except perhaps among the embittered intellectuals of Eastern Europe, have I seen so many people chain-smoking. Mrs. es-Said—we are in her office—says she smokes three packs of English-made Rothmans each day.

We joke about this for a while, two recalcitrant addicts anxious to reform but, because of our limitations, our life-styles and professions, incapable of doing so. Mrs. es-Said is the head of Dar al-Hilal, one of the biggest publishing firms in the Middle East, founded ninety years ago by the Zaidan brothers and now socialized. "Not nationalized," Mrs. es-Said says, rather sharply, "the right word is 'socialized.' We are not government-controlled."

In the one-party state under Nasser, Dar al-Hilal was owned by the Arab Socialist Union. Now 50 percent of the profits are distributed to the workers. The rest is reinvested in the company. The firm publishes eight mass-circulation weeklies and books of all kinds, 9 million copies a year. The majority are textbooks, and almost half of them are sold to other Arabic-speaking countries.

Like many Egyptian intellectuals, Mrs. es-Said is concerned over Egypt's sudden isolation within the Arab world because of the peace with Israel. She thinks that Begin's inflated, aggressive rhetoric is partly responsible for that isolation. Mrs. es-Said went to Washington with President Sadat for the peace-signing ceremony at the White House—she is a close friend of Mrs. Sadat. "I came home furious," she says. "Why did Begin have to spoil the great occasion by making such strident references to his paratroopers and their so-called liberation of Jerusalem?" Other Israeli public figures don't annoy her so much. "They say the same things, but they say them sweetly. They do it without insults. They are not abrasive. They don't bring us trouble with the Arab states every time they open their mouths. We can listen to them and even respect them as we disagree. They give us hope that if we continue to negotiate, we can find a compromise."

Don't you invest rhetoric with too much meaning? I wonder, not for the first time since I am in Cairo. "Rhetoric is important," insists Mrs. es-Said. Again, this is not the first time I hear this view.

Don't you overestimate the importance of form, as against content? I ask. "No, style and form are very important."

More important than deeds? "You can't separate the two. Not at this stage, when we are trying to make peace without cutting ourselves off completely from the Arab states."

"Style and form and gestures are everything in the Near East," said an English diplomat whom I met at a party last night. He said this in a nasal, slightly condescending tone. I said that T. E. Lawrence thought the Arabs were rather responsive to ideas: "Arabs could be swung on an idea as on a cord," he wrote in *The Seven Pillars of Wisdom.*

The English diplomat looked annoyed. "Ideas?" he said. "Rubbish! What ideas? There are no ideas here. Form is everything in this part of the world. You'll have to learn that, now that you are becoming, so to speak, part of it. . . ."

Should I report that tedious conversation to Mrs. es-Said? No, I cannot. Mrs. es-Said twists a new cigarette into a long silver holder. She wears her hair short and straight. Two thousand employees work for her at Dar al-Hilal, in a land and society where males are enjoined in the Koran: "Your wives are your fields. Go in, therefore, to your field as ye will." She looks back with relish on the great changes in the position of Egyptian women that have occurred in her own lifetime. In the 1930s she was one of the first five women who forced their way into Cairo University. When she first began working for a newspaper she had to write under a male pseudonym.

In the old days, she had many friends from the Jewish community of Cairo, which has since dispersed. In Jewish families girls were less likely to be treated like perfumed chattels. She would like those friendly relationships to come back—together with the Cairo Jews. "They didn't have to migrate," she says. "It is unfortunate that they did."

In passing I learn that you don't have to be Israeli to have a body-guard supplied by State Security. Amina es-Said also has guards, one at the office and one at home, around the clock. She has been with President Sadat to Jerusalem. Every editor who joined Sadat on his peace mission to Jerusalem must have a bodyguard, she says. "It's not pleasant," says Mrs. es-Said, "but you can never tell." Yussef Sabei, editor in chief of *Al Ahram,* was assassinated in Cyprus last year by Palestinian terrorists. They vowed to kill everybody who had gone on that trip, including the President himself.

YUSSEF IDRIS, the novelist, was a leftist in the early 1950s. In 1954 he called Nasser a tyrant. He was imprisoned, beaten, and locked away in a desert concentration camp for two years. Later, when the communists and Nasser made up, and the Soviet Union became Egypt's main provider, Idris made his peace with Nasser, but in his writing he never followed the mode. Just as he never wrote in the genre of socialist realism at the time he was pro-communist, so he did not adopt the style of patriotic "Arab socialism" that was expected of writers in the days of Nasser, in return for considerable creature comforts. Until a few years ago he was a practicing physician. When I first call on Idris in his office at *Al Ahram,* a visiting Japanese professor of literature is sitting with him. Idris is talking about writers and intellectuals in government. "Let us put them in power," he says grandly. "It is high time. In Egypt as well as in Israel."

"But are they tough enough?" wonders the visiting professor.

"Listen to me," snaps Idris. "I spent two years in a concentration camp, until 1956. I tell you, the weakest of all were former army officers and police. They broke under the first blows."

I am fascinated by Idris. Many of his short stories have been translated into Hebrew. They are marked by a haunting, Kafkaesque quality and existential dread that one so often finds in Czech or Polish literature of the post-Stalinist era. His protagonists wallow in deep depression; the sky is often dark or cloudy, or it is raining. Nightmare plots are laid out in seedy police stations or cafés, where crimes are committed that no one understands, and the innocent an-

swer charges and are found guilty. Some of his stories are thinly
veiled attacks on the politicians who involved Egypt in destructive
wars. Many of his protagonists seem to cry out for an end to the vicious circle of war and poverty.

A friend of mine who met Idris at a conference at Princeton in
1976 told me that during a discussion Idris had jumped up and said,
"I have been listening to fine talk for days, trying to tune in and
enjoy the idyllic beauty of these lawns and parks. It's a piece of
Eden—but we come from hell! A hell of hunger, disease, and war!
How can I think like you?"

Elsewhere he has written that he wished "all of Egypt's problems
were as simple as the crossing of the Suez Canal in 1973 . . . you
could put your finger on that. But the things from which we really
suffer we can't even define."

He is the author of controversial, anti-Nasser, anti-war short stories and plays. Some of them were at first forbidden by the censors.
In a superb little story, "The Operation" (1971), a renowned surgeon, Professor Adham (a portrait of Nasser), performs a fateful
"operation." (In Arabic, as in English, the same word serves for the
surgical and the military kind.) A vain and shallow man, anxious to
display his virtuosity, the Professor does not first check whether an
operation is necessary, and the patient dies. There follows the bitter
disenchantment of a young doctor, Abdul Rouf, who had considered
the Professor his leader and supreme guide.

Idris's physical appearance is striking. He looks the way writers
should but rarely do. At fifty-two, he is handsome, tall, with a head
of gray curls over a long, furrowed face. He is impatient with nonsense, you can tell by the thin lines of weariness around the bright
blue eyes. He speaks admiringly of an Israeli scholar, Sasson
Somekh of Tel Aviv University, who has translated some of his
work into Hebrew and published a critique of him. "Somekh is very
good. He understands my work better than any Arab critic does."

It is perhaps that enemies understand one another better than,
say, friends? Idris laughs: that might well be. "But truly, I never
looked on any Israeli as an enemy," he says. He says that in the

early 1970s he wrote a short story in which he foresaw events as in a dream: the 1973 war, the return of Egyptian self-confidence and dignity, Sadat's dramatic mission to Jerusalem, and the peace, as well as the fury unleashed by that peace among the other Arabs. The name of the story was "Innocence." I promise Idris that I will read it.

"In Arabic?"

No, I am loath to admit, in the Hebrew translation.

"There you are," he cries. "That's the problem! We don't speak each other's language." The Japanese professor nods approvingly. The lines of his mouth, finely drawn, are pressed together in a thin smile; *his* Arabic is much better than mine. In Israel it is mostly specialist "Arabists" who read Egyptian literature in the original. In Egypt, too, only the "professionals" read Hebrew literature. (The Japanese professor is also a professional Arabist, but then Japan is thousands of miles away from here.)

Idris says, "We don't read one another's books. This is very unfortunate. We must make up for that as quickly as we can. And don't believe for a minute those cries of 'Peace! Peace!' you hear in the streets of Cairo. With equal ease they will scream 'War! War!' I know. I've heard them."

Idris is not happy with the peace treaty. What has it achieved? Not enough, says Idris. For the moment, all it has accomplished is the "Israelization of Egypt."

What's that?

"Very simple. Instead of one beleaguered ghetto in the Middle East, we now have two, Israel *and* Egypt." Even though he is very anxious to meet Professor Somekh, Idris will not travel in the near future to Israel.

"No," he says, "I can't go. Not until you bring justice to the Palestinian people."

Well, yes, I say, I agree the Palestinians deserve a fair deal. But, in the meantime, Sadat went to Israel, didn't he?

"Of course," says Idris. "Sadat doesn't have to ask anybody. He is a dictator. But I am a writer. Don't you see? A writer stands for reelection every day of the year, I can't go to Israel just like that. *I must be able to take my readers with me.* And they won't go as long as you rule over a million Palestinians against their will."

I HAVE SINCE READ "Innocence," the short story Idris spoke about. Dark and suggestive as a mythic dream, its theme is a curious hallucination, written in the first person. There is always a danger in reading too much politics or psychology into a surrealist, many-layered work of art. Yet I was invited to do so by the author himself, who said it was a premonition of peace. In his politics prior to 1972, Idris had been rather militantly but never viciously anti-Israel. In this story, the overwhelming impression is a twisted love-hate relationship with the "enemy," who appears as a "one-eyed general," clearly Moshe Dayan.

The story is rich with Jungian archetypes. The "one-eyed general" is standing in a boat, very near to shore, and smiling. The boat rocks in the water, up and down; it is the rise and fall, says the narrator, of a "tremendous temptation." The general looks flabbier, fatter, less ominous than in his pictures in the newspapers. The narrator hardly sees the "black stain" on his eye because of the "smiling satisfaction" on his face. The narrator sees "no claws, no spearheads," nor any "treacherous daggers," in that face; he sees only the smile. He pays no attention to the "stain."

". . . The general's smile, the boat, the invitation . . . the invitation stands. It continues, is renewed, a light caressing wind." The general laughs. His teeth seem worn with age, "but there are no incisors, no incisors."

Again, "the smile, the boat, the invitation." As the general's boat draws nearer, the narrator jumps into it, "eagerly, with passion." He reminds me of Catullus: "I hate and love, maybe you wonder how that can be. I know not, but feel it happening, *and I am in torment.*"

"The lashes of his one eye winked a light greeting," writes Idris. The expression on the general's face is that of a man unwilling "to embarrass me. He seems aware that I will not shake his hand. I just want to look at him, that's all." Why shouldn't one look? There is no "abomination" in that; "my heart is pure as white woven linen."

The narrator cannot shake that hand, the hand of "snakes and scorpions." The rays of the sun are diffuse. "They are coming in from every direction, but the feeling of twilight remains." The general looks satisfied. The narrator wonders whether he is happy or indifferent "that I've finally arrived." The narrator feels as though he were "on the other side of the moon."

There follows a series of confused, violent happenings on the shore. A woman's face appears in the dark. It may even be that of the general. The narrator views it all through his "back eyes." The woman is "my type," he writes, her hair is soft and flowing, her lips not innocent. "The eyes large, eager, radiant . . . I know for certain that if my hand only so much as touches hers, I shall never be able to retrieve it." The woman speaks. She speaks reason. "Her mind blinds my eye, swallows me, floods me with images of life."

The mind of the narrator, conversely, is the "thread of a cobweb" torn by the particles of a thousand words. The general reappears. "I am afraid to touch, deadly afraid." The end of the general's walking stick emits "a radiation that subdues everything. . . . I groan. No, I did not touch, I was not defiled. I was just looking, that's all. I am still pure as white woven linen."

Crowds have lined the shore. There is the unexpected appearance of the narrator's "own son," barefoot, wearing a nightgown, with wild unruly hair. The boat touches the wooden jetty. The narrator is paralyzed by the look in his son's eyes. He cannot come ashore. At first he thinks that the gun in the boy's hand is a toy. It points directly at the narrator's heart. The boy's face is that of a "judge," the eyes are those of a "hangman." His mouth intones the verdict.

The narrator screams, "No! I didn't touch! Son, I touched nothing, you maniac. . . . The muttering stopped. The lips are pressed together. . . . The bullet in my shoulder . . . the second crushes my chest. I still hear its thunder. The third I do not hear at all."

The complexities implicit in this story are rarely, if ever, present in Israeli fiction. Instead one finds a towering sense of guilt toward the Arab opponents and former inhabitants of the area that is now Israel. Guilt has been one of the main features of Israeli letters over the past twenty years. It contrasts sharply with Israel's official surface image of self-righteousness. I think of Hannah, the ecstatic protagonist of Amos Oz's novel *My Michael*. Hannah achieves a Dionysian kind of bliss in the arms of Halil and Aziz, Palestinian twins, terrorists and bomb throwers. The twins, in Oz's novel, seem part of the "natural," i.e., Arab, environment. A. B. Yehoshua's allegorical novella *Facing the Forest* is the account of a "subversive" crime, the delirious destruction of a national forest planted on the ruins of a Palestinian village by its watchman, a torn intellectual and student of the Crusades. In "Innocence" by Idris the nightmarish turbulence of Oz or Yehoshua meets something of a parallel.

ON THE RADIO I happen to tune in to the Voice of Peace, broadcasting from "somewhere in the Mediterranean." The fare is jazz interspersed by commercials. The Voice of Peace is a pirate station broadcasting from a ship floating a few miles beyond Israeli territorial waters. It is run on a nonprofit basis by a foundation and broadcasts a mélange of music and peace slogans in Hebrew, English, and Arabic. An old friend of mine, Abie Nathan, has been floating the ship on a shoestring for several years, hoping, as he puts it, to generate "mutual understanding and compassion." Abie Nathan's career as a peacemaker began flamboyantly in 1966 when he mortgaged his popular café-restaurant in Tel Aviv and bought the *Shalom I*, a monoplane which he flew to Egypt on a one-man peace mission. He was turned back by the Egyptians and later prosecuted by the Israelis for taking off without clearance.

There is a lot of static. The sound is weak, barely audible in my hotel room on the twelfth floor. But it is nice to hear Abie's voice. I'm told that along the coast, in Alexandria and Port Said, the reception is nearly perfect. Hattam, the young social worker, says that during the summer he and his friends in Alexandria often listen in. They like the music. Abie Nathan has succeeded, says the cynical Hattam, in bringing young Egyptians and young Israelis closer to American jazz.

YUSSEF HATTAM is embittered by a chance encounter he had with some rough Israeli students in Greece last year. Nor does he like what he reads about Israel in English and French newspapers. He challenges me to a discussion.

"Israelis are terribly arrogant vis-à-vis Arabs," he says. Even Israeli doves, he says, always tell us what to do, rather than do something themselves about the Palestinians.

Israelis are arrogant, I tell Hattam, I admit that. But their arrogance is directed not toward Arabs in particular but toward every non-Israeli. They have been conditioned to be tough and rough by their experience. Many of them have lived through horrors.

"Yes, yes," glowers Hattam, "it's a backlash. To the Nazis."

No, it is not that.

"Yes. Israelis have assumed a Nazi mentality. They rely on force. Hitler also relied only on force."

No, I say, and we argue back and forth with some vehemence. I ask him not to generalize and to remember that persecution has never been a school for tolerance. Egyptian hostility and anti-Semitic war propaganda shared in the formation of current Israeli attitudes. I do not convince Hattam, and come away with forebodings. When the borders open to mass tourism, the first encounters will settle the stereotypes on both sides for a long time to come. Some Egyptian intellectuals, on the other hand, have an all too rosy image of Israel as a land of gentle Freuds and Einsteins, playing chess with one another in corner cafés. I am afraid they will have a rude awakening.

Others remember only the few rich Jewish businessmen who always left large tips, or the few highly cultivated Jews who played a certain role in Egyptian society before the wars, rather than the great mass of poor Cairo Jews who also had to flee the country after 1952. They mention a Madame Kitawy, who was lady-in-waiting to the Queen; a Jewish pasha who was the royal chamberlain; or another who was a minister of finance. I foresee problems when they discover we are just a lower-middle-class people.

And yet one of the pleasures of talking to Egyptians is that so far no one—including Hattam—has told me that *because* we are Jews we must set the world a moral example. In Europe one is still told this all the time; once I even heard it from a German who served as a judge under the Nazis.

MORE EXISTENTIAL PHILOSOPHIZING from D.Z., a poet. We sit on little chairs at Al Fishawy, a popular bohemian café wedged into a narrow passageway in the old Cairo bazaar. In the huge wall mirrors every image is thrown back and forth, as in a tedious argument, and multiplies to infinity. We sip black tea, and talk. D.Z. is a passionate talker.

"We don't grant you any moral motivation and you don't grant us any," says D.Z. "Begin even said Egypt never had any *reason* fighting you! In other words, not only were we beaten in battle, not only did we lose a hundred thousand lives and ruin our economy, but according to Begin, we were also stupid. We did all this for no reason at all!"

That's not what he meant, I say defensively, although it is true, these were the words Begin had used. There is little empathy for *them* in most of us. With our lack of empathy, how can we expect sympathy from Egyptians for our own moral motivation? How will we ever convince them that Israel was created not just because there was a dire need, also because it was just? From D.Z. I gather that there is only one new development in the attitude of Egyptians: the outrage over the establishment of Israel has begun to wane. Perhaps they are beginning to forget it; perhaps it is only drowned temporarily in a sea of blood.

What kind of encounter, then, is possible between Israelis and Egyptians at this stage? The only kind, D.Z. says, is existential. The one quality we share at this moment, as humans, is what Albert Camus called "solidarity against death." We agree on an anti-suicide pact, says D.Z.

D.Z. no longer sees us as Macbeths, but as Meursaults, the existential protagonist of *The Stranger* by Camus. Like Meursault we have committed a crime—but what is the meaning of crime, says D.Z., in a world devoid of supreme values? There are only anti-heroes in this plot. In an immoral world there are no heroes, D.Z. says, but no fury either.

D.Z. lost an arm in one of the Egyptian-Israeli wars. With the other he is now writing an abstract novel, he says. No plot, he says. In Israel we love to find "moral" justifications for every claim we make; perhaps this stems from the arrogance Hattam complains about. From D.Z. and others I learn an important lesson. If we attempt at this stage to talk to Egyptians in moral terms we risk being considered hypocrites. We are always more or less in the dark about other people, and about ourselves. But it is among foreigners that we realize the extent of this ignorance.

D.Z. TELLS ME A STORY about the impossibilty of forgiveness. A wise ulema overheard a woman's prayer. She said, "Oh, please, God, do not let me die until you have forgiven me for my sins."

The ulema turned on her. "Wicked woman!" he cried. "You ask God for immortality, not for forgiveness." He meant, says D.Z., that God would never forgive her.

DR. LAILA ABOU-SAIF, well known in Egypt and abroad as a theater director and as a leading feminist, recalls the unpleasant hassle she had with the police during the late sixties. She had just returned to Egypt from the United States with a collection of long-playing records, among which was a rendering of Handel's *Israel in Egypt*. It was confiscated. Dr. Abou-Saif was sharply questioned by the police. After sundry protests, interventions, and explanations, a police agent was given the task of listening to the entire recording in order to ensure it included no single word of "Zionist propaganda."

It seems such difficulties are not yet over, as she had hoped they would be, after the signing of a peace treaty. In a little theater not far from Al Azhar Mosque, Dr. Abou-Saif has tried—and failed—to produce a play by the nineteenth-century Egyptian-Jewish playwright Jacques Zanua. Could it be that her failure stems from the government's hypersensitivity to the feelings of religious fundamentalists? Zanua, who died at the turn of the century, had been a well-known Egyptian nationalist, but because he was a Jew his plays were banned in Egypt after 1948.

At first Dr. Abou-Saif had no trouble; the rehearsals in the state-owned theater proceeded according to schedule. But then someone protested, and almost overnight Dr. Abou-Saif found herself without a theater, without actors, and without a budget. What happened? Is Zanua still banned in Egypt because he was born a Jew? Or because his play, in the spirit of secular nineteenth-century liberalism, ridicules the Islamic institution of polygamy? Or simply because of the proximity of the theater to the Mosque of Al Azhar? Is it Dr. Abou-Saif's highly controversial role as a militant feminist? She herself still does not know the real reason. A dangerous wave of religious radicalism is mounting among the masses, says Dr. Abou-Saif. She is herself a Copt—and it frightens her very much.

AN EVENING WITH Yussef Idris, charged with unexpected drama and awe. We had arranged to drive out to Husseiniya Mosque to see the thronged ceremonies held there in celebration of the annual feast of Hasan and Husein, two martyrs of early Islam. In view of what happened later, I still wonder why Idris agreed to come along in the first place.

Soon after 10 P.M. we reach the wide road leading up to the mosque. A friend of Idris's, Dr. Mohammed Shalaan, a professor of psychiatry at Al Azhar University, is at the wheel. The road is crowded thick with people. Many of them, it seems, have come in from the countryside for the occasion. We crawl slowly through the crowd, hardly moving. Suddenly Idris is seized by an attack of agoraphobia. In a panic, he exclaims, "Get me out of here! Get me out of here! I can't stand it!"

Shalaan stops the car. I am sitting next to Idris in the back and follow his outburst with awe. He is trembling. I cannot help feeling that this is one of those rare and frightening moments when a flash of lightning strikes in the dark; in its weird glow the contours of some terrible ambivalence come into view. The dense crowd streams by. "I can't stand it," Idris groans, still shaking; "get me out of here."

What would his biographers have made of such a scene had Tolstoy been struck with nausea as the throngs of muzhiks flocked through the gates of Optina-Pustyn Monastery? Idris, perhaps the greatest modern novelist in Egypt, writes of Egypt and the Egyptians with love. He is like a man who suffers from vertigo but is condemned to live on a high cliff.

Dr. Shalaan says soothingly, "Relax, please relax." He looks out at the crowd and adds, "They are believers."

"I hate their superstition!" cries Idris. "I hate their misery! Their ignorance! Take me out of here! I can't stand it!"

"I love them," says Shalaan in a muted voice.

"You love them because you are rich!" exclaims Idris. "You come from a feudal family. It is easy for you to love the poor. I come from the poor. I hate it. I hate it! Please, take me out of here."

With some difficulty, Shalaan turns a corner and speeds up the road to the naked desert hills of Al Muqattam, beyond the city. We get out of the car. Idris breathes deeply. There is nothing but silence and darkness in the void. In the distance the city lights glitter in the haze.

IV

LEAVING CAIRO IN THE morning—the ever-oppressive feeling of a huge, uncountable mass. It is still very early. The streets are teeming with people. Thousands are waiting at the bus stops. The traffic is slow and heavy and tangled at the main intersections. Everything moves along at a crawl. Street vendors offer for sale rolls and black tea in little glasses.

The main highway to Alexandria runs north along the broad corniche that was cut in Nasser's day through the slums alongside the Nile. Suburban trains, belching trails of smoke, roll slowly south, so crowded that dozens of passengers are riding on top. I watch the fearsome scene with trepidation. But Mr. Afifi says, "Don't worry. They are used to it."

Mr. Afifi is an official of the Ministry of Agriculture. We are heading north toward the Nile Delta, to visit some villages there. The Nile is a lizard-gray. Cargo boats are sailing by in both directions. Women are washing clothes in the turbid waters of an inlet. Mud huts alongside everywhere, and many new construction sites as well. "Apartment houses," says Mr. Afifi, "new factories." Much of the work is done by hand. The larger building pits are dotted with human figures, scenes by Brueghel—or Hieronymus Bosch—teeming, purposeful conglomerations of people, like ants crawling in the dust, doing today as did the ancient Hebrews, "hard labor, in clay and bricks."

After a drive of half an hour or so, through busy industrial suburbs and residential areas built in old clay or new stone, the landscape changes. It is a little less crowded at first; then comes the open country. The land is flat. The sooty gray tones of Cairo give way to colors: dark browns, pinks, and violets, and suddenly a green so rich and deep as to suggest a Central European countryside.

The Nile Valley, at the narrow southern tip of the Delta: a fertile, enormous hothouse, where the sun shines all the days of the year and where it hardly ever rains, but there is plenty of water, and plants grow in a rich luxuriance, amazing in its strange, fragrant plenitude. There are no seasons here. Instead there is perpetual toil. "The peasant is nailed to the land," says Mr. Afifi. "It is his cross."

The desert is still very near at this southern point, and dimly visible in the east. The valley is narrow. God promised Moses to take him out of Egypt and bring him to a good and a wide land. The emphasis must have been on *wide*. Canaan was undoubtedly more wide than good. I look amazed at this thin strip of civilization along the river Nile. It is even narrower than I imagined, more vulnerable, a mere thread. All life here seems to hang on it. In a pamphlet issued by the government I read that only 4 percent of the territory of Egypt is settled, or tilled. I try to visualize what this figure means. It means that the tilled area of Egypt is little more than one and one half times the area of Israel! This small area is supposed to support 40 million lives. So much for bookish figures. No book conveys as full a meaning of this shocking fact as the visual encounter with this narrow valley, in which men, women, and children over the centuries have scratched out bits and pieces of life with their fingernails. Beds of vegetables. Cotton fields. Orange plantations. Groves dense with mangoes and bananas. A fine blue morning mist hovers on the canals. And everywhere one looks in this most overpopulated countryside: people, men, women, and children, in the fields, walking alongside the road, or outside their little red mud houses.

It seems less a population explosion than a persistent, irreparable leakage. There is a scent in the air. Simonne Lacouture, in a beautiful little book on Egypt,* quotes an Egyptian who says, "Flowers without a fragrance we call European." I don't see any flowers. But the scent is there. At this time of the year the corn ripens. The melon fields are planted. The clover is trimmed. And in the great avian exodus of the spring the swallows and storks fly north in the sky, in dark revolving clusters.

We pass large fields of clover and wheat. To this region migrated the starving Hebrew nomads in search of food—"in the garden of God that is Egypt," as it is called in the Bible—and in the Koran. Here they came when there was "dearth . . . in all lands; but in all the land of Egypt there was bread." And other nomads came after them. One senses what the Arab conquerors must have felt in the seventh century when they entered the Delta from the desert. Green and gold pastures, rivulets, orchards—some so enchanting, the Arab general Amr is said to have refused to enter them in order not to anticipate the joys of paradise.

In this moist hothouse of warm and fertile soil surrounded by desert, the human race invented agriculture, architecture, science, geometry, art, monotheism. All one sees now is a great multitude of nimble dark humans. Their eyes are clouded by trachoma. Children, skinny to the bone, are raking, sowing, pruning, hoeing, digging ditches, while other beasts of burden, the fly-infested cows and buffalo, go round and round in endless circles, pumping water for the fields. The ravens that dart through the humid air look well fed.

The cattle that work the water wheels are a problem, explains Mr. Afifi. Because they go round and round all day, they produce little or no milk. But they are indispensable, he says. The water must be pumped up continually. The farmers are too poor to install machinery. I think of a story told of Stalin. He was lecturing the graduates of a Soviet military academy and quoted, with some approbation, a dispatch from a certain Red cavalry commander who had just lost seven troopers and their mounts: "Seven horses lost at ford." Why did he mention the lost horses, not the dead men?

* *Egypt,* trans. Veronica Hull and Phil Ableman (New York: Viking Press, 1963; London: Vista Books, 1963).

"Anyone can make a man," said Stalin, "but which of you boys can make a horse?"

EVERYTHING IS FLAT. The smallest hill, here or there, is in all probability a pharaonic or Roman mound. The land around it is like a table or, as Lady Duff-Gordon wrote in the nineteenth century, "a palimpsest in which the Bible is written over Herodotus, and the Koran over that." And over the Koran one sees the more recent addition, in large script, of President Nasser's *Philosophy of the Revolution*. High steel pylons, sprouting six or eight legs like Martians in the H. G. Wells novel, and strung with electric wires from the power stations of Aswan, stalk across the flats from horizon to horizon. Each bears a white placard in Arabic and English: "Danger —High Tension."

ENCHASS IS A VILLAGE in the district of Sharkieh. We are twenty-five miles northeast of Cairo. "Village" in this part of the world means a cluster of twenty to thirty thousand people—a decent-sized town elsewhere. Enchass appears to occupy relatively little land: land is so scarce here. The village is a dense hive of crude clay bricks, mud and straw. Until a few years ago, the fellah made his own bricks from Nile mud. Since the completion of the high dam at Aswan, little silt remains in the river, so the fellah must use other, more expensive materials. Before the Nile was dammed, some of the houses would wash away during the great flood. Enchass now nestles safely alongside a little canal. "Men, women, and children of Egypt. The miracle has been wrought. You have built the dam" (Nasser, 1965).

A few children are playing in the grass. Actually, they are tending the young cotton plants. The fruit of the small frail plant is well within reach of the hands of children, and in every corner of the fields children are at work. Machinery is used only for plowing. "Cotton," says Mr. Afifi as though quoting a well-known text, "is a gift made to Egypt by its children."

Cotton, wheat, rice, clover, corn, and vegetables are grown in rotation. Crop rotation, says Mr. Afifi, was introduced only after the land reforms of 1952 and 1960. Until then only wheat, cotton, and some vegetables were produced. The land reform, begun in 1952, is more or less completed now. Each farmer may hold only fifty acres. None of the peasants of Enchass had any land of their own before the reform. "The difference between a landless and a landed peasant is the difference between a two-footed animal and a man" (Colonel Mohammad Naguib, 1955). The land here was parceled out to landless farmers in plots of two to five acres. A farmer earns about forty dollars a month, says Mr. Afifi.

Mr. Afifi has a friend in this village, Abdul, who oversees the regional cooperative. We visit him in his new house, which is made of cement and prefabricated blocks. Abdul is a gaunt, round-faced man of about thirty-five, a veteran of the 1967 war. He shows me the boots in which he tramped through the sands of Sinai in 1967, for eight days, he says. The officers fled in trucks over the paved roads.

"I am not bitter at anybody," he says as we jump the ditches under the mango trees and taste the strawberries that are grown here for sale in Cairo. They are a little dry. At the far end of the field there are a few olive trees, as gnarled as the faces of the farmers who own them, and like them they produce a small, often bitter, fruit.

The fellah's wife pours black powdered tea into a small pan of boiling water. The men sit around a table, sipping the dark concoction. The black tea of Ceylon, introduced by the British in the last century, is expensive. China tea is cheaper, says Mr. Afifi. But, he adds sadly, all efforts to substitute China for Ceylon have failed. Simonne Lacouture writes in *Egypt* that the black tea "is the opium of the Egyptian people. The fellah, often ill and undernourished, is cheered by the drug of this strong beverage. A third of his income is spent on this counterfeit nourishment . . . [which is] the most durable triumph of English colonization in Egypt."

With a resignation similar to that which he applies to the drinking of Ceylon tea, Mr. Afifi speaks of the Aswan Dam and all its works. It has put an end to the floods, of course, and produces a great amount of electricity—much of it still unused—but at the same time the entire ecological balance has been upset. No one as yet has discovered how best to redress it. "In this country," says Afifi, "when you solve one problem, seven new ones crop up." If he could begin again from scratch he would build a different dam.

As for the wars, he says, "Everyone is fed up. *Tired.*" Hunger and weariness as a *social* quality distinguish men from beasts. But does fatigue spur? In the early days of the Russian revolution the Bolsheviks refrained from nationalizing the cabs in Petrograd. When someone asked Alexander Berkman for the reason, the famous anarchist answered, "It's obvious. Men can go without food, but horses cannot. When you don't feed them, the stupid beasts die!"

MR. E——, IN A SPORT shirt open at the neck is surrounded by Egyptian officials wearing warm woolen suits. Mr. E—— is a United Nations expert on Egyptian agriculture. He is a native of Alexandria, born of Greek parents who lived in Egypt before the wars: hence his fluent Arabic. He visits Egypt two or three times a year to supervise international grants in aid. He speaks of plans and plants and pests and is a very pessimistic man. Forty percent of the Delta population suffer from bilharzia, a disease that debilitates its victims.

"The main problem is population," he says slowly, in a calm voice. He is not a man of many words; the engineer in him tells him that waterworks are mightier than words. Industry and agriculture don't catch up with the birth rate. If only the birth control pill had been invented twenty years before penicillin, instead of the other way around . . . Even if birth control could now be put into effect, how do you feed 40 million mouths from this arid land? As it is, the population will reach 60 or 70 million within a generation.

Isn't it possible to increase the area under cultivation? But it is being increased all the time, says Mr. E——. Three hundred seventy thousand hectares (about 925,000 acres) of new land were made arable in the past twenty-five years; that's 20 percent more than in 1954. Yet at the same time urbanization took away more land from agriculture than was added with so much effort: 400,000 hectares (about 1 million acres). In other words, a net loss. At the same time, the rural population grew by 60 percent.

There is still a great possibility of making the desert flower. Egypt is, after all, the classic land of desert reclamation; the technique was invented here some millennia ago. And yet even the great Nile is not an inexhaustible source of water. There is enough water left in it to irrigate some 800,000 more hectares (2 million acres). What about afterward?

I tell Mr. E—— that some Israeli engineers have been talking about buying Nile water to irrigate the Negev desert.

"A pipe dream. The Egyptians need every drop of it." In Greece, he says, 9 million people live off four times as much cultivated land as 40 million Egyptians.

What, then, is the solution? Some say there is none. Mr. E—— thinks the solution is industrialization. The trouble is that so many new industries are what he calls capital-intensive (aluminum, or plastics). They offer employment to a limited number of people only.

Later, in the village of Dhamurieh, Mr. Afifi and I stand at the edge of a field of clover. The field is dotted with figures dressed in flowing robes, bent low over the ground like so many worms of paradise in the Garden of God that is Egypt. I give Mr. Afifi a short résumé of Mr. E——'s pessimistic views. He says nothing, but his shoulders sag. We look out across the green flats, peopled with stained tans and reddish browns and occasional stripes of black and white, and I suddenly think of those Russian dolls made of colored carved wood, trapped one inside the next, a box within a box within a box.

MOHAMMED MAHMUD AL-SALHI, Secretary of State for Agriculture, is seated at his desk in the old Ministry of Agriculture building in the heart of Cairo. The heavy old-fashioned desk, in dark, stained wood, is loaded with books and brochures It was occupied until 1936 by a British commissioner. The walls are hung with charts and pictures of President Sadat. At the far end of the room is a long table, large enough to host a mammoth conference.

Mr. al-Salhi is in his early sixties. His silver mustache is clipped. The black eyes are sparkling; the smile, open. *T'faddalu, t'faddalu,* the Arabic equivalent of *s'il vous plaît.* "Coffee?" Coffee.

"Sweet or medium?" Medium.

The pleasant ritual, languid, always graceful, that precedes every interview in Egypt. "Cigarette?" Thank you.

"You are very welcome."

Thank you very much. I am the first Israeli he has met in thirty-four years. "It is a pleasure." A pleasure. In 1945 Mr. al-Salhi spent a week in Tel Aviv on a problem of veterinary control; cattle and meat were at that time imported into Palestine from Egypt. In Tel Aviv he lodged with a well-known dentist, what was his name, he is sorry he has forgotten. Like most Egyptians, he too had been startled by President Sadat's peace initiative. Yes, "thoroughly surprised." But it is a good thing, a very good thing indeed. Mr. al-Salhi envisages great forward strides in Egyptian agriculture as a result of this unexpected peace. It will release funds that were before devoted to defense.

He speaks hesitatingly on the nature of any future Egyptian-Israeli relationship. He knows this is dangerous ground. Like other government officials, he will not tread on it before Sadat shows the way. He is quite familiar with the success of Israeli agriculture. Ah yes, it is very intensive. Yes, very high yields in certain crops, perhaps the highest in the world. The average yield of an orange grove in Israel is 96.5 tons per hectare, as against only 15 tons in Egypt. Yes, he has heard of the winter crops that have turned parts of Israel into northern Europe's winter vegetable garden and are an important source of foreign revenue. In Geneva once, Mr. al-Salhi attended a lecture on farming techniques in an irrigated Israeli desert area. He speaks about it quite vividly. But he does not refer, even obliquely, to the possibility of Israeli technical aid. This is very clearly a sensitive issue, wrapped in layers upon layers of feelings and pride. We have a lot to learn from one another, I say, feeling my way forward, carefully. "Yes," he says vaguely. "Thirty-four years is a long time." And that's it.

Agriculture is probably the most promising of all possible fields of cooperation between Israel and Egypt. Israel is likely to offer some sort of aid soon, but will it be accepted in the near future? At the very least a great deal of tact and patience will be needed to surmount the walls of suspicion raised in thirty years of war. The Egyptians also have bitter memories of condescending Russian and East German advisers. But two or three thousand young Israeli kibbutzniks might well come and live in remote Egyptian villages and work with the fellahin, not over them as the Russians and East Germans had done. I am thinking that many now jaded Israeli "pioneers" would perhaps consider this a national, a moral, a personal challenge. But seeing Mr. al-Salhi's guarded face, I do not pursue it.

"Another cigarette?" Thank you. Diplomatic Mr. al-Salhi suggests a visit to the Cairo Museum of Agriculture, where many important objects are displayed, old and new, including an ancient crib very much like that of Moses.

WHEN SIMHA DINITZ, the former Israeli ambassador to Washington, returned to Israel from the peace negotiations at Camp David, he was asked whether they had discussed technical cooperation between the two countries, exchanges of experts and the like. Dinitz said no, "not yet, it is too early." Was there a possibility in the future?

"Of course, a great one."

Would it be only one-sided?

"No, mutual."

"How?" said a brash reporter. "We can teach them a lot, in agriculture. But what can they teach us?"

Dinitz gave him a sharp look. "Diplomacy," he said.

THE COUNTRY OF STATE control *par excellence*. From Joseph the Provider, to Mohammed Ali, from Lord Cromer to Colonel Nasser, to President Sadat. One key is the canals, the clockwork mechanism of the opening and closing of locks. When Napoleon came to Egypt he very quickly grasped the meaning of the canals for the theory of government. Whoever rations the water rules.

Another key is the shape of the land. Egypt is a man-made island surrounded by desert. Its political system is stamped by its geography. I look up the Nile Valley south of Beni Yousef at the narrow banks on each side of the river. The fertile strips on either side are not more than ten miles wide. Farther south they narrow to three, then two miles. The plain is sown with cotton, beans, and corn; it is brimming with mud houses, palm trees, scents, and the ashes of countless generations. Sensuality, slavery, and force grow harmoniously here. Beyond this narrow sheath of green lies nothing but desert. The whole country can be controlled by a few gunboats, says Lacouture. North of Cairo, in the Delta, the shape of the land equally commands obedience. "There are no woods for the rebel to hide in, no way out but the desert, where life is impossible. . . . Here nothing escapes the master's eye."

GLIMPSES OF THE MASTER. His portraits are everywhere: on hundreds of thousands of banners, placards, floats, and triumphal arches in every city and village. They are an inescapable presence, always larger than life and the transmutation of a system, a principle of government. Endlessly repetitive, in wood and tin sheets, in cloth or papier-mâché, along and across every main thoroughfare, on every city square and public building. In profile and full face, in dark formal business suit, and in bright sportswear. Anwar al-Sadat in uniform, with a field marshal's baton, or without; as an admiral, as a general of the army. Smiling and serious, saluting and deep in thought. And always colossal. The supernatural magnification of images, as a political technique in the service of the state, is an Egyptian invention as old, as authentic, as the discovery of the principles of hydraulics. Witness the gigantic statues and bas-reliefs of the Pharaohs and their wives at Luxor and Abu Simbel. "All this bulk is incomprehensible and repugnant to me," Nikos Kazantzakis wrote in 1927 after a visit to Upper Egypt. He echoed a different civilization that had made man, not giants and outsize gods, a measure of all things.

Anwar al-Sadat occupies a place in Egyptian life that is hard to imagine. He is the Chief of State and Supreme Commander of the Armed Forces. He is both *Zaim,* a symbol that emanates the mysteries of power, and *Rais,* the man who gets things done, the Boss. His daily routine reflects the Zaim rather than the Rais. He seems to be forever moving, from one official residence to another. There are more than a dozen. The remoteness of some of these residences, usually called rest houses, is emblematic of the way he runs his government. Artfully aloof from the details of daily management, he pretends to be preoccupied—as De Gaulle did—only with the larger tides of history. His style is a far cry from that practiced in Israel. The Israeli Prime Minister so fills his day with partisan and parliamentary maneuvers, problems of bus strikes and teachers' wages and farm subsidies and sundry threats of resignation from ministers and senior civil servants, that often the "larger tides" of history are submerged and occasionally ignored under the pressure of managing and surviving politically in a modern welfare state.

The daily routine of an Israeli Prime Minister is marked by a constant stream of visitors pleading for this or that special cause. Sadat sees relatively few people. He rises late. He is said to begin work at ten or eleven and finish at two or three in the afternoon. The rest of the day he spends alone, reading, or walking in his garden; or in the company of close relatives. He is very much a family man. His married daughter and her husband live with him, as did his aged mother-in-law until her death in 1979. He has no "social life" and few close friends. His diet is rigidly sparse, interspersed by long periods of fasting. As a rule he is either by himself or in front of huge masses. Somewhere in between these two poles he forms his sense of reality. He addresses the crowds as "my sons," refers to "my army," "my ships," "my land," "my oil wells," or "my relations with the Saudis."

Charisma in a person is a strange quality. It strikes some as an affront, a slap in the face, while to others it is a rare and wonderful perfume. On the edge of Heliopolis our car is halted by the police. Sadat is visiting the nearby University of Ain Shams. The entire quarter has been cordoned off. Double rows of armed guards in black uniforms line the streets. With their backs turned to the President's road of approach, they face the large crowd along the avenue. Sadat is due to arrive at any moment. The waiting crowd is mostly students. The atmosphere seems calm. The students appear remarkably well behaved, even serene. It cannot be the same "affability" that Edward Lane in *The Manners and Customs of the Modern Egyptians* (1836) described as "a general characteristic of Egyptians of all classes." Violent student riots have been a regular feature of Egyptian life during the past two decades. The last riot, in 1977, exacted a toll of almost one hundred dead. Today the universities are said to be again a major focus of unrest, aroused by both the religious fundamentalists and the communists.

I move with the slow human stream toward the plaza where Sadat is scheduled to speak. His motorcade arrives, flanked by motorcycles gleaming in the sun. A dozen plainclothesmen on foot are running ahead in the heat. Sadat travels in a big open limousine. Not many mass leaders take such a risk today; even in the smaller democracies the people's representatives shield themselves behind steel armor and reinforced plate glass. The crowd roars. Sadat is standing upright in his car and acknowledges the applause. *B'ruh, b'dam, nifkid ya Sadat!—With soul and blood we redeem you, O Sadat.* The traditional chant of obeisance whips up the throng to an ecstasy of enthusiasm. The future masters of arts and doctors of philosophy push close to touch the body of the car as though it were a precious charm. The big car halts. Sadat steps out solemnly, like a pharaoh descending from his barge. The crowd parts. He lifts both hands. *B'ruh, b'dam.* A band is playing folk music. Sadat mounts the rostrum. The crowd falls silent. He stretches his hand out over Egypt. It seems a mere gesture, quite brief. He withdraws it; a pair of horn-rimmed spectacles has been placed in his hand by a well-trained aide. One has the feeling that if he suddenly bent his knees a chair would find itself under his lowered seat, with such efficacy and silence as to suggest no human intervention.

His speech lasts for almost an hour. He is not by any standards a "good" public speaker. His predecessor addressed the masses in a voice pitched with emotion. Nasser's speeches often overflowed with high-sounding patriotic rhetoric: "Brothers in glorious Arabism," "In the name of the Arab Nation," "Heroic brothers in arms."

Sadat, by comparison, speaks in a low, soft tune. *"Bis millah"* ("with God's help"), he says haltingly, and stops. The invocation *Bis millah* precedes every public utterance by Sadat, whether he is giving a speech in Arabic, English, or German, or just answering a question on Dutch television—at official negotiations too, apparently. I have heard from an aide to Begin that during the negotiations over the terms of the peace treaty President Sadat would listen patiently to an argument by Prime Minister Begin, then begin his reply with a small cough and say, *"Bis millah,* Mr. Prime Minister, I am very disappointed . . ."

"Bis millah," he tells the students at Ain Shams. "We are not only celebrating the end of thirty years of war, suffering, and losses in lives and material resources. Today we celebrate the regaining of our freedom of choice. The freedom of our lands. The freedom of our will. Let us start building the future as civilized, free men, in peace."

He emphasizes that word *peace.* It rolls slowly off his tongue, *Saalla-am.* The masses cheer enthusiastically. While they cheer, Sadat pauses. The reading glasses are perched halfway down the strong broad nose. He peers over them at the crowd below. I remember Yussef Idris saying that the crowds would scream with equal facility for war. ("Believe me, I have heard them," he said.) I recall a speech by Sadat on April 25, 1972:

"We shall not only liberate the Arab lands and Jerusalem and break Israel's pride of victory," he said then, "but we will return [the Israelis] to the state in which the Koran described them: to be persecuted, suppressed, and miserable. . . ."

Today he repeats the first part of that statement, the liberation of the Arab lands and Jerusalem, but not the last. The invective is reserved for his Arab colleagues. His aim, or at least the means, have changed. He *reasons.* "How can we regain our land, and our Jerusalem, if we do not negotiate with Israel as civilized parties?" he argues. "We sit with the Israelis and discuss our problem with them step by step. The first step is to set the Palestinians on their way to full autonomy. Is this treason?" he asks. "Is it?"

Shouts of "No!" from the crowd.

"So why do the ignoramuses attack us?" The Palestinian problem, he explains, was created when Palestine was partitioned, in 1948, between the Arabs and the Jews. The intransigent Arab leaders would not create a Palestinian state. (He does not mention that the leaders of Egypt were among those intransigents.) And so Israel was able to occupy the whole country. The same intransigent "rejectionists" are now opposed to the Egyptian-Israeli peace treaty. They threaten Egypt, they isolate it in the Arab world. But they are not able to do it, Sadat says. "They are retarded dwarfs," he says. The crowd cheers wildly. Most of the speech is devoted to explaining the treaty with Israel. The treaty, says Sadat, will enable the Palestinians to determine their own future. Nobody else can exercise that right for them. The remainder of the speech is an attack on religious fundamentalism.

"I will not tolerate the abuse of religion for political causes [as in Iran]," he says. "We have no time for internal squabblings of this kind . . . no time for the abuse of Islam . . . we must rebuild the country from the ravages of war and work hard to reap the benefits of peace . . . we must not lose time. [The fundamentalists] are trying to keep us from it. They claim the government is corrupt. They say it must be rebuilt on this or that ideology, on Khomeini, or what have you. Theirs is an easy way out. Executions, secret trials, and so on. . . . They want women to wear the veil again—like a tent." (Laughter.) "But women must build the country alongside the men. Religion must not be surrendered to the fanatics."

Again there are loud cheers, but not so loud, it seems, as before. The ceremony ends. The President retires to a hall with members of the faculty. The crowd streams back along the broad avenue. The guards are withdrawn. Not more than a few dozen traffic policemen remain to disentangle the cars caught up in a chaotic jam. The thick mass streams by. I am struck again by the phenomenon of this mass. There seems to be an inner harmony in this beehive. It functions by some hidden rhythm—or trail of scent—and a disciplined, even good-natured tolerance What happens when that rhythm is disrupted, or a new queen bee arrives? Army ants (*Labidus praedator*) lay a scent trail, which they follow by the myriad. If disrupted, all havoc breaks out. They begin to fight one another, or rotate in circles endlessly, until the last one drops dead.

In the Bible a great deal is made of the seven lean and the seven fat years of Egypt. Judging from the external evidence, and the public rhetoric of its leaders, many Egyptians now see themselves on the threshold of great plenty. Fat years are coming, partly through large-scale aid from the United States, and partly through the diversion of local resources from military to peaceful purposes. But what if American aid will not match that which is being withheld by the Arab states? Or be larger still, as many Egyptians hope? What if, after the seven fat cows have risen from the Nile, seven lean ones follow? As I write I wonder why it is that in Egypt I fall so often under the spell of these primeval archetypes and I ask myself: Is this rhythm dependent only on economics?

F.L., an Egyptian newspaperman I know, swears it is. He tells me an Arab tale. A man wrote to his beloved: "Send me a vision of you in my dream."

She wrote back: "Send me a thousand dinars and I will come in person."

But F.L. is a cynic. I find him altogether too rational. Egypt has a strange effect on me. The rational dimension I so cherish elsewhere somehow seems inadequate here. The result is endless foreboding. I try to fight it as one fights ingrained prejudice. I am not sure I succeed.

ON THE WAY BACK from Ain Shams University we pass Nasser's private residence, on a side street in Heliopolis. There are two policemen in a booth outside the medium-sized suburban villa. They protect—or perhaps watch—the late leader's family. Nasser's daughter, Odda, was recently stopped in the street by security men while distributing leaflets against the Sadat regime, which she considers corrupt, and against the peace treaty, which she regards as treason to the Arab cause. The leaflets were seized. Ms. Nasser was sent home.

The late leader himself is buried nearby in the newly built Gamal

Abdel Nasser Mosque. A modern structure, its odd eclectic style combines Western elements with Eastern frills. It rises high alongside a dusty railroad track. It reminds me a bit of some of the Jewish Reform synagogues I have seen in America. The large marble block over Nasser's tomb is inscribed with a passage from the Koran. It is the same passage Sadat had read over the radio announcing Nasser's death: "O peaceful soul, go back willingly to thy God and thou wilt be received. Go back among the believers into My house." Then, surprisingly, Sadat overthrew much of the late man's inheritance.

The caretaker says that few people come here these days.

A COURTIER. Dr. Boutrous Boutrous-Ghali is the Minister of State for Foreign Affairs: a slim, good-looking man, politic, cautious, and meticulous. The strong, pale, nervous face is long and gloomy. A striking face, the reincarnation, almost, of the delicate wooden statue of a Fourth Dynasty nobleman on the shelves of the Cairo Museum. He is a former professor, catapulted by Sadat to the Foreign Ministry from academic life, and a Copt, that is to say, in all probability a descendant of the ancient pre-Arab population of Egypt. Educated in France, quite obviously a first-class mind. Serious, polished, elegantly dressed. During the recent peace negotiations, when the informal Israelis and Americans undid their ties and removed their jackets, Dr. Boutrous-Ghali kept his on, saying on one occasion that "staying buttoned up gives me self-confidence." A curious combination of Coptic gravity and Galli charm. His English is perfect, with a slight French intonation, except for the *r*'s, which he rolls musically, like an Italian tenor.

I have been warned that in the whole of "official Cairo" I would not find a more pessimistic man. He certainly takes a bleak view of almost any subject. His pessimism stems not only from the difficulties of the moment, but from a bleak overall view as well. The immediate problems are quite obvious. It is all very well for Sadat to concern himself with War and Peace and History and Civilization writ large, but Boutrous-Ghali's job, after all, is to look after the small print. Sadat displays a supreme indifference to the ugly crisis between Egypt and the Arab countries—"the long quarrel of the East," in Gibbon's phrase—but the daily management of that crisis is up to Boutrous-Ghali. He and his colleagues in the Foreign Ministry work continuously to keep a very dangerous situation from worsening.

The strains are showing. Dr. Boutrous-Ghali is a professor who has been placed in a very difficult public position. His two predecessors resigned in protest against the policies of Sadat. Rumor has it that Boutrous-Ghali was chosen because as a Copt—the Copts are a minority in Egypt—his loyalty to the President seemed assured.

The peace treaty with Israel has placed Egypt in a very delicate situation, says Dr. Boutrous-Ghali. Israel could help to improve it. But what is Israel doing to help? What? Little or nothing! He is a dramatic speaker: a graduate of the Sorbonne, with that canonical prejudice of certain French intellectuals always on the lookout for easy dividing lines between angels and devils. Israel, he says, does not appreciate the Arab dimension in Egyptian history, politics, culture, and economic life. "We are not only Egyptians, we are also Arabs." Egypt cannot afford to, Egypt will not live in isolation, as another ghetto like Israel. Egypt has made a great step forward toward peace, but Israel is ungrateful and insensitive. It rewards Egypt for this breakthrough by making her difficulties greater. Israel creates new settlements in the occupied areas of the West Bank, Gaza, and the Golan Heights. "Suppose that on the day the first Egyptian ambassador arrives in Tel Aviv another ten settlements go up? How do you think Egypt will look?" The Arabs accuse Egypt of having betrayed the Palestinians. Israel must help Egypt to prove that the opposite is true. The Palestinian problem is the very heart of this conflict, and there will be no peace unless that problem is resolved. Time is pressing, says Dr. Boutrous-Ghali. The experience of the French in Algeria is uppermost in his mind. He constantly refers to it. "The greatest mistake of the French in Algeria was that they always gave too little, too late."

But doesn't the resolution of the Palestinian problem depend first and foremost on normalization between Israel and Egypt, I suggest. Time may change all the perspectives. Everything may look different after a year or two of *real* peace. Perhaps after a year or two of normal relations with Egypt, Israel will no longer regard the establishment of a Palestinian state as apocalyptic.

"No, no, no! There is no time!" The lines in Boutrous-Ghali's face are sharply drawn. We are moving in a vicious circle. He makes it very clear that in his view *real* peace can come only after the resolution of the Palestinian problem, not before. The elements of normalcy—trade and tourism, cultural exchanges—can be realized only gradually, in a slow, long-drawn-out process. "Where on earth have such things come to pass so quickly? After such enmity?" he exclaims. He draws on this and that historical example. "For normalcy we need at least a generation."

But his longer-range view is even bleaker. Wherever his eyes turn he foresees the rising of dark clouds. This civilized, sophisticated, cosmopolitan scholar of international renown, the Foreign Minister of Egypt, sees the very existence of the nation-state as a great danger. He is as much against the Israeli nation-state, with which he has just made peace, as he is against the nation-states of Egypt or Syria, Lebanon or Jordan. He does not believe in absurd artifacts like Kuwait or Abu Dhabi. How could he? He is a federalist by conviction. "Maybe that is outmoded. But it is my belief!" Only evil will come out of the continued existence of nation-states in the Middle East, terror and more wars, one more destructive than the other—not only wars between Israel and the Arabs but among the Arab states as well. By the end of the century, there will be more than 80 million Egyptians. How are we going to feed them? The Middle East will have to form a federation in order to survive. But he is not sure it will; in fact he doubts it very much. Hence his gloom.

In his office there is a map of the Middle East on which Israel is still blacked out. Israel, he thinks, must join his proposed federation and integrate fully into the area. How does one "integrate"? By accepting the *nature* of the area, he explains. That nature is Arab, of course. In the past, before he became Foreign Minister, Dr. Boutrous-Ghali occasionally spoke publicly of the need to bring about the "Arabization" of Israel. He once told my friend Michael Brecher, a professor at McGill University of Montreal: "More than half of the population of Israel is of Middle Eastern origin. They *are* Arabs anyway," but governed by a European elite, alien to them and to this area.

In 1975 he wrote that whereas Marxism and capitalism are reconcilable because they share the same moral and intellectual roots, Jewish nationalism and Arab nationalism are irreconcilable because they represent diametrically opposed ideas.

Before I take my leave I ask Dr. Boutrous-Ghali if he still believes in that statement. "Did I write that?" he says absent-mindedly. "Ah, I have written so much."

IN A CAFÉ ON Tahrir Square, where I am sipping a lemonade in the afternoon, I am approached by an old man dressed in a black galabia. A sharp face, like a knife's edge. The eyes are bleary, the lines of his mouth deeply drawn. The smile somehow gives a different effect from each corner of his mouth. He is selling paper charms against the "evil eye" and little Korans and wooden beads. If you rub them, he insists, they will guard you against all manner of trouble. He swings a charcoal incense burner on a chain, and as he spins it he all but vanishes in a cloud of smoke and dust. A sorcerer, says a boy at a nearby table. "Once there used to be many in Cairo. This gave us a bad name."

Now the old man takes some salt, or sand, from a little box. He throws a handful onto the pavement, with an outstretched hand, like Moses turning water into blood. "Allah Akhbar," he says. The traffic roars by. Almost everyone in the café gives him money. I buy a little booklet from him containing certain holy phrases, which, he says, should be recited for safe travel, by car or by air.

Tewfik al-Hakim, the great Egyptian novelist, writes that "the experience of a long past is so deeply imprinted upon Egypt it has become an instinctual, almost unconscious, feeling."

IN THE EVENING I read some of Dr. Boutrous-Ghali's past writings on the Arab-Israeli conflict. He has thought about it a great deal. On both sides the "conflict" has been an obsession of intellectuals for decades, and the casualties it has left in the academic world are numerous, if less bloody than on other fields. The novelist Naguib Mahfouz has described the obsession in *Karnak* (1974), where conversation turns around this one theme, day in, day out, year after year—make peace or make war with Israel, in this manner or that—until one of the protagonists exclaims, "Let us find another subject or else we'll all go out of our minds!" In vain. Soon they return to the regular theme, "to kill it and be killed in it," endlessly.

Before he joined Sadat's staff, Boutrous-Ghali was a director of the Cairo Center of Strategic Studies. In this capacity he was called upon to brief visiting scholars and journalists. As one reads the available record—it is ample—one is fascinated to see how, very gradually, this determined intellectual foe of Israel—he was a veritable doctrinaire of conflict—became in the years after Sadat's trip to Jerusalem one of the main architects of peace, working assiduously, marshaling his great charm and learning in the intricate field of international law, in order to bridge the differences and difficulties and arrive at a common formula.

Boutrous-Ghali fascinates, as intellectuals in politics often do. For years he considered Israel an unmitigated evil. His smooth generalizations were made more palatable on occasion by a judicious use of the subjunctive. His former views are still upheld by Sadat's foes within the Egyptian intellectual community. But although in the labyrinth of power as practiced today in Sadat's Egypt, Boutrous-Ghali is first and foremost a disciplined, loyal Minister of State, he is also no Conte Mosca—Stendhal's cunning Chief Minister in *The Charterhouse of Parma*—nor a Prince Hamlet, nor "an attendant lord, one that will do / To swell a progress, start a scene or two, / Advise the prince; no doubt, an easy tool, / Deferential, glad to be of use, . . . / Full of high sentence, but a bit obtuse." The opposite is true.

In his preface to the collection *Palestine in the Year 2000,* published in 1975, Dr. Boutrous-Ghali wrote: "The struggle between Zionism and Arab nationalism is a struggle between ideologies totally diametrical: racist seclusion and imperialist domination versus anti-imperialism and openness. . . . it is easier to overcome the contradictions between Marxism and capitalism than between [Zionist] imperialism on the one hand and the [Arab] war of liberation from imperialism on the other. Moreover, between the Soviet block and the American there is an element of equality that facilitates the arrival at détente. There is no such element of equality between the Arab homeland and the Zionist state." It is true that a certain balance of power was established between the two sides in the 1973 war. But this, Dr. Boutrous-Ghali wrote, did not end the "struggle between Arab quantity (one hundred twenty million Arabs from the Persian Gulf to the Atlantic Ocean) and Israeli quality (military and technological superiority, maintained by the international Zionist movement). Therefore, it may be said that despite the use of the oil weapon, the Arab-Israeli confrontation resembles that in South Africa and Rhodesia between the racist minority (of whites) and the black African majority. . . . In Kenya, Algeria and Mozambique the imperialist struggle was ended not by détente between the majority and the minority, but by the liquidation of the racist minority or its assimilation."

Another record of Dr. Boutrous-Ghali's thinking in the past is the tape of a long discourse he delivered in 1975 to Professor Brecher and a group of visiting scholars from Canada and the United States, and of the discussion that followed. At that time he greatly shocked his visitors with his apparent notion that *culturally*—let alone politically—there was place in the Middle East for Arabs only, and for no others. In the vast area between the Persian Gulf and the Atlantic Ocean everyone had to be Arab, or risk continuing strife. The politics of narcissism could not have been carried further than they were by the present Foreign Minister in 1975. He seemed at that time to be saying that "only Arabs are beautiful" in the Middle East. Jews could live there too, but they must not be too conspicuous, they must assimilate. Brecher and his colleagues argued with him vehemently and at length. They could not understand why Germans and Italians could strive for European integration without wanting to assimilate the Danes and the Dutch, but according to Boutrous-Ghali the Middle East had to be "Arab" only.

Boutrous-Ghali explained himself at equal length. He spoke disparagingly of the Israeli "Establishment" as foreign—"Polish,"

"German"—and imbued, in his view, with the "mentality of white settlers." Integration with such people was impossible, he thought; the entire area should be a monolith, perhaps not one of faith but of language, one nation, one people. Everything non-Arab was marginal, in his view, subsidiary, if not downright dangerous. (And all this from a Copt! The phenomenon is not entirely new, perhaps. Some of the most ardent nineteenth-century German nationalists were Jews.)

Still, Boutrous-Ghali felt there might be a solution. How? If a common denominator could be found between Israel and its neighbors. What could that be? Well, Israel could become an Arab country. Most Israelis were immigrants from Arab countries anyway; their birth rate was higher, so this was the wave of the future. But, asked the Canadians, weren't the so-called Arab Jews of Israel generally more intransigent and militant than Israelis of European origin? (Within two years this segment of the population would be a main source of votes for Menahem Begin's ultranationalist Likud party.) Not necessarily, thought Dr. Boutrous-Ghali at that time. He seemed to imply that their intransigence was implanted in their minds by the ruling elite of Polish, German, and Russian colonists: he continued to compare them to the French settlers in Algeria. Wasn't there a basic difference between Algeria and Israel, Brecher suggested. The French, after all, went to Algeria from metropolitan France and could return, but Israel was born of persecution and homelessness and powerful historical memories, if not rights. Perhaps, said Boutrous-Ghali, but the "image" of the two was nevertheless the same. The ruling elite in Israel had lived like white settlers among the natives, and its attitudes had been similar, he claimed, to those of the French colons in Algeria. A sophisticated European community had come in and pushed out a less sophisticated non-European population. Dr. Boutrous-Ghali was ready, however, to grant Israel a limited form of autonomy within the Arab federation, similar to that of the Armenians in Lebanon. . . .

The tape reveals a great deal of heated discussion between Boutrous-Ghali and the visiting professors: hardly one note of agreement. Listening to it now, one wonders at subsequent events. One clue can perhaps be found in the concluding passage of Dr. Boutrous-Ghali's contribution to the volume *Palestine in the Year 2000*. There he speculates on whether Israel will finally agree to merge with the "Arab homeland," or whether in the year 2000 Israel will be the "Hong Kong" to an Arab "China." Will it be an Arab-Jewish "state" (in the limited American sense of the word *state*) within a United States of Araby? Or were all of these concepts of no use, "and the struggle will continue for decades, with a fifth, a sixth, a seventh Arab-Israeli war"?

Could it be that Dr. Boutrous-Ghali now aims at making Israel into an Arab-Jewish Hong Kong? Professor Brecher has suggested another possibility; he thinks Boutrous-Ghali's insistence on cultural integration could be the alibi needed to make peace more palatable to the Arabs. By stressing "integration" the alibi conveniently delays "perfect justice" to a distant future, an end of days when all divergent souls will fuse in mystic unity. Boutrous-Ghali spoke of the waning of Israel as a culture, as a nation, on the eve of making peace with Israel. It would be pleasant to speculate that he was speaking like Khrushchev in 1960, who, even as he told America "we shall bury you," was laying the groundwork for détente.

The oddest thing in all this talk about the ultimate "Arabization" of Israel, by Boutrous-Ghali and others, is that it recalls the romantic origins of Zionism. At the turn of the century some of the leading advocates of Zionism dreamed of a Jewish renaissance in Israel as Easterners, not as Europeans. One branch of Zionism was definitely Europe-weary. As a mood it survived well into the long civil war between the Palestinian Arabs and the Palestinian Jews. The late Arthur Ruppin, head of the Zionist colonization department, wrote in 1923 that the true meaning of Zionism was the "return of the Jews to Palestine, to reintegrate into the [Arab] family of Near Eastern nations . . . in which they were born . . . to establish a progressive *Kulturgemeinschaft* together with their neighbors of close kin. Let the peace-loving Jews and with them the peace-loving Arabs (in as much as they are not yet infested with the European poison of national particularism) get up and raise the flag of peace among all men."

The idea was pursued later by Martin Buber and others. Dr. Boutrous-Ghali, by the way, is married to a Jewish woman. He is an engaging man, far from heartless; his brilliance and wit charm even when one disagrees with him. I am told he wrote some of the most moving parts of President Sadat's speech to the Israeli Knesset.

JOSEPH KRAFT, the American columnist, is experienced and shrewd. He is not as emotional as I am about Egypt and the Egyptians. Kraft has come to Egypt often during the last decade. He "knows everybody" apparently quite well, the President, his main advisers and ministers, Dr. Boutrous-Ghali, and many other prominent Egyptians. Kraft and I have been friends for more than twenty years. He is in Cairo and staying in the same hotel—that is, whenever he is not rushing from one confidential briefing to another as befits a great American journalist. He has tête-à-têtes with Mr. and Mrs. Sadat, the Minister of Interior, or of Defense, the Chief Ulema of Al Azhar, the American Ambassador, and even with some of the embittered politicians-in-demise of the time of Nasser. They hate Sadat with a venom and are perhaps plotting his downfall. Most of these old politicians are opposed to the peace treaty for reasons both personal and principled. Most have so far refused to receive me. Mohammed Heykal, Nasser's chief propagandist, now living in near-total isolation, splendid only in a material sense, granted me thirty seconds on the telephone to say that he cannot see me. No, it is impossible. The other day, when I tried to call another prominent opposition leader, the hotel operator told me that his telephone was not working, or perhaps that it was disconnected because of his "undesirable politics."

In the evenings I often go upstairs to Kraft's room. We compare notes. I tell him my concerns and ask for his views. I envy his experience of Egypt and admire his good judgment and keen sense of politics and human affairs.

Kraft is stretched out on his bed. He suffers from a bad back. He sips ice water and calmly gives me his view. The opposition to Sadat is marginal, he says. The support for Sadat's policy of peace is near-unanimous, says Kraft, especially where it counts most, in the armed forces. Sadat has given this country a rational sense of purpose, for the first time in over twenty years of crazy experiments and adventures, at home and abroad. Perhaps he is overestimating the material or political support he will gain from the United States as a result of the peace. And perhaps he underestimates Begin's obdurance and staying power. But unlike Nasser, who dragged this country from one disaster to the next, Sadat is able to show tangible results. He is getting back his occupied territory without shedding a drop of blood; living standards, at least in the cities, are rising somewhat, although through God knows what financial and budgetary maneuvering. "Sadat doesn't really give a damn about the Palestinians," says Kraft, "but he feels he must do something for them" in order to restore his standing with the other Arabs. He can't stand those either, but he needs the other Arabs for political, emotional, and economic reasons. The remittances of 1½ million Egyptians working in the Arab countries amount to almost $2 billion a year. That is one sixth of the gross national product. Until recently Saudi Arabia and the various Gulf States gave Egypt more than $1 billion annually in direct aid.

Kraft is not upset by Dr. Boutrous-Ghali's past statements. "It still compares rather well with some of the stuff written by American academics during the Vietnam War." He reminds me of an important fact. Israeli academics go to Harvard, or Berkeley, and finance their projects with grants from the Ford or Rockefeller Foundation. But the Egyptian academic world is closely linked with the Arab states; Cairo is, after all, the intellectual center of the Arab world. Hence the unease among local academics toward Sadat's peace initiative. Yet Boutrous-Ghali, Kraft thinks, is wholeheartedly in favor of Sadat's peace, though it has cut him off from his former academic milieu.

Late at night Kraft and I go down to the hotel lobby. It is deserted at this hour, except for several secret service men who sit in a far corner. They look up from their card game and nod affably. We cross the lobby and go up a broad marble stairway to the gambling casino that forms part of the hotel. There is a similar establishment in the nearby Hilton. Both are open ostensibly only to foreigners.

It is past midnight. The roulette and tarok tables are still surrounded by gamblers and kibbitzers of both sexes. The muffled air smells of scented face powder. The women are heavily jeweled; some have blond or aluminum-colored hair. The players seem to be German and French; some come from war-torn Lebanon, others from Libya, Saudi Arabia, and Kuwait. According to the newspapers, direct flights between Cairo and the Arab capitals have been suspended as part of the boycott of Egypt. But the tourists and gamblers from those countries are still here.

A young man, hardly more than a boy, bends over a roulette table. Slim and tense, he balances a cigar between two thin, nervous fingers. There are heavy rings on both of them. He wears a gray, shiny Cardin-type suit with thin elongated lapels, a crimson shirt, and silver tie. It is whispered that he is a Kuwaiti prince. He reaches into his breast pocket and pulls out a thick wad of fresh bank notes. He hands the entire package to an adjutant, a man of about forty, who goes off to acquire chips, for the young man seems to be losing rather heavily. He puts down his cigar and takes a sip of whiskey.

At the other side of the table I recognize another player behind his stack of chips, who appears to be steadily winning. It is S——, an international businessman from Tel Aviv. He tells me he is here on business. No, he can't say what. But it is serious. I had not known that at this early stage businessmen from Israel were being granted Egyptian visas. S—— smiles mysteriously. There are ways, he says, in straightforward Hebrew, as he adds another stack to his growing pile of chips. He is obviously having good luck tonight. And he seems to be getting on fine with the prince from Kuwait, who manipulates his cigar and his losses with insinuous, conscious grace.

I stand around, a bit too self-consciously no doubt, the poor man's Somerset Maugham. Dr. Boutrous-Ghali told me yesterday that nothing could be worse than a premature influx of overly energetic Israeli businessmen into Egypt. It could be very damaging if they tried to make quick and easy deals and cash in on the heavy investments the United States was expected to make in Egypt. I have heard other Egyptians voice similar concerns, in more urgent terms. "To see the nakedness of the land ye are come," said Joseph to his brothers when they went to Egypt from Canaan to buy food. ("Nakedness" does not convey the full sense of the original Hebrew *erva*, which means private parts, genitals.)

The Egyptians, I am afraid, have an exaggerated view of the shrewdness of Israeli businessmen and entrepreneurs, and they seem to overestimate the power of our economy. They ought to take a closer look at the latest statistics. But of course Boutrous-Ghali is correct in asking Israeli investors to proceed slowly, at least in the first stages, and to show as much tact as possible. It is true, unfortunately, that as soon as the guns fell silent too many prospective Tel Aviv carpetbaggers were beginning to hear their cash registers sing.

V

THE OFFICE TOWER OF *Al Ahram* rises thirteen stories over the
shacks of a run-down section in central Cairo. The prestigious,
semiofficial Egyptian daily, once the voice of a short-lived French-
influenced bourgeois liberal movement, was founded early in this
century by an enterprising Lebanese family. It was "socialized" in
the 1950s following the Free Officers' coup d'etat. The flashy tower
was built by a new editor in chief, Mohammed Heykal, the brilliant
high priest of Nasserism. Heykal is now in disgrace, a lonely and embittered man. The gaudy monument of his heyday remains one of the
landmarks of Cairo. Its architecture is a cross between postwar Italian vulgarity and Russian socialist realism. It reflects the taste of the
late President Nasser, some would say his megalomania and that of
the ruthless cabal of militarists, propagandists, sycophants, policemen, and informers that surrounded him. Everything about it is
massive and monumental. In the large oil paintings and frescoes, a
great many workers and peasants are flexing their muscles and soldiers in heroic poses are roaring for the attack.

Heykal's former suite, designed to awe a visitor by its size alone,
takes up much of an entire floor. Mussolini had a similar office in
the Palazzo Venezia; like Heykal, he was a man of smaller stature.
The walls are wood-paneled and hung with precious tapestries. An
intricate system of closed-circuit television enabled the occupant to

observe his visitors unseen as they fiddled nervously in the an-
teroom, waiting to be received. Heykal's great swiveling chair,
behind the mammoth desk, is now occupied by Ali Hamdi al-
Gamal. He is a journalist rather than a participant in the power
game surrounding a tyrant's court. This office is now little more than
the heart of a great publishing empire, of newspapers, books, and
magazines distributed throughout the Arab world. The daily circula-
tion of *Al Ahram* is about 800,000. The newspaper is printed by the
most modern, computerized machinery. Elsewhere in the building
are reference libraries said to be among the best in Egypt, as well as
various research centers equipped with electronic computers and
staffed by scientists and experts in many fields. Their work ranges
far beyond the requirements of the publishing house. Dar Al Ahram
—the House of Al Ahram—is a place of employment, perhaps a si-
necure, for intellectuals of all opinions. Some are temporarily in disgrace (the term commonly used is "They are on the shelves").
Little they write is published, but all are drawing considerable
salaries.

Dr. Louis Awad, perhaps the greatest literary critic in the Arab
world and a former university professor, is a good example. He supports the peace treaty. But as a former leftist who somehow came
into disfavor with Sadat, his reviews are not published in *Al Ahram*.

He can be interviewed, though. He thinks that the renewed meeting between Egyptians and Israelis will create an interesting cultural
situation. Before Israel became a state, Egyptian Jews were closely
linked with the cultural life of Egypt. They brought their knowledge
of French and German culture into the artistic life of the country.
They were innovators, accelerators in the process of Westernization.
"They loved Egypt," says Dr. Awad, "but their presence here was
cut short by the revolution and the wars. I for one would like very
much to see them again.

"I am not a nationalist," says Dr. Awad. "I am a secularist." He
is a humanist first and foremost, and a Copt. He regrets that Nasser
pushed Egypt headlong into premature experiments of unity with the
Arab countries. He himself visited an Arab country for the first time
in his life only in 1974. "We are part of this Arab sea, but we have

an identity of our own." Dr. Awad believes in Egypt's uniqueness as a civilization. Egypt should look not only east to Damascus and Baghdad, but north to Europe, and aspire to be a Mediterranean country. The wholesome process of Westernization could be given a new push now, he hopes. He does not expect too much, though, from the new links with Israel. He is a sober, well-informed man. He knows that in Israel, too, there is provincialism. But Israel is nevertheless closer to Europe and to the mainstreams of Western civilization; perhaps its impact upon Egypt will be "helpful." It can hardly be more, he fears. There are no Jeremiahs in Israel now, just as there are no Ikhnatons in Egypt, only varying degrees of mediocrity. Dr. Awad is a friend of Tahsin Bashir. Like Bashir, he thinks that both countries are, in a way, sick.

"Egypt resembles an iceberg," Dr. Awad wrote in 1969; "only one eighth is above sea level. Seven eighths are submerged in the depths. One eighth of our lives takes place in the light of the twentieth century, seven eighths in medieval darkness. . . . In the nineteenth century we went through pangs of birth . . . but [the renaissance] was stillborn, and when another embryo was formed in the womb, it was aborted."

This violent image of stillbirth and abortion recurs elsewhere in modern Egyptian letters. Naguib Mahfouz, in his play *Child of Pain* (1970), described the bourgeois period in modern Egyptian history under the corrupt monarchy as an experiment that ended in stillbirth, and the Nasser revolution as the cause of a terrible bloodbath. I ask Dr. Awad if he has any intention of visiting Israel in the near future. "No," he says grimly—he is otherwise a soft-spoken man— "I will not set foot in that country so long as there is a single Israeli soldier in occupation of Egyptian soil."

BY FAR THE MOST fascinating place in the *Al Ahram* tower is the sixth floor. Each Thursday morning novelists, poets, and critics of modern Egypt gather here in a suite of offices put at their disposal in the days of Mohammed Heykal, who loved playing the enlightened potentate:

The aging Tewfik al-Hakim, now in his eighties, the "doyen" of

Egyptian letters, author of *The Soul Regained* (1927), which described Egypt's first national renaissance in 1919, and chairman of the Writers' Association. The gentle Naguib Mahfouz, best known for his evocative *Cairo Trilogy,* a panorama of three generations of life in the city, written in the manner of a nineteenth-century *Bildungsroman* (Mahfouz has been compared to Dickens). Tense and sharp-tongued Yussef Idris, whom I had met before, and whose surrealist forays into the realm of sex and violence, coercion and despair, make him, I think, by far the most interesting and innovative Egyptian writer at the present. The essayist Hussein Fawzy, and others.

When they were first given their rooms in the tower, the censorship office—since abolished—was located conveniently nearby. Fortunately, censors rarely understand literature; it seems that in the worst days of repression Hakim, Mahfouz, Idris, and others were able to publish allegorical attacks on the regime with apparent immunity. Hakim wrote *The Embarrassed Sultan,* an attack on the lawlessness of the Nasser regime. In another story, *Everything in Its Place,* he exposed the prevailing apathy and corruption. In *The Bank of Worries* he attacked the brutality of the Nasser security police, and the great network of informers who were making Egypt into a "wired state" of torturers and power-hungry sycophants.

In his *Giver of Life and Death,* Hakim condemned the Soviet penetration of Egypt that was turning the country into a Russian colony; in *The Thief and the Dogs* and *Miramar* he denounced the corruption and cupidity rampant among the leading potentates of the state.

The Man Who Lost His Shadow Twice, by Naguib Mahfouz, was another allegorical work that attacked Nasser's secret police. I have already mentioned his play *Child of Pain,* with its implied message that under King Farouk, Egypt's attempt in renovation ended in stillbirth, and under Nasser, in bloodshed.

When I first visited the sixth floor of *Al Ahram* on a Thursday morning, I was struck by a prevailing sense of relief, and a certain optimism. It recalled the mood of Polish and Hungarian writers one met in Warsaw and Budapest a year or so after the death of Stalin. Some of the occupants of the sixth floor had been imprisoned under Nasser for their views. The worst is over, Hakim, Mahfouz, and Idris seemed to be saying, but guardedly. A lot remains to be done. Will the regime allow it?

"For my part," says Mahfouz, "I'll try to do my best."

As in Eastern Europe, where writers and artists were pampered by the totalitarian regimes and in the end turned out to be spearheads of liberalization, so in Egypt, during the past twenty years, the best poets and novelists have been at odds with the government, except during relatively brief periods. Hakim, Mahfouz, Fawzy, and Idris never complied with demands for a "constructive" literature mobilized in the service of Nasser's revolution. Their obligation as artists, as they saw it, was to provoke society, not to blindfold it. When that proved impossible in what had become a police state, Hakim fell silent. Mahfouz turned to films. Idris developed an arcane style of symbols and codes.

When the pressures for "mobilized" art were applied again in 1965, Idris wrote: "The greatest service art can render the revolution is when it itself becomes a revolution. . . . Those who try to make art an instrument to glorify the material achievements of the revolution understand neither art nor revolution."

Some twenty of the best Egyptian novelists, poets, and critics, led by Hakim, Fawzy, and Mahfouz, had been militating for a settlement with Israel for some years. In 1970—some say even earlier— they gathered into something like a small peace movement. By 1971 they were in heated discussion with both official spokesmen and hard-line Egyptian and Arab intellectuals. The discussion was not public, but according to foreign witnesses, by 1972 the exertions of Hakim, Mahfouz, and the others had become common knowledge in Cairo. Their message was never published, but they were nevertheless attacked for it in the newspapers. The peace movement, such as it was, was noted in Israel at the time. In retrospect it seems odd that only a handful of non-establishment academics paid any serious attention to it. As the years went by, the writers' peace movement embraced additional leading literary figures in Egypt. In 1977 Sadat himself gave it form, became its chief architect and official spokesman. But they had articulated it first.

Their rationale, given in various degrees of intensity, was that Nasser's foreign wars had depleted and ruined the country. Only in peace would Egypt "catch up with the caravan of the world," as Hakim said, and realize its "civilizational task" and "true destiny." Mahfouz went further. He said in an interview given to a Kuwaiti newspaper (and withheld from publication for almost two years) that peace and the building of civilization were more important than the liberation of occupied land.

"We sacrifice humans and send them to die in wars. Why, then, do we not sacrifice land, if that sacrifice is necessary toward an even greater aim?" Asked if he had any new vision of Egypt's problems, he said bluntly, "I have no new vision. All I know is that we must make peace. . . . *Hallas!* [Enough!] Let us make peace with Israel."

The left-wing writer Mohammed Sid Ahmed, in his 1975 book *When the Guns Fall Silent,* which could only be published abroad, in Beirut, called for a policy of détente between Egypt and Israel similar to that between the United States and the Soviet Union. He claimed there was no way to solve the problem by force. The two sides must choose between peace and mutual suicide.

The Libyan ruler, Muammar al-Qaddafi, on a state visit to Cairo in 1972, was shocked to discover that some of the leading writers of Egypt—for that matter, of the entire Arab world—were ready to "betray the sacred cause," as he put it, and make peace with the enemies of God. The discovery occurred at the headquarters of *Al Ahram.* In Heykal's office, Qaddafi was introduced to Hakim, Mahfouz, Fawzy, Idris, and several other well-known writers. A long discussion ensued. The writers voiced their opinions.

"It was a very heated discussion," Mahfouz remembers. Qaddafi would not give in. He cited chapters of the Koran to reinforce his argument. The writers remained firm. Qaddafi became incensed. Heykal tried to soothe him:

"They are only writers, you know. Writers are always so imaginative," said Heykal, according to Mahfouz. But Qaddafi would not be placated. Unable to imagine that some men make up their minds independently of the dictates of government, he surmised that in all probability they were echoing the voice of their masters, perhaps even that of Sadat himself. He swore he would take the matter up with the Rais, who indeed a short time later, in a speech at Alexandria University, attacked the "defeatist" poets and novelists as "men of little faith, who would like to recognize the facts [Israel]," but did not mention Hakim by name.

Earlier that year (1972) Hakim had privately distributed his now famous *Manifest of the Reawakening* among friends in Egypt and abroad. The title of this document referred back to Hakim's major work, *The Soul Regained* (1927). That book had been a great favorite of Nasser, who said that it had helped to turn him into a revolutionary. Hakim and Nasser seem to have been quite close during the first years of the revolution. In 1954, when the Minister of Education moved to dismiss Hakim from his job as director of the National Library, Nasser was outraged and dismissed the minister instead. Nasser's admiration for Hakim was reciprocated by the writer, at least until 1963. By 1967 Hakim seems to have become thoroughly disgusted with him. At one point the writer was treated roughly by Nasser's police and accused of being a foreign agent. The reason for this was a private letter Hakim had written to his former idol protesting the appointment of Heykal as Minister of Propaganda.

Nasser's death in 1970 produced one last spurt of what might be considered affection for Nasser by Hakim. He publicly proposed to erect a great statue in Nasser's blessed memory. Two years later he expressed regret at having made this rash proposal and suggested that Tel Aviv might be a more appropriate home for such a statue, since few people had done so much to ruin Egypt as Nasser.

Though the *Manifest* was privately circulated, excerpts soon appeared in the Lebanese press. The tract became a public sensation in Egypt, too, as the newspapers began to attack the "defeatist novelists," led by Hakim, who were variously called, "right-wingers," "left-wingers," "pro-Americans," and "agents of Moscow." In the *Manifest,* Hakim comes out with an impassioned condemnation of Nasser. Nasser's revolution, he claims, had been nothing more than a coup d'etat. He decries Nasser's tyranny, his cult of personality, arrogance and high-handedness (as in the nationalization of the Suez Canal), the reckless squandering of national resources, the misinvestments (including the High Dam at Aswan), the endless wars with Israel and in the Yemen that had left Egypt a ruin, in a state "impossible any longer to bear." The *Manifest* is a very emotional document, written, apparently in some haste, by a venerable old man, embittered as much by Nasser's recklessness as by his own failure to recognize it sooner. With the billions squandered on war and foreign intrigues, Hakim wrote, every one of Egypt's four thousand villages could have been rebuilt and brought up to the level of villages in Europe.

Nasser's worst crime, however, was in causing Egypt to lose its proper "awareness of self." The *Manifest* was Hakim's appeal to his fellow countrymen to wake up; they must regain the liberties they had lost; insist on freedom of speech, free criticism, and free elections; demand the curtailment and public control of all repressive government agencies.

It is not easy today to disentangle the true chain of cause and effect that has led to so many changes in Egyptian life since the early 1970s, and eventually, to peace. We know that in the winter of 1972–73 the writers, again led by Hakim, went a step further. Hakim and twenty others submitted their views in a written memorandum to President Sadat. The memorandum was followed, apparently at the President's request, by a long meeting with him, and with his Minister of Culture and Education. The new "awareness" that Hakim was calling for in his *Manifest* was, of course, spreading anyway throughout Egypt. It was a natural result of the new freedoms ordained by Sadat, just as the new freedoms in Eastern Europe were reimposed from above by Khrushchev's de-Stalinization of Russia. One of the immediate results of Sadat's rise to power was a relaxation of the stringent rules of thought control. It seems that the writers made good use of that. Today, Mahfouz says, "it is a good feeling for a writer to know that he was somewhat ahead of the politicians, and perhaps even influenced them a little."

Hakim said on March 3, 1973, "The writers' group has arrived at the conclusion that its duty is to strew roses for Sadat on the road to negotiations with Israel." Sadat, it seems, had taken that road rather reluctantly at first, rather tentatively. Hakim and Mahfouz urged Sadat not to stray from it. Even after he had begun to speak of peace, Sadat at no time excluded the option of another destructive war, as he was shortly to prove in October of the same year.

What seems certain now is the fact that, long before that war, soon after Sadat had come to power in 1971, a certain dialogue developed between the regime and the writers led by Hakim. They were by no means a representative segment of the Egyptian intellectual class, yet they included the most illustrious names in modern Egyptian (i.e., Arab) letters. Sadat at first resented their intervention and called them "defeatists." But as he gradually moved closer to a policy designed to extricate Egypt from Nasser's heritage of disastrous social experiments and war, he began to find them more useful. He was alone among the leaders of the Arab world in his tentative search for peace. He needed to legitimize his peace policy—peace as one option—and was able to use some of the most prestigious men of letters in the entire Arab-speaking world. His peace initiative, although it came so suddenly in 1977, was not born in a day. It must have germinated within him for a considerable period. It was the result of many influences. Peace might have come anyway, without the writers' intervention, as a result of the military stalemate. Perhaps it would not have come as soon. Hakim and his friends did not take their cue from President Sadat; that much is clear. Sadat was a relative latecomer to the cause of peace. If anything, he took his cue from them.

"THERE ARE A GREAT MANY WRITERS," Günter Grass writes in a little pamphlet that I greatly cherish, "who, far from presuming to be the conscience of the nation, occasionally bolt from their desks and busy themselves with the trivia of democracy. Which implies a readiness to compromise. . . . A poem knows no compromise. But men live by it. The man who can stand up under this contradiction and act is a fool, and will change the world."

Nietzsche put it differently: "A very popular error, having the courage of one's convictions. Rather it is a matter of having the courage to attack one's convictions."

TEWFIK AL-HAKIM is an old man now. His back is bent. He is wearing a beret. He has a high, domed forehead, a strong nose; the white mustache is clipped straight over the upper lip. An imposing head. He says there has been some agitation in the Arab countries to ban his books. But except for a few isolated instances, the agitation seems to have come to nothing. "They cannot really impose a ban on Hakim," says Mahfouz, gallantly. "Not if they wish to read. It would be like cutting Tolstoy out of the Russian language."

Hakim has also heard that his name has been placed on a special blacklist by the Palestinian terrorist organization that murdered Yousef Sabei, editor of *Al Ahram,* in Cyprus in 1978. "I could have opted out of these exhausting fights. But I have quarreled for years, with strangers and with friends. Otherwise I would not have been myself." He might have played the role of *Tkia* (pretending another faith), a convenience permitted to Moslems *in extremis*—if life depends upon it. But at his age he preferred not to. He is eighty-one.

Hakim thinks that Egypt will go on playing a central role in Arab culture. Few Egyptian writers have been as critical of the Arabs as Hakim has been in recent years. He has complained that the oil-rich Arab countries have lured away many Egyptians to teach in their schools, run their universities, and publish their literary and scientific magazines; and yet, not infrequently, Egyptian teachers and technicians are made to suffer humiliations in the Arab countries. He says that Egypt must begin to look after its own interests. It must stop being a beast of burden for others: the opportunists and cynics in the rejectionist states. They have taken Egypt for a ride too often in the past, only to serve their own selfish interests. Egypt should adopt a kind of neutral position in the Middle East, like that of Sweden in Europe.

Hakim is pleased, perhaps also a little amused, that his books are widely read in translation in Israel. He has been in touch with one of his translators, who happens to be Abba Eban. Hakim and Eban first met in Cairo during the Second World War. One of Hakim's works, *The Tree of Wretchedness,* serves as a basic text to teach the rules of Arab syntax in Israeli schools. A Hakim play has just opened in an Israeli theater; Hakim has read the reviews. His favorite critic is Dr. Sasson Somekh of Tel Aviv University: "Somekh understands Egyptian literature better than most." He hopes that more Israeli books will be translated and published in Egypt. An Israeli play ought to be produced in Cairo before the two national soccer teams meet. But Hakim is afraid it will be the other way round.

Naguib Mahfouz's office is next door. He is a frail-looking man, his smooth dark hair is combed back above the forehead, the large dark glasses over his eyes cover a good part of his face. It looks almost as though he were wearing a mask. He soon takes the glasses off. The eyes behind them are warm and brooding. His shrewdness and candor remind me of Brecht's character Herr Keuner, the intellectual poised between—and occasionally crushed by—the conflicting dictates of state power and conscience. I ask Mahfouz whether those writers who scorned Nasser after his death had also opposed his policies during his lifetime. Had they always been against war, or did they lose faith only after the wars ended in disaster?

The question is probably too direct. Mahfouz is also a little hard of hearing. I must repeat my question. He nods gravely. But he does not evade the question.

Undoubtedly there were both kinds, men of principle and opportunists, he says. Hakim certainly never belonged to the latter. "Hakim was our leader," he says. "We followed his call." And when Hakim said in his *Manifest* that he had lost his "awareness" during Nasser's heyday, this was just a figure of speech. Hakim had never lost his awareness, as he so clearly showed in his books. They prove where he stood. Hakim rebelled against tyranny as best he could under difficult circumstances. There was a dictatorship, after all. While it was not so repressive as the communist dictatorships of Eastern Europe or the tyrannies in Syria and Iraq, the pressure was very real. Police surveillance was effective. No, no, Hakim was no

Abbé Seize, who after the French Revolution could claim only that he had managed to survive it. "Hakim wrote," says Mahfouz. "He argued all the time."

Mahfouz says he would like very much for Israel now really to become "part of this area in which you have been trying for a century to strike roots."

What do you mean, "become part"?

"It is mostly a question of feeling. One can live in one's own house and feel alien. Or one can be at home in a strange place. In both cases it affects behavior. Once upon a time the English and French were our enemies. Now we are friends."

Isn't it a bit more complicated between us? "Yes. Because of the *land*." Liberated land, occupied land. All this talk about land, always. "We love land more than people." Mahfouz thinks this is a moral outrage. Writers and artists must combat it, in Egypt and in Israel. Land is inanimate; it is neither free nor enslaved, only people are.

Mahfouz says, "Do justice to the Palestinians. You Jews of Israel were a homeless people, you ought to be able to understand the Palestinian's bitterness and distress. What has happened to the Palestinians is what happened to the Jews. Half the way to an equitable solution is empathy. Historically it was the country of two peoples: the Jewish and the Palestinian. Let them partition it."

He is writing a new novel, he says, inspired by the most recent events but not reflecting them. As soon as it is published he will send a copy to Dr. Somekh of Tel Aviv. Like Hakim, Mahfouz is full of praise for the Israeli critic. Like Idris, he claims that no other critic understands his work so well as Dr. Somekh. He has not met him, but they have corresponded. What is it that Somekh has understood? "Other reviewers and historians of Egyptian literature have seen a kind of history or sociology in my work. Not Somekh. He has understood the main thing."

Which is? "Man's battle with time."

MAHFOUZ ASKS IF I read Arabic. I say no, I can only speak it a little. He asks why. I say I studied Arabic in high school but never had much opportunity to use it. You can begin now, he says. I say I am afraid it is too late, quoting a line by the Israeli poet Yehuda Amichai—and Mahfouz laughs. When he laughs, his eyes tear. Amichai wrote after the 1967 war, during which the Israelis had captured East Jerusalem:

> It's not time that takes me away from my childhood,
> But this city and everything in it.
> *Now to have to learn Arabic . . .*

Boutrous-Ghali also spoke of languages the other day. I had asked him how best to develop cultural exchanges between the two countries. "First of all," he said, "you people have to learn Arabic. . . ." But not the Arabic slang spoken by Jews from the Arab countries, he stressed, nor the patois of the Palestinian fellah—that is, the Arabic that Moshe Dayan speaks—no, not that, but classical Arabic. As he said this, Boutrous-Ghali made an impatient little gesture with his hand—patrician Copt that he is, the pharaonic vizier.

Mahfouz and Idris are agitated by the great problem of language in contemporary Arabic letters. The difference between the classical, written word and the spoken word is increasing. Some Arab writers have tried to overcome the difficulty by devising an intermediate language, a mixture of classical and demotic words. Idris's dialogue is purely demotic, and so are large parts of his narratives.

To a lesser degree this is also a major problem of modern Hebrew letters. There are other similarities of language that give rise to thought. Both Hebrew and Arabic are emphatic languages to a degree that no European language can match. In both languages the tenses are somewhat vague. The number of verbal forms is limited: no conditional, no subjunctive, no past absolutes, no participle or gerund; no sequences, only events. The labyrinthine devices developed in both languages to overcome this classic handicap lack precision. Classical Hebrew and classical Arabic evaded historical time through use of the prophetic perfect. Both languages took on certain prefixes that reverse the future into the past and bring the past into the future. Even in modern Hebrew there is but a single present tense, no past perfect, no subjunctive, and only a very roundabout way to imply a conditional. In modern Hebrew and Arabic, it is impossible to say as precisely as in French or English, "The Israelis thought they *would* hold on to the occupied territories as long as there *was* no peace." In modern Hebrew or Arabic one says, "The Israelis thought they *will* hold on to the occupied territories," etc.

In the Romance or Teutonic languages, the conditional *would* suggests a problem, an uncertainty dependent upon some contingency that might or might not occur. I wonder if peculiarities of language have not contributed over the years both to Arab intransigence and to Israeli reluctance to understand that peace is a drawn-out process that cannot be achieved in one stroke of a pen. In both languages, time sequences are obscured by the classical emphasis on events. This facilitates the writing of great poetry with a stunning economy of words. But what does it do to political thought?

D. V. Segre, in *Israel: A Society in Transition,* writes that the Hebrew verb structure may explain to some extent why it is so difficult for responsible opinion in Israel to make a clear distinction between past, present, and future on any issue connected with collective Jewish feelings. Could not the same be said of Arab culture as well? Segre is a noted political scientist of Italian origin; in Italian there are at least fourteen tenses—eight in the indicative mood alone, four in the subjunctive, two in the conditional—and possibly six forms in the infinitive, participle, and gerund.

Since there is no clear past historic (or absolute) in Hebrew or Arabic, the relation of events that have occurred at different times in the past remains obscure. A man thinking in Hebrew or Arabic finds it easier to imagine that Mohammed, or Solomon, or Saladin, or Masada, happened or acted only yesterday. The grammar enables whole centuries to be cut away and creates an illusion of uninterrupted continuity.

I joked about this with Hattam, who said that maybe we ought to abstain from sending Arabic-speaking Israelis to Egypt or Hebrew-speaking Egyptians to Israel. Instead we should continue to speak English or French to one another. It would give us a greater choice of nuances and tenses. Sadat and Begin have, in fact, spoken to one another entirely in English, and so have most of the negotiating diplomats. But we are still each thinking in our own language.

EVEN WHEN EDUCATED Egyptians support the peace treaty, as many do, still I have not met one who expressed even a remote desire to visit Israel. The only people who have told me they would like to come soon were an elevator boy in the hotel, a truckdriver who wanted a job with an Israeli company, and a man in a shop who cashed my traveler's checks and said he would like to work as a teller for an Israeli bank. Among intellectuals and writers I notice a certain lack of curiosity, even indifference. The opposite seems true in Israel. It is, after all, we who have just broken out from isolation, not they; we, not they, have emerged from confinement, as it were, and are anxious to see what life is like beyond the wall.

Hattam would rather visit London, or New York. Idris would not go, since he cannot take his readers with him. Dr. Awad is held back by the presence of Israeli soldiers in the Sinai. Mahfouz says, "But I never go anywhere, except for a few months in summer to Alexandria!" Hakim travels only to Paris, where he has an apartment.

Hattam says that Egyptians are stay-at-homes by nature. "Herodotus came to Egypt," he says, "but who has ever heard of an ancient Egyptian who visited Greece?"

I AM READING Mohammed Sid Ahmed's *When the Guns Fall Silent* (1975) and recognize in his reasoning the rationale behind much of what I have heard from many peace advocates here. Sid Ahmed's arguments strike me, who have been longing for genuine rapprochement with our Arab neighbors, as being a bit too "functional." He supports peace as a "mathematician," not a moralist. He describes societies as though they were machines. And yet I know that such is the logic behind all détente.

Mohammed Sid Ahmed is a former communist, the scion of a rich feudal family. Hattam says he is like a character in a nineteenth-century Russian novel: the aristocrat with a social conscience. And yet the one thing he seems to lack is *empathy*. Sid Ahmed spent time in jail under both King Farouk and President Nasser. In the 1960s, when Nasser made his peace with the communists, Sid Ahmed became a regular contributor to *Al Ahram*.

"The time has come to contemplate what until now we have not dared to contemplate," he writes, "détente (and peace) with Israel." The reasons he gives after this promising opening are mainly negative. The disadvantages of war, he says, simply outweigh its possible advantages. Peace is possible now—he still hesitates to call it desirable—because of the "balance of terror," and also because (Arab) money is in need of (Israeli) technology. All conflict in the Middle East still relates in one way or another to what Sid Ahmed calls "the Zionist threat." Peace, he argues, will not abolish the contradictions between Israel and the Arabs; it means merely their rearrangement. Peace is nothing more than the "least harmful" possibility available to all parties. Israel has a "functional" role to play in the area, says Mohammed Sid Ahmed. All the same, he looks forward to its disappearance; he is hopeful that détente will gradually cause the withering away of the Jewish state as a distinctive culture, through assimilation into the Arab world. For even if it is not an "instrument of imperialism," Israel remains, in Sid Ahmed's eyes, "a foreign body."

At the same time he is very critical of Arab and Egyptian life. "We still live by the logic of tribal society," writes Sid Ahmed. This tribal thinking threatens to increase, for if Arabism has gained a new dignity in recent years, this was a result of mineral wealth, not because of any intellectual or physical effort, or even human suffering. Elsewhere he has complained that there has been a greater exodus of Arab wealth to the West—Arab playboys in London, Arab investment in European banks and California real estate—than an influx of real wealth to the Arab world.

Mohammed Sid Ahmed has thought of an interesting way to safeguard the future borders between Israel and its neighbors against aggression from either side. He proposes the establishment of a belt of heavy industry alongside the border where Arab money and manpower could combine with Israeli technical expertise. The combination might generate interest on both sides never to expose this profitable belt to the danger of destruction.

But, he adds, such a belt cannot by itself prevent war, just as the industrial zones on the French-German border never did. He maintains that real peace can be achieved only after the dismantlement of the national character of Israel, within a "secular" state in the whole of Palestine. This is not Hakim's point of view, nor that of Idris or Mahfouz. With all its support of détente—a rather depressing tract.

TEA AT A YOUNG architect's house, in the country. We drive out on the road toward the pyramids, past gaudy nightclubs and bars and cabarets. Farther out, the narrow asphalt strip follows a silent canal into the flat, open countryside. The architect, Ismail, studied in Italy. He works for a local construction company. His garden is shaded with date palms and overgrown with rose bushes and jasmine and red and yellow oleander. The sun filters through the branches and leaves. We sip tea from heavy earthenware cups, glazed a deep red, which are made in a nearby village. Ismail speaks with great feeling of the terrible housing shortage. At least a million new houses are needed, and yet only a few thousand are constructed each month. No money. Somehow we come to speak of Mohammed Sid Ahmed's *When the Guns Fall Silent*. I tell him my reaction to it.

Ismail speaks Italian fluently; he is a great lover of fourteenth-century architecture and poetry. He cites Petrarch:

> Pace non trovo a non ho da far guerra
> E temo e spero et ardo e sono un ghiacco.
>
> (Peace I find not and for war I have not the means.
> I fear and hope; I burn and am an iceberg.)

After tea a friend of his arrives, like Ismail an architect. Unlike Ismail he has been unable to find work in Egypt. There are at least twice as many trained architects in Egypt as can be employed locally. Nabil works for an architectural firm in Kuwait. He has been designing offices and houses for rich Kuwaitis during the past four years. The price of a five-room house on a little suburban plot in Kuwait, he says, is more than half a million dollars. The pay is not

bad, he says, although he receives only two-thirds that of his Ku
waiti colleagues. Advancement is difficult; the Kuwaitis leave littl
doubt who is master and who is servant. As an Egyptian "foreigner
in Kuwait he has been exposed to occasional insults and humilia
tions; these have become more frequent since President Sadat bega
negotiating with the Israelis. It is virtually impossible for an Egyp
tian to be naturalized as a citizen in Kuwait. Nabil comes home t
Egypt once a year. This time he had to fly via Athens; direct flight
from Kuwait to Cairo have been discontinued—temporarily, h
hopes, but he is very worried about his future.

Ismail is also worried. He is afraid that Israeli architectural firm
might come and corner the Egyptian market. His words echo a pre
vailing sense of inferiority, irrational but ubiquitous. It will tak
some time to dismantle the cliché of the Israeli as either a militar
superman or a crook in business.

Later, on the drive back to Cairo, we pass the Mena House Hote
It nestles luxuriously at the foot of the great Pyramid of Cheops, an
rather incongruously, with its laced towers and windows and ram
parts inspired by the summer palace of an Indian maharajah. It wa
built as one of the way stations in the British Empire. The hote
menu still lists curries of all kinds, as in the days of the sahib.

As we come back through the pyramids road, the nightclubs a
lit up and crowded. Tourists surge out of buses into a belly-dancin
establishment. Ismail does not like belly dancing. He says it is an in
elegant Turkish taste. I wonder at the appellation "Turkish.
Weren't the Turks rather puritan in their interpretation of th
Koran, with much the same attitude as the English Protestants to th
Bible? No, it was the Turks, Ismail is adamant, the Turks and thei
lecherous corrupt pashas, whom they sent out to rule Egypt. Th
costumes are paste nineteenth-century French, a designer's idea c
the East. Bedecked in jewels, with their bare navels, the dancers sug
gest slave girls vibrating their hips for the enjoyment of voluptuou
potentates.

IN THE PAST FEW DAYS, after some pleading on my par
the security measures have been relaxed. It is enough if I tell m

guard where I am going. Then I am off on my own. It is a great relief, especially for my Egyptian acquaintances. They are embarrassed
by the presence of a security man awaiting me outside. I have a new
guard, however, a Major Sherif. He is in his late twenties, the son of
an army officer. Sherif, a law school graduate, makes less than
eighty dollars a month, a high salary in Egypt. But a two-room flat,
he says, costs forty thousand dollars. He has been married for three
years, he tells me, but still lives with his parents. His wife, also a
university graduate, could not find a job in Egypt. A few months
after their marriage she went off to one of the Gulf States. She is
working there as a receptionist-clerk in a hotel. Major Sherif has not
seen his young wife in more than two years and is very sad and
lonely, he says. His wife, he says resignedly, lives in the "museum of
my memory."

MUSEUMS. The famous Cairo Museum is a depressing place, a
vast storehouse rather than a display of antiquities and works of art.
The treasures are crowded on the floors and shelves, inadequately
lit, some unmarked and covered in dust. The authorities must be as
overwhelmed by this mass as is the casual visitor. Several conspicuous copies bear witness to the ravages of centuries. The originals,
stolen or sold, are in European or American museums. But what
treasures!

Sherif, who is here with me, says that a few years ago there were
still sandbags in the halls to protect the exquisite objects in their
old-fashioned glass cases from possible damage during air attacks.
Spectacular treasures—carved pharaonic chaises, beds, tables,
wooden statues—are piled up on the vitrines, some on top of one another, as in a used furniture shop.

There is that same breathless feeling of massive density and stag-
nation as elsewhere in Cairo. And, in this maze of alabaster, granite,
and carved wood, the same powerful impression of infinity. The
identifying numbers are fading. An awe-inspiring warehouse, an
attic filled to the brim with the most exquisite objects, it suggests
that too much has happened here for too long in too little space.
The Thutmoses arm in arm with their wives and mothers, thin

waists, curiously long toes; the delicately carved sphinxes, half lion, half human, to denote divine wisdom as well as bestial strength. The beauty of all these remote rulers is perhaps so appealing because relatively little is known of their history.

The mummies are in a special room upstairs. The visitors' fascination for the morbid is shrewdly exploited and one is made to pay a separate fee for the pleasure of inspecting them. The small room, like a mortuary after a sudden disaster, is tightly packed with dead bodies. It is crowded with curious visitors. Nearby the fantastic collection of jewelry and artifacts and delicate frescoes makes one wonder what has been added by later civilizations. The superb realism of Ikhnatonese sculpture, bordering on the grotesque, chills one to the bone. The sacred cows, the gilded, magnificent carved horses: the Bible says that Solomon brought his horses from Egypt, as well as at least one of his thousand wives. "I have compared thee, O my love, to a company of horses in Pharaoh's chariots." There is a fine stele of the Middle Kingdom: "Ho, ye living ones upon earth who shall pass by this stone who love life and hate death . . ." The treasures of Tutankhamen are in a special side room. "No more than fifty may enter." There are more than one hundred souls inside, and still more are pushing to get in.

All these great works of art, the more staggering to look at and admire when one remembers how old they are—Europe was still forest and swamp, the ancient Hebrews a pack of hunger-dazed nomads wandering in the Mesopotamian desert! All these noble thoughts, of art, of life and god, one sun god— and *cui bono*—as Aldous Huxley once wrote. The theologies and passions—what has become of them? The fossilized remains are here. The tourists look at them, and at what else? And outside the museum, all that squalor, all those questions to which no one seems to know even the beginnings of an answer; and the problems, as Yousef Idris says, "cannot even be defined."

The tourists come in hordes, smelling of suntan lotions and deodorant. They only half-listen to the well-worn litany of their guides. When Aldous Huxley was here in 1954, he was shattered. He had never felt such a sense of the tragic nature of the human situation as he experienced here—and in Jerusalem. The horror of a history in which the great works of art, the philosophies, and the religions were no more than little islands in an endless stream of war, poverty, famine, frustration, squalor, and disease. "One sees the misery of the Egyptians," he wrote in a letter to a friend, "huddled about the pyramids, and the hopelessness of the inhabitants of Jerusalem for whom the holiest of cities is a prison of chronic despair punctuated by occasional panic when the hand grenades start flying. And it must always have been like this—little islands of splendour in a sea of darkness—and then during the times of trouble, darkness unmitigated for a few centuries."

KAMAL AL-MALAKH, the noted archaeologist, chides me for my subservience to Huxleyan melancholy. Emotionalism has habitually marked the reaction of many a Westerner who visited Egypt. Some rave like children about Egypt, or like Huxley and Gérard de Nerval before him, see only black suns of despondency rising daily in the luminous plain of the Nile.

Mr. al-Malakh lectures me on the "true" spirit of Egypt. He wears an elegantly cut dark suit. His bright eyes are set in a square face. He is a very attractive man and a staunch supporter of the peace. "It should have happened a long time ago," he says. He is the man who found the famous sun boat of the Pharaoh Cheops at the base of the Great Pyramid, and was one of the organizers of the Tutankhamen exhibit in Washington, New York, and other cities of the United States. He is a popular writer on archaeology and art, the author of a biography of Tewfik al-Hakim, and a great patriot of the Nile Valley. A Niliote, as they say here. Like many a Niliote, he is not particularly fond of the Arabs. They are Bedouins, in his eyes, like the Hyksos.

Yes, Egypt is very poor. But essentially it is a land of peace, he says, which is more than can be said of most countries! "This is why we feel we belong to time, and not only to history. Other peoples

have been dissolved by time. But not the Egyptians." They civilize
their conquerors, he says in a tone that suggests he does not exclude
the most recent ones. He smiles. We sip our coffee. A very Niliotic
approach, this, I reflect. Even the Moslem conquerors in the seventh
century, says Mr. al-Malakh, became pacific as soon as they settled
here. After capturing Cairo at the head of 3,500 cavalrymen
(mostly Yemenites), their general, Amr, told his troops, "The floods
of the Nile have fallen. The spring grazing is good. Go out with
Allah's blessing and enjoy the land, its milk, its flocks, and its herds.
And live in peace with your neighbors."

Mr. al-Malakh goes on to speak passionately of the true, historic
spirit of the Land on the Nile. The days of Nasser, with their gran-
diloquent illusions, are over. In terms of foreign policy they may
have been little more than an episode. Historically, the Land on the
Nile, a flat country of hardworking peasants, abhors war; it is
insular, it hates foreign adventures. It is a small green slice of land
surrounded by desert. Its inhabitants know instinctively that if you
venture into the desert you die. With few exceptions (the adventurous kings of the New Kingdom, from 1580 to 1320 B.C.) the only
wars Egypt ever fought were defensive: when a threat appeared on
the Eastern border—the only gateway to Egypt. When there is no
threat from the East, through Sinai, Egyptians crave only to be left
alone in peace. Speaking of Nasser's dream of an Arab empire cen-
tered in Cairo, Mr. al-Malakh says, "An imported idea! Doomed
from the beginning. This country has never been the heart of an empire, except under foreign rule. The Fatimids did not originate here.
Saladin was a Kurd. We don't consider him an Egyptian." True
Egypt has always been the world center of Islam because of the University of Al Azhar, but a spiritual center, not a political one.

When he speaks about ancient Egyptian history, Mr. al-Malakh's
eyes acquire a certain gleam. He is more at home—certainly more
comfortable—in past glories than in the present squalor. He listens
patiently to my objections, then goes on to refute them with the im-
mutable rules and abstractions he distills from geography and history. One of the first things Israelis must do, says Mr. al-Malakh, is

become acquainted with Egyptian art. Israel must invite the Egyptian Council of Archaeology, of which he is an officer, to send a representative exhibit of Islamic, Coptic, and pharaonic objects to Jerusalem; perhaps even the Tutankhamen exhibit after its tour of American cities. This will give Israelis a better idea of the real Egypt than a thousand articles in the newspapers. He dwells on this for a while. Let us exchange exhibits and books before we exchange businessmen, he says. He, too, is suspicious of Israeli businessmen. Although we need one another economically, let the businessmen come later. He would also like Israel to participate in the forthcoming Cairo film festival, of which he is one of the organizers. He is a many-sided man. "But don't send a political film!" he warns. "And send your people to see Luxor and Aswan! Abu Simbel! The Valley of the Kings!" he adds enthusiastically. I find it difficult to resist his charm, and tell him the experience of my friend Shalom Cohen.

Cohen, an Israeli, was able to visit Cairo before the peace, on the strength of his connection with a French newspaper. One day he flew up to Luxor to visit the Valley of the Kings. For two days he went around with a local guide, who was aware of Cohen's identity. At the end of the second day they reached the temple at Karnak, where a fresco on the wall depicts a row of Hebrew prisoners of war captured by a pharaoh during his sack of Jerusalem. (This is perhaps the event described in II Chronicles 12: ". . . in the fifth year of king Rehoboam Shishak king of Egypt came up against Jerusalem, because they had transgressed against the Lord, With twelve hundred chariots, and threescore thousand horsemen: . . . And he took the fenced cities," and Rehoboam humbled himself before this pharaoh, who took away the treasures and Solomon's shields of gold and many prisoners as slaves.)

When Cohen and his guide arrived at the fresco, the guide, who until that moment had spoken Arabic and English, suddenly said triumphantly in Hebrew, "You see, Mr. Cohen"—and it was clear that he had been awaiting this moment—"what you did to us also we did to you. Once we took Jewish prisoners to Luxor, and once you took the sons of Luxor as prisoners to Israel." He himself had learned Hebrew as a prisoner of war in Israel.

"There you have it!" cries Mr. al-Malakh. "It shows the past here is not just artifacts and remnants—it lives!"

JEWS AND EGYPTIANS may yet achieve great feats together, Mr. al-Malakh thinks. He admires Freud's little book on monotheism, which claims that Moses was an Egyptian—inspired by Ikhnaton, the husband of the beautiful Nefertiti. Her face still launches a thousand tourist buses each day to the Cairo Museum, where a replica is sold. The original—smuggled out of Egypt early in this century—is in Berlin.

VI

I WEAVE AS QUICKLY as I can through the crowd on Suleiman
Pasha Street. Suleiman Pasha (alias Colonel de Seve) was the colorful European mercenary who in the nineteenth century had modern-
ized the Khedive's army, and had gone native and married an Egyptian woman, siring, I am told, a great many children in and out of
wedlock. In the 1950s, Suleiman Pasha Street, like others named
after foreigners, was renamed after the banker Talaat Harb. But
most Cairenes still call it by the old name.

Suleiman Pasha—or Talaat Harb—is one of the main shopping
streets of Cairo, perhaps the most elegant. This was once the heart
of the "European city," the Cairo of Greeks, Italians, Englishmen,
Jews, Armenians, Frenchmen, Copts, Maltese, who played such an
important role in the city's commercial and cultural life before the
revolution. The epithet "European city" is still occasionally applied.
As elsewhere, the common mania of revolutionaries to rename
streets and squares comes up against the inert conservatism of a people with an unusually long memory.

It is seven in the evening. Groppi's famous pastry shop, once the
favorite meeting place of foreigners, rich Egyptians, and bohemians,
is crowded with clerks from nearby offices and banks, sitting with
their girl friends. The shop windows are brightly lit. They display,
somewhat shabbily perhaps, a variety of Egyptian-made shoes and

clothing, where in the early 1950s Greek and Jewish traders were still offering expensive French and Italian imports to the small class of beys, pashas, and foreigners who could afford them. Simonne Lacouture, in *Egypt,* gives a vivid description of a fine lady who instructs her chauffeur to stop the Rolls before a shoe store.

"The chauffeur signalled, and the salesgirl hurried out to fit Madame's shoes inside the car, without her even having to descend. But there has been a Revolution," Lacouture adds dryly.

There are also a great many more people here now. The general impression is solidly middle-class. The goods, if not of the best quality or latest design, are relatively low-priced, perhaps a third less than in Europe or the United States. The stores are full. Boys and girls, some with long hair and in blue jeans and high-heeled shoes, stroll with their arms around one another. This, too, I am told, is a great change from the past. Some of the bigger stores, although nationalized now, still carry their old Jewish names: Ben Zion, Cicurel, Shamla, Gaby.

At Groppi's I turn right, down a side street, where the old English Turf Club used to be (it was burned during the anti-British riots in 1950), and arrive at a busy intersection. There are bookshops on three corners. The books are mostly in Arabic, but there are a good number of technical texts in English and French. The crowd hurries by. I turn into Adly Street. It is quieter at this hour. On the right, upstairs in an old office building, the windows of the local office of the Palestine Liberation Organization are still lit. Directly opposite the PLO is the dark, ramshackle façade of the last remaining Jewish synagogue in Cairo.

Inside, it is the hour of the Sabbath evening prayer; a few old men and a small boy are huddled in their seats. The unsynchronized wailing chant of male voices echoes through the otherwise empty chamber. As I enter, the men briefly turn around. In the dim light I notice the lined, bearded face of an old man; his narrow shoulders are wrapped in a white prayer shawl. Then the sounds of the dirge, a mixture of sobs and exhortations, continue as before.

When the prayer is over, a short while later, we retire to a bench in the corner to talk. The bearded old man has removed his prayer shawl. He has put on another garb, a drab sheet of cotton, worn thin, half Arab robe, half old-fashioned European cape. He is a re- tired postal clerk, he says, the last of his family in Egypt. The rest migrated in the 1950s, some to Italy, others to France and Israel. Before then, he says, there were almost one hundred thousand Jews living in Egypt. Today, perhaps three hundred. "Fewer, fewer!" says another man. "And they are almost all old." He doubts whether there are more than two or three young Jewish males of marriagea- ble age left in the entire country. "In ten or twenty years, it's over."

"Yes," echoes the old man in the cape. "Everybody left when the hard times came—thrown out with the other foreigners."

"But we aren't foreigners," the other man retorts angrily. He is a former schoolteacher. His two brothers and their children left for Is- rael, via France, "after the war." (He does not say which.) Their shop was looted and then taken over by the state. "As 'enemy prop- erty,'" he says. "But we are Egyptians!" True, many Jews were foreign nationals, he says, but they did no harm to anybody. On the contrary. Who supported the opera? Who developed the trade? The Jewish community dated back to Hellenistic times, it "was founded under the special protection of Alexandre le Grand himself," says the old man, shifting to French. He speaks it much better than Eng- lish. *"Nous sommes plus Égyptiens que les Arabes,"* he adds, empha- sizing every syllable.

Life was very hard for Jews, especially during the wars. But things have improved in recent years, he says. The old-age home in Alex- andria is permitted to accept aid from an international Jewish relief organization.

It is getting late. The members of the small congregation hurry out into the lighted street, which is suddenly thronged with people. There are stalls selling fruit juices outside, and pyramids of green watermelons stacked up on the ground. The old man leaves last and locks the gate. The prescribed minimum of ten men for a formal prayer service is rarely filled at Adly Street synagogue, except when tourists are here.

"The Jews have eight synagogues in their quarter in Cairo," Ed- ward Lane wrote in *The Manners and Customs of the Modern*

Egyptians (1836), "and not only enjoy religious toleration but are under a less oppressive government in Egypt than in any other country of the Turkish empire."

But, further on: "They are held in the utmost contempt and abhorrence by the Muslims in general," far more than the Christians, and jostled in the streets or beaten "for merely passing on the right hand of a Muslim." Jews scarcely ever dared "to utter a word of abuse when reviled or beaten unjustly by the meanest Arab or Turk; for many a Jew has been put to death upon a false and malicious accusation of uttering disrespectful words against the Koran, or the Prophet." They were generally considered so unclean "their blood would defile a sword. For this reason Jews were not beheaded," Lane wrote, but hung out of the window of a public building to starve and dry to death in the sun.

A more recent observer, the English writer Harry Hopkins, in *Egypt the Crucible* (1969), speaks of the comfortable though at times "acrimonious domesticity" of the Jews, Moslems, and Christians in Egypt. Many Egyptian Jews now living in Israel say the same. Some of them have in recent years published nostalgic memoirs of their lives in Cairo and Alexandria. Naguib Mahfouz has blamed Nasser personally, as well as the chauvinist revolution generally, for the deterioration in community relations after the 1952 coup d'etat. The Copts have suffered, too. They make up some 8 percent of the population. In an oft-quoted interview Mahfouz gave in 1975 ("The revolution has ruined us and we must make peace with Israel") he spoke at some length of the intolerance toward the Coptic minority brought about by the Nasser dictatorship. Historically, Mahfouz said, Egypt had been a tolerant society; "there has never been a Thirty Years' War here as there was in Europe." With Nasser began the discrimination against the Copts: "A dictatorship cannot respect minorities. It is based on personal trust, not on talent. When the tyrant is a Moslem, whom can he trust? He trusts only Moslems."

For many Jews the almost immediate result of the first Egyptian-Israeli war was not simply discrimination but arrest, confiscation of property, in some cases expulsion, and the sudden spread of anti-

Semitic propaganda. The state of Israel was conceived by its founders as the antidote, the solution to the anti-Semitism from which Jews had suffered for centuries. By an unexpected irony the very establishment of Israel, at a time when anti-Semitism in Europe was discredited and waning, caused the same disease to spread over parts of the world where historically it had been more or less unknown. Jews who had lived for millennia in Egypt, Iraq, Yemen, and North Africa were forced to emigrate only because they were Jews. Under the new nationalisms the darkest, most militant, most obscure elements of Islamic tribalism were revived. Other minorities were also affected: Armenians, Kurds, Cypriots, Greeks, and Italians, none perhaps so cruelly as the Jews. The War against the Jewish Enemies of Islam was officially enjoined by Nasser's "saintly revolution of the armed forces," as a sacred duty of the faithful; he who lost his life battling against them was promised the glorious rewards of a holy martyr in heaven.

PASSOVER EVE. The strange feeling of being in Cairo in the first place is augmented by the odd sensation of being here on the day marking the Exodus from Egypt—and in the home of an old Jewish-Egyptian family. *How is this night different from all other nights,* Jews all over the world would be asking tonight as they assembled for the Passover Seder. I am invited to share it with the N—— family. Their home is a comfortable five-room apartment, located in a good middle-class section of Cairo. N—— is a man in his late fifties, a graduate of Alexandria University, self-employed and relatively well-to-do. He is married to a slim, gray-haired woman with a rather sad face. Her family has been living in Egypt, "forever," she says, a family of rabbis, and traders in spices and wood. She can trace it back, she says, almost to the days when Maimonides was Saladin's physician at the court of Cairo. N—— and his wife attended French mission schools, as did many of the better-off Jewish children in Egypt. Their two teenaged children are now going to state schools. "The old days are over," says N——.

The family gathers around the table at eight o'clock. But first they watch Sadat's televised fireside chat to the nation. Sadat talks for over an hour. He speaks without notes from his study in the presidential villa near the Sheraton Hotel. He talks in a calm, benevolent sort of way, mixing promises with fatherly exhortations. The news tonight is that he is not content with having the peace treaty with Israel ratified by his hand-picked Parliament only. He will ask the people to ratify the treaty as well—by national referendum. Let the rejectionist Arab leaders "who used Egyptian blood in order to raise the price of oil fourfold—let them see for themselves!" he says, that such is the will of every Egyptian man and woman. These midgets, says Sadat, warming to his theme, these miniature rulers, these hypocrites, some of them so corrupt they dare not show their faces in the streets! No, he is not going to place the fate of the Egyptian nation in their hands. He is going to make peace and get back Egypt's land. "I challenge them! Let us see them do what I did."

Furthermore, he announces elections for a new Parliament within two weeks. And, for the first time since 1952, freedom to form new parties. The one-party state is at an end. A new era of liberty dawns, and so on.

"Rubbish," says N——, who happens to be one of the founders of the Communist party of Egypt. The party is officially suppressed, though it manages to lead a marginal existence as the Progressive Union of Egypt. N—— has served time in several Egyptian prisons and desert concentration camps. It is natural that he is a bit dubious about Sadat's promises. Only the other day the Union's office was raided by the police. No one was arrested, but a stack of leaflets attacking Sadat's "hallucination of prosperity" after peace was seized by the police. "They used to oppress us in the name of war. Now they oppress us in the name of peace." N—— speaks about this with apparent nonchalance. He has been through more difficult days. He says, "They accuse us of spreading fake news to confuse and agitate the people. We only say the truth."

Still, it is true that this night is different from others. N—— admits that he feels relatively safe for the first time in years. He is not afraid of being put away for weeks, or months, in preventive custody. Both N—— and his wife have close relatives living in Israel. Yes, they left Egypt in 1954, when things were getting difficult for the Jews. Yes, life was very hard after the 1948 war and under Nasser. N—— admires Nasser, though. "A great man," he says. "A very great social reformer."

In 1948 the Communists of Egypt had been the only political party that opposed the war against Israel. (The Soviet Union had, after all, been one of Israel's chief sponsors.) For this, N—— and some of his colleagues had been imprisoned. And now? What does N—— think now of the peace that has finally been signed?

Well, after four wars and one hundred thousand casualties on both sides, N—— and the Communists of Egypt are against the peace treaty. Isn't it a tragedy, I say, given the past record of the Egyptian Left as the only political body who opposed the war from the beginning?

Yes and no, N—— says. But "yes, we are against the treaty," he adds, a bit reluctantly, perhaps, and with a self-conscious smile. "It's true, I don't like this peace very much." Why?

"Because this is Sadat's peace. It is not real peace. It is a Pax Americana. Imposed by multinational corporations." N——'s wife looks sullen. She says nothing.

The table is laid in the spacious dining room, next to the library. Through the windows, a fine view of the city. The wine is Egyptian —Cleopatra Red. The matzoth are from Israel; none are baked in Egypt today. *This is the bread of affliction which our ancestors ate in the Land of Egypt:* select portions of the Haggada are read by N—— and his children, in French. *This year we are slaves, next year free men,* or *In every generation a man must see himself as though he had come out of Egyptian slavery.* So much of the Jewish ethos is compressed, encapsulated in the little book of the Haggada, a shorthand code; the other holy books seem almost footnotes.

When Israel went out of Egypt . . . N—— has had many an opportunity to get out. He has chosen to stay, at no small price of hardship, discomfort, and suffering. *This year we are here. Next year in Jerusalem.* But N—— is not a Zionist. For this reason he was against the establishment of Israel in 1948. Afterward he was sorry to see that Israel had become, as he puts it, an instrument of imperialism. *We were slaves of Pharaoh in Egypt.* N—— believes in human rights under socialism. As a young man at the university he resolved that he was an Egyptian, though at the same time an avowed Jew. "I am very proud of our heritage." Does he believe in God? There is a brief silence. "I . . . I . . . don't know."

Clear soup with dumplings is followed by delicious boiled beef. The conversation is in English and French, but the members of N——'s family address one another in Arabic. N——'s daughter is engaged to be married to a Moslem. The shelves in the library close by are filled with books on Jewish subjects pressed in between Lenin and works by contemporary French and Italian Marxists. There are mezuzoth on all the doors. N—— speaks four languages fluently. *Pour thy wrath upon the heathen that have not known thy name.* As a proud Jew, N—— has been active during the past ten years in helping to restore a modicum of civil rights to the few Jews who have remained in Egypt. He remembers a time when his children came home from school traumatized by teachers' remarks that all Jews were enemies of God, had assaulted Egypt and Arabism, and therefore deserved to die. The anti-Semitic propaganda of the Nasser days, however, is over. N—— says he had always protested against it. His last achievement in the field of civil rights, he says, was the restoration a few years ago of the passports of Jews for foreign travel on an equal footing with other Egyptians. Confiscation of Jewish property—not that there is much left—has also stopped. *Our ancestors were slaves to Pharaoh in Egypt but God brought us out from there, from slavery to freedom. In every generation every man must see himself as though he himself has come out of Egyptian bondage*

N—— says he is fully resolved to stay on in Egypt. "I belong here," he says, he intends to continue the fight for human rights, for workers' rights, and against economic exploitation. In the past twenty-five years he has spent a total of five and a half in jail, mostly because of his political activities as a left-winger, but at least twice because, as a Jew, he was suspected of sympathizing with Israel. Did he? On the contrary, he says firmly. In 1956 he was so incensed by the tripartite Anglo-French-Israeli aggression against Egypt that he presented himself as a volunteer to the Egyptian

Army. He was ready even to fight against close members of his own family who were at that time already in Israel.

But he was rejected. The excuse the Egyptian Army gave was the same the Israeli Army uses vis-à-vis Israeli Arabs, N—— says with a sly smile. They did not wish to embarrass him with a *crise de conscience*. Immediately afterward, however, he was detained and held in prison for three months. The same happened in 1967. Again he volunteered to serve in the Egyptian Army, was rejected, and was arrested, this time for six months. *We were slaves . . . in Egypt,* but God has not yet brought us out to freedom. N—— hopes very much that life will be easier from now on, but he isn't sure.

Coffee is served in tiny porcelain cups. N—— is slender and good-looking. His pleasant eyes dart back and forth around the table, and when he is amused, as he often is, his pale cheeks acquire a ruddy flush and he breaks out into a loud infectious laugh. A likable man—though enigmatic; on many occasions in the past he could have moved to, say Paris, where such views as his, when fervently held, are both chic and even a lucrative source of income. N—— laughs as he says this. His wife looks at him across the table. Her eyes are dark and clouded. N—— believes that his place is here. He is a believer. Behind every ephemeral moment he seeks the absolute. There is something very old, very Jewish about N——. I sip my coffee, feeling also the wine I have drunk, looking at N—— and thinking that although he is an Egyptian and not a Polish Jew, he is a character straight out of one of the Isaac Bashevis Singer novels I love so.

A PECULIARITY OF EGYPT: people rarely say no to you here. It is not that they always give you a straightforward yes. When they want to say no they have a gentle, roundabout way of doing so, through deflection or procrastination.

For example, the very friendly, always smiling officials of the government press center who help me to arrange meetings within and outside of the government. I do not trouble them too greatly, for I do not seek the "big names" that other foreign reporters want to meet. I am not looking for interviews at all but rather for informal meetings to acquaint myself, as best I can, with people in different walks of life. Whenever I ask the press center to arrange a meeting with a person known to be opposed to the Sadat government the answer is never no. But neither does a meeting emerge. I am told the man has been contacted. There is no problem at all, the time and place remain to be fixed. Then I hear nothing. I call to inquire, and discover that the file has been misplaced or the secretary is out. She will call back as soon as she comes in. But she doesn't.

If this be a convention, the less-subtle, no-nonsense Israelis will find it difficult to adapt quickly. Moreover, Israelis have been conditioned by their history to think that no may mean yes, if only a certain amount of tenacity is employed. Every Israeli political debate—always exhortative and didactic—every labor conflict, every trade union negotiation, further accustoms the Israeli not to take no for an answer. I know that this contrast in style has already caused many a misunderstanding between the two sides during the peace negotiations.

The Palestinian issue serves as a case in point. Egypt's no to the annexation of the Gaza Strip and the West Bank is firm but muted. Almost every conversation with Egyptians leads up to this theme. There is little chance of avoiding it. It is always the same, either as plea or complaint. I hear it from nearly everybody, politicians, officials, intellectuals, journalists, or the casually encountered man in a café. Major Sherif of the State Security Service also talks about the Palestinians. This is perhaps natural, since when he is not accompanying an Israeli visitor he is tracking down potential Palestinian terrorists in their Cairo hideouts.

But so also do the luminaries of the original Egyptian peace movement, the writers Idris and Mahfouz and Hakim. Try as one may, one never gets away from it, one always comes back to the same theme. Not in a strident manner and never very insistently, for the consummate politeness and rules of hospitality, even of the most opinionated intellectuals, usually preclude any direct affront. There are subtle means of making points tenaciously, through roundabout routes, remarks and general reflections on the nature and origin of conflict. When the frills are cut away, what they all seem to be saying is: the Palestinian issue is the heart and crux of the conflict that has divided us in the past thirty years and still divides us today. The peace treaty with Israel has been signed, yes, and it is a very good thing too. But without a resolution of the Palestinian problem it cannot be a real peace. The Israelis must try to win over the Palestinians to the cause of peace. How? By granting them the right to self-determination on the West Bank and in the Gaza Strip. But do the Palestinians want to live in peace with us, I ask.

Answer: They will, they will! It is up to you! You must win their confidence! You must invest in them! Egypt cannot do this for you! It is your problem, not ours!

These are reasonable suggestions, no doubt. When I hear them, I sometimes ask my interlocutors why, if this is really something between us and the Palestinians only, why then did Egypt vote against the United Nations partition plan of 1947 that stipulated the establishment of a Jewish and a Palestinian state within a divided country? Why did the Egyptian Army invade Israel, with the avowed purpose of preventing that resolution from being carried out? There could have been a Palestinian state many years ago! The two states might have learned to live with each other. We might have avoided thirty years of bloodshed and ruin. And why didn't Egypt grant self-determination to the Palestinians of the Gaza Strip, which it had controlled until 1967?

When I ask these questions—they are not altogether idle—I try to be as tactful as I can. There is little sense in reopening now all the old wounds. We have all made blunders. The Palestinian problem is real, I know that very well. But I do try to make my perplexities clear.

The answers range from guarded regret for the blunders of past Egyptian governments to the frank statement that Egypt's policy in 1948 had been morally and politically correct; only later on was it shown to be "impractical" or prohibitive, because of its great cost. Some rationalize the Egyptian intervention of 1948 as the outgrowth of inter-Arab feuds rather than as innate hostility against the establishment of a small Israeli enclave in the Arab East. Others simply say, "The situation has changed."

One elderly Egyptian recalls Ismail Zidky Pasha, the Egyptian statesman who pleaded with King Farouk in 1948 to avoid a military adventure in Palestine. There is a certain nostalgia in his tone. Zidky Pasha was one of several Egyptian statesmen at the time who doubted the wisdom of the King's Palestine policy. None was as firm as he in warning the King against involving Egypt in a quarrel that was not Egypt's. For this, Zidky was denounced as an agent provocateur, a spy for America and the Jews, a traitor. He died a few years later, a sick, broken man.

Mussa Sabry of *Al Akhbar* halfheartedly blames Nasser. Nasser, he says, continued the King's policy, which the Free Officers had at first shown little tendency to pursue. It was, after all, in the trenches of Faluja, during Farouk's disastrous Palestine campaign, that the Free Officers first got to "thinking of our problems," as Nasser recorded in his *Philosophy of the Revolution,* and resolved that the real problems were in Egypt, not in Palestine. I say Sabry blames Nasser "halfheartedly" because at the same time he insists that Nasser never really wanted war with Israel . . . no, not even in 1967! Nasser was only bluffing, says Sabry. Nasser expected to get away with the blockade on Israeli shipping in the Strait of Tiran, expelling the United Nations, and massing his troops and tanks in the Sinai, without provoking a war. Nasser blundered into that war by accident, quite unintentionally, Sabry insists. Nasser was confused. Nasser miscalculated. Of such stuff, Sabry seems to be saying, history is made. I should believe that Nasser was the legendary ram whom the shepherd was fattening for the slaughter, and only because he was fatter than the rest was seen as a great leader and genius in the eyes of the flock, and in his own eyes as well. Meanwhile events take their own course; the ram has little effect on them.

Besides, he adds, wasn't it Israel—not Egypt—who fired the first shot in that war? Dare I tell Sabry—of whom I am becoming very fond—that this argument seems about as sensible to me as the claim that Britain and France were the aggressors in World War II because they had first declared war on Germany? This, in fact, had been Ribbentrop's pious argument to the French ambassador. Should I tell Sabry that Nasser *wanted* war? And said so himself, but did not realize how inept his army was? Of course I do not. For what point is there to acerbate feelings? Moreover, I fear the learned Mussa Sabry might throw Tolstoy's *War and Peace* at me to support his theory of blundering generals and kings in the course of history. But he doesn't. He changes the subject, and says in a soft voice that he would like to take me to an important art exhibition that has just opened in Cairo. The artist, Munir Canaan, is a friend of his, and a very nice man.

FIKRY MAHRAM EBEID is the secretary-general of President Sadat's National Democratic party. He takes the common view that Egypt's Palestinian policy had been correct, but the cost proved prohibitive in the end. Mr. Ebeid says that the wars cost Egypt $58 billion. With that money, he says, echoing Tewfik al-Hakim, every single village in Egypt could have been reconstructed.

"We love the Palestinians," he says, but what are they really doing for themselves? What are the other Arabs ready to do for them. "Of the one hundred and sixty thousand Palestinians who have died in the wars, one hundred thousand Palestinians were killed by *Arabs,* in Jordan or Lebanon."

Sadat's disillusionment with pan-Arabism strongly influences Mr. Ebeid's position. When he, or President Sadat, publicly decries the rampant corruption of certain PLO leaders, it immediately fuels the wishful thinking of many Israelis. I think about this a great deal and wonder whether we are properly attuned to the complexities that make up the orchestration of Egyptian policy. Sadat may indeed inveigh against the corruption and cupidity of the present Syrian, Iraqi and Palestinian leaderships, in a perhaps naïve hope that they might be replaced. But that does not mean, as many Israelis would like to think, that he "does not give a damn about the Palestinians . . . that if we hang on long enough to the occupied territories, Sadat's no to annexation will become a reluctant yes." This, I am afraid, is a mistake. The Egyptian no will continue to be a quiet one, as long as Israel is still in the process of returning to Egypt the occupied territory of Sinai. But once the withdrawal is complete, what is to prevent Sadat from abrogating the treaty because of Israeli noncompliance on the issue of Palestinian self-rule? Or, at the very least, from postponing the process of normalization?

When Naguib Mahfouz publicly stated that he was ready to sacrifice land for the sake of civilization, he was viciously attacked in the Arab press ("Mahfouz sells out the Palestinians"). But in that same statement he made it very clear that by "sacrifice" he meant only those parts of Arab Palestine, as he called it, which were Israel proper, not those occupied during the 1967 war. Mahfouz is for compromise, not for capitulation.

BY CHANCE, I RUN into Dr. A——, a Palestinian activist from the occupied territories. He materializes one afternoon out of the multitude on Tahrir Square. I have known Dr. A—— for some years. He is what I would call a moderate man. By "moderate" I mean that he would be content with some form of Palestinian self-rule in the territories that would not be a "sham," as he puts it, "not another Bechuanaland." He travels back and forth between Israel and the Arab states regularly. He is on friendly terms with important political figures in Israel, as well as in Cairo, Amman, and Beirut.

Dr. A—— is as surprised to see me in Cairo as I am to bump suddenly into him in this crowd. He is a man of small stature, rotund but solidly built, a little like Napoleon in some of his more flattering poses. Dr. A—— is a man of independent means, the graduate of a famous European university—he does not practice his profession. He takes a keen interest in many things besides politics: art, horticulture, archaeology. This makes him easier to befriend. For even when neither wants it, conversation with so many other Palestinian activists on the West Bank inevitably turns to the common theme: politics, nothing but politics, tense, frustrating verbal wars of attrition between conflicting views that seem to allow for little reasonable compromise. With Dr. A—— I find I can also quarrel or agree about architecture. We share an interest in the subject. This helps to bring us closer as human beings.

We embrace and retire to a nearby café. He looks frustrated and depressed. He wants to talk. I think I understand his depression. A moderate Palestinian nationalist (there are not many), he is one of the few Palestinian leaders who have called for the recognition of Israel and welcomed Sadat's peace mission to Jerusalem. He feels frustrated by the obstinate refusal of other Palestinians to join in Sadat's efforts and, at the same time, by what he fears is Sadat's reluctance to stand more firmly behind them. One frustration feeds the other.

He is pleased to be in an Arab country, though, away from the occupation, which, he complains, is becoming "more brutal" all the time. At the same time he is worried by what he has heard here. He has had a series of meetings with Egyptian government ministers. They have been trying to reassure him, he says, but he is not reassured. He is, in fact, rather upset with the Egyptians for rushing into this peace treaty without first securing a more specific Israeli commitment on the question of Palestinian independence. He tells me of a meeting with one of President Sadat's chief ministers.

"I asked him, 'Why didn't you write into the treaty clear guidelines for Palestinian self-rule? In the same way that you insisted on the exact timetable of the Israeli withdrawal from Sinai. Now it is too late.'"

The minister, says A——, put his hand on his breast. "'I swear to you,' he said, 'believe me, the cause of Palestine remains very close to my heart. I promise you we shall not abandon your interests.'" There were tears in his eyes, says A——. The gesture was very dramatic, but it left A—— unconvinced. "Another high official, in the Foreign Ministry, agreed with everything I said. He told me, 'Make sure to tell everyone upstairs,' meaning Sadat himself." But A—— does not trust Sadat anymore.

"I told his minister, 'You signed this treaty without thinking about us. Don't be surprised that the Palestinians are now refusing to join the negotiations as you had hoped. You signed! Now *you* deliver something concrete to us.'"

He does not really believe they will. He is afraid that as a consequence the entire edifice of peace may collapse. "In our lifetime we won't have such a chance again," he says. "There are too many madmen around." He is flying home in a few days, via Athens. On the West Bank many people refuse to talk to him because he wants peace with Israel and initially supported Sadat's efforts. Is he going to rescind on that now?

"I feel sick," he says. He is also concerned because one of his nephews has just been arrested as a suspected PLO agent and faces possible expulsion by the Israelis. A—— is a very lonely man. He is caught in the middle—on a bridge. The trouble with being a bridge, said Jan Masaryk, speaking of Czechoslovakia's role between East and West on the eve of the cold war, was that everybody steps on you. As we leave the café, a madwoman in Tahrir Square is shouting at the sky.

DR. A—— SAYS THAT among ordinary Egyptians he is encountering much antagonism, even hatred, toward Palestinians. Some people have told him, "You are the cause of all our misery. Because of you there is such a housing shortage in Egypt." Palestinians are regarded in Egypt as deracinated parasites, pushy and loud, says Dr. A——. Palestinians are said to cheat on taxes. The number of Palestinians attending Egyptian universities is said to be "disproportionately high" at a time when there are not enough classrooms and dormitories for Egyptians. They are said to be a nation of "millionaires" who have enriched themselves at Egypt's expense. It all sounds a bit like the accusations leveled in the West at the turn of the century against Polish Jews. Dr. A—— shows me this week's issue of *Al Siassi*, a popular political magazine; there is an article on the front page entitled "The Truth about the Palestinian Millionaires," which lists the names and addresses of rich Palestinians who live in Egypt, complete with estimates of their wealth. The material was quite clearly leaked by a government agency.

"The Palestinians own the biggest shops and businesses in the most expensive quarters of Cairo. Les Grands Magazins Nani, 42 Talaat Harb Street. Proprietor: Mohammed Hussein el Sharfa. Capital, 1.5 million pounds." And so on.

While Egypt suffers from a grave housing shortage, continues *Al Siassi*, Palestinians (including a number of PLO leaders) occupy "11,985 furnished luxury apartments at rents ranging from 150 to

1,500 pounds a month. Where does the money come from?" Over twelve thousand Palestinian students are enrolled in Egyptian universities, complains *Al Siassi*. Many choose medicine, pharmacology and engineering, and when they conclude their studies, the ungrateful pack prefers to work elsewhere, outside of Egypt. . . .

Dr. A—— says, "We are the new Jews, don't you think?" The traffic on Tahrir Square is roaring by. The arguments are beginning to revolve in circles and leave one dizzy.

MUSSA SABRY, as he had promised, takes me to see the exhibition of paintings by Munir Canaan. Sabry thinks very highly of him. And the reason he takes me to see Canaan's work is, I suspect, that he would like to give me a holiday from politics. Yet he speaks of hardly anything else. He says he is quite disappointed with Prime Minister Begin as a man. When he asked Begin what Israel was ready to do in return for Sadat's recognition of Israel, Begin, says Sabry, answered condescendingly, "My dear friend, we didn't ask you to recognize us. . . ."

Munir Canaan's exhibition is in a little palace by the Nile. We drive there in Sabry's Mercedes limousine. In the back there is a push-button radio telephone. Sabry's bodyguard sits in the front seat next to the driver. We enter the grounds through a spacious garden. Canaan is at the door. He is a husky man. The show is a retrospective of his work during the past twenty-five years and will soon go on loan to a gallery in Paris, Canaan says.

He creates powerful collages in burlap and reed and strong earth colors, as well as delicate abstract paintings in white on white and pale pinks. Style and technique are the same that one sees everywhere in the West, "but I did these things years before Rauschenberg," cries Canaan. The sense of decay in colors and texture is purely his own. He points at a square collage of driftwood and sand, a delicate intersticing that barely holds together. "It's like Egypt," he says. "Take out a pin and the whole thing collapses."

A sense of exhaustion throughout. Lawrence Durrell (who was obsessed by the effect of geography on the personality) says it was this sense of exhaustion and the climate that made people want to get away from Egypt—the stifling, devitalizing feeling that comes from being so near to the desert in a land so flat there is not so much as a molehill for miles around. And yet this crude achromatic monotony produced such great visual art, full of refined affectation and color, and it still produces the remarkable canvases of Munir Canaan.

Such works are their own confirmation, absolute, indisputable. Unlike ideologies, they are not polemical. Durrell disliked Egypt. In *The Alexandria Quartet* he raided an incestuous city of the mind, a fantastic place that never existed. Durrell felt in Egypt like the banished Ovid in Romania. But when Durrell says that "even *small-time* Egyptian clerks [to Durrell it was quite a "rich country"] used to take themselves off to Paris once a year . . . to let some air into the system," I wonder how many *big-time* non-European clerks there were in his time.

Canaan says he could not work anywhere but here, even though the life of an artist is very difficult in Egypt. Few people have an interest in modern painting. Fewer still are prepared to buy. Canaan supports himself as an illustrator for Sabry's *Al Akhbar*. We talk about Rauschenberg and Klee and Durrell. Color is like music, Canaan says, he can hear it with his ears. For an entire evening I am able to engross myself in something other than politics.

WHAT SENSITIVE EGYPTIANS, like Yussef Hattam, must deal with in the new times that are coming: Hattam has secured a recent issue of the Israeli English-language newspaper, the Jerusalem *Post*. It includes an extensive report by three special correspondents who accompanied Prime Minister Begin to Cairo. The emphasis is on the squalor and dirt and the telephones that don't work. Not a word on any other aspect of Egyptian life. Instead there is the patronizing attitude of:

> Cairo itself is crying out for a Teddy Killek [the mayor of Jerusalem] to do some tidying up, water the scant gardens, post trashcans and get people to use them. . . . I thought only [*sic*] of what Avraham Yoffe [head of the Israeli National Parks] could

do if entrusted with landscaping around the pyramids and sullen sphinx. He could turn a miserable dustbowl and garbage dump into a garden fit for a spectacle.

Hattam is naturally upset and accuses the *Post* of condescension and, of course, arrogance. He has no patience with the objections I offer. It does not matter that there really is a garbage dump by the Great Pyramid. This Hattam does not deny: it is the tone he resents. On that I cannot challenge him. We sit on my terrace in the evening light, talking.

When Hattam was a boy, his father, a customs inspector, was molested by British soldiers in the Canal Zone. They left Hattam's father lying in a ditch and walked on, singing "King Farouk, King Farouk, Stick your bullocks on a hook."

After this incident, Hattam says, his father was never the same again. All these neurotic shadows that are thrown by the past on the peoples of the two countries, Egypt and Israel! (Tahsin Bashir says they are both "sick"; how can you make peace between such people?) In Israel the shadow of persecution falls on the discussion of almost any public theme; an aggressiveness explodes, merely from living too long as pariah in a sealed pressure cooker. In Egypt, the shadows are cast by the enslavement, repression, and humiliation suffered at the hands of Mamelukes, Turks, and British colonial administrators.

In his memoirs, Anwar al-Sadat tells the story of the village of Denshawai which, he says, traumatized him as a young man. Denshawai was a little Delta village, a few miles from Sadat's native Mit Abul Kum. The inhabitants raised pigeons in round, tower-shaped pigeon houses of whitewashed brick. In 1906 a party of British officers came to the village to hunt the pigeons. In the resultant melee one villager was beaten to death, four more were wounded by gunfire, a Captain Ball was severely beaten and later died of concussion and sunstroke. Although it was clear that the "sportsmen" had no right to come and shoot the peasants' pigeons, the British viewed the incident as an instance of dangerous nationalist and religious fanaticism. The penalty, meant to be exemplary, was medieval. A special tribunal sentenced four villagers to death, two to life imprisonment, six to seven years in prison, and nine others to fifty lashes each. The scaffold, writes Sadat, was erected on the village square even before the sentences had been passed. The hangings and floggings were carried out in public; the inhabitants of Denshawai were forced to watch.

The incident seems to have bred a generation of Egyptian rebels. Bernard Shaw wrote about it in *John Bull's Other Island:* "Try to imagine the feelings in an English village if a party of Chinese officers suddenly appeared and began to shoot the ducks, the geese, the hens and the turkeys, and carried them off asserting that they were wild birds, as everybody in China knew, and the pretended indignation of the farmers was a cloak for hatred of the Chinese, and perhaps for a plot to overthrow the religion of Confucius and establish the Church of England in its stead."

Hattam tells me that Dr. Boutrous-Ghali's grandfather had been the presiding judge at the trial of Denshawai. Hattam does not remember whether this was why Boutrous-Ghali's grandfather was assassinated in 1910. As a collaborator with the British—and a Copt—the grandfather, Boutrous Ghali Pasha, had been a very unpopular man.

LIKE JERUSALEM, CAIRO has an English-language daily newspaper, *The Egyptian Gazette*. Arthur Koestler's extravagant theory that the Jews are not really Jews but Khazars is popular with its editors. Speaking of Israel's long-standing demands for territorial change (a "secure border"), the *Gazette*'s editorial has attacked "Begin and his rough crew of land grabbers . . . it is absurd for a 7000 year old nation to discuss territorial changes with a collection of Khazar Jews, who just about have enough claim to Arab land as Eskimos to Tanzania. . . . With effort perhaps Mr. Begin can be made to see that his ancestors and indeed those of all Eastern European Jews are not the ancient Hebrews but the Jews of Khazaria, that eighth to thirteenth century kingdom esconced between Christian Byzantium and the Arab Caliphate. When the kingdom was smashed by the Mongols, the Khazars, who had converted to Judaism from phallus worshipping, fled to what is now Eastern Europe. . . . The real Jews [must not] be confused with Begin's converted from phallus-worship lot," according to *The Egyptian Gazette*.

VII

THE EGYPTIAN PARLIAMENT is called the People's Assembly. The name, given to it during Nasser's days, recalls Egypt's
affinity in the past with the "people's democracies" of Eastern
Europe. Like Eastern European parliaments, the People's Assembly
is still largely a rubber stamp for executive decisions. The 360
members are carefully (s)elected by the regime. The assembly is a
convenient place to observe the potentates of state. The security
measures are less stringent than those of the Knesset, where visitors
are X-rayed and bodily searched for weapons, and are allowed to
follow the proceedings through loudspeakers only, from behind a
thick plate of armored glass, a precaution introduced in spite of a
public outcry long before the upsurge of Palestinian terrorism.

The People's Assembly plenum meets under a dome of muted
cream and golds, in a round hall of pleasantly intimate proportions,
built in the French neoclassical style of the *fin de siècle*. It has seen
the painful birth and demise of Western-style parliamentarism in
Egypt, with its attendant violence and assassinations. The deputies
crowd together on green upholstered benches. Most are in dark
business suits; a few are wearing long galabias.

President Sadat has just concluded a speech of three hours, in
which he urged the Assembly to ratify the peace treaty. *"Bis millah,*
in the name of Egypt my mother, Egypt my father, my faith, in the

name of this holy soil, of every child, every mother, every father," peace is great, it is good for the future of civilization.

The session is carried live on television. Sadat is given a long standing ovation. "Bless you for all your good deeds!" cries out one deputy dressed in a long burnous. "Peace is one of the names of Allah!"

Sadat withdraws to a side room. The deputies file out slowly to the antechamber, where they stand about in small clusters. Dr. Boutrous-Ghali, clutching a file of papers and looking very professorial, explains a fine point to Vice-President Mubarek. The Prime Minister, Mustapha Khalil, tall, square-faced, a former engineer, says it is not true that he boycotted Begin's visit to Cairo, he had simply been indisposed. He feels sure the treaty will work. But Israel must be "more flexible" on the Palestinian issue—"and more rational: if you will pull out the Bible every day to claim some hill town, the Arabs will pull out the Koran! Where will all this end? This is a political, not a religious problem." Unlike Boutrous-Ghali and officials of the Foreign Ministry, the Prime Minister is not filled to the brim with fears and suspicions.

Osman Akhmed Osman, a major building contractor and former Minister of Housing, is a chief proponent of the theory, widespread in Egyptian business circles, that building contracts are more profitable than cannons. His son is married to Sadat's daughter, and he is shaking hands all around as though he had just concluded a successful business deal.

Osman Akhmed Osman says he would like to do business in Israel, but not too soon; his interests in Kuwait and Libya are too large, he risks difficulties if he moves too quickly too soon. He is already involved, indirectly, in the restoration of the Mosque of Al Aksa in Jerusalem. "If Begin has any sense," he says, "he'll offer the Palestinians full autonomy. He risks nothing. The Palestinian organizations will go on fighting one another and never accept his offer anyway. Not in a thousand years."

Dr. Sufi Abu Taleb, Speaker of the People's Assembly, also stresses the Palestinian problem. It is the heart and crux of the matter, he says, echoing what Sadat has just told the Assembly. And yet clearly he has very little patience with the self-appointed professionals of the Palestinian cause. They hurt the very people they set out to save, the misdirected terrorists and their even more dangerous high priests, the intellectuals, the vicarious heroes prepared to fight to the bitter end from the comfort of their luxurious offices and hotel suites; the cynics and manipulators of the various PLO splinter groups, more eager to preserve their organizations and their bank accounts than to serve the cause of the Palestinian people. That cause, he thinks, should be taken up by the inhabitants of the occupied territories. They must take their fate into their own hands. How? By working with Egypt, Israel, and the United States to implement the treaty. A bomb here or a bomb there is not going to liberate their land. What if they don't cooperate? "They will, they will, I assure you, they will." What if not? "In that case, let them go to hell."

In a corner, off by himself—discouraging conversation—is the dark-faced, saturnine, bearded, slightly sinister-looking Mohammed Hassan Touhami, Sadat's adviser and emissary to many a secret assignation. It was Touhami who secretly met with Dayan in Morocco to begin hammering out an agreement even before Sadat flew to Jerusalem. He prefers to remain behind the scenes. No, he is very sorry, he will not talk. It is against his principles, his method of work, he also shies away from photographers. He is said to be a religious mystic. One morning, during negotiations at Camp David, he told an Israeli diplomat that during the night he had had a strange dream. In his dream, Sadat was in mortal danger. He, Touhami, hears about it, he soars through the air to his rescue. He reaches Sadat and saves his life. On another occasion he is said to have told his colleagues that the Prophet Mohammed appeared to him in a dream and told him it was right to make peace with the Jews.

Meanwhile, President Sadat has left the building. The reason for the deputies' delay in the antechamber is that nobody leaves the Assembly building before Sadat. In the street outside, the trumpets sound, a military guard of honor salutes the departing President. His car moves up the narrow street. The roads ahead have been blocked and cleared of traffic. The bridge over the Nile is lined with special militiamen. Nearby, the vast Tahrir Square is black with stalled traffic. On the sidewalk a blind fiddler is leaning against the wall, as in a picture by Hogarth, oblivious to the commotion. He passes a short, rounded bow over the three strings of his pumpkin-shaped instrument. The throbbing sound is all but swallowed in the noise, but his little collection box is filling with coins.

A LONG WALK THROUGH the pyramid area at dusk. I take the back way from the sphinx up the steep slope to the Pyramid of Cheops. According to Munir Canaan, the painter, it is the more dramatic route, as though the other lacked morbid drama and pathos. In the mauve light the air smells of dung and hot stones, and sand fading into dark. The pyramids stand on a barren plateau overlooking the city. The city is barely visible because of the pollution in the air. From behind, the Great Pyramid seems even more massive than from up front. It is surrounded by muleteers and ice cream vendors. The tourists mill about. The grounds are strewn with refuse. The wind is blowing empty plastic cups down the rocky ravine. Some visitors are slowly making their way to the top, like steady insects. The Great Pyramid is a taste that takes some time to get used to. When Gustav Mahler was shown Niagara Falls, he searched for words to please his hosts. Finally he sighed and said, *"Endlich fortissimo!"*

There is little new that one can say about the pyramids. They reminded Nikos Kazantzakis of the pyramid-shaped mountain of skulls in a famous painting that portrays war. These plundered tombs of ancient god-kings, built by thousands who labored and died under the lash, are so designed as to make mere mortals feel small, insignificant, insectlike. Man is not the measure, as in Greece where even the mountains seem anthropomorphous, not the center of creation but only another form of physical substance. This feeling is a modern one: Roquentin feels it as he contemplates the tree in Sartre's *Nausea,* one of the great moments in contemporary literature. It is the celebrated existentialist sickness that hits you here, the horror and revulsion caused by the realization that under the veneer of individual manifestation there is ultimate reality, matter—infinite and vicious.

"Nowhere on earth have I felt such violent and sensuous contact of life with death. . . . Everything takes on a superhuman symbolic value because nowhere as here in Egypt can you see so clearly before you that life is a tiny island built on the infinite ocean of death." Kazantzakis wrote this in 1927. In Egypt I find myself strongly drawn again to Kazantzakis. He was the quintessence of intellect infused with passion. Egypt had a magnetic attraction for this modern man in search of his soul. The observations and vignettes of his Egyptian journal later became major themes in *Zorba, The Greek Passion,* and the semiautobiographical *Report to Greco.* From Kazantzakis there runs a line to Camus, whose thinking he seems to have anticipated by a decade. "What is our obligation?" Kazantzakis wrote in a letter from Egypt. "To look at the chasm . . . without hope and fear," to wage "the quixotic, despairing campaign" of a Sisyphus, or a "green leaf in the Nile Delta," for immediately beyond is the dead desert.

THE TOURISTS CRAWL into the entrance of the pyramid. A narrow shaft leads through to the empty burial chamber. A German-speaking tour guide lectures through a megaphone. He speaks of heights and measurements—two and one half million cut stones; Napoleon said they were enough to build a wall nine feet high around the entire area of France. The guide speaks of depths and weights and gods. There were a great many gods, gods of the living and of the dead, bulls and cows and at the same time gods of the sun and of the stars.

Inside the narrow shaft the air is damp. The guide speaks of eons. Three thousand five hundred years, five thousand years, seven thousand. Tourism began here in 700 B.C.: a million graffiti testify to this fact, including the classical verses of a Greek poet in the days of the Ptolemies, and in a later age, that of Edward VII of England.

"At the foot of this monument, everything becomes insignificant," the guide says, quoting a German authority. The tourists wipe their perspiring foreheads with tissues.

To think that only two weeks ago a pale, elderly Jew stood here in the shaft between the fading graffiti, a native of the little town of Brest Litovsk in the swampy eastern region of Poland, here he stood, surrounded by the courtiers and sorcerers of a present pharaoh. To think that he was welcomed here with all the pomp due to a visiting potentate, and then uttered words of appreciation for all the depths and weights and values of a great and ancient civilization, words that were kindly received, even with satisfaction and some pleasure, and greatly improved the cool atmosphere of an unprecedented state visit.

To think that fewer than forty years before, that same pale visitor had himself escaped an insect's death in the gas chambers of Poland by fleeing to a neighboring country, to join what was then an isolated community of splenetic pioneers living out a dream of individual and collective redemption in a bare land; to think this visitor now officiates as Prime Minister of that land, a sovereign state which has just signed a treaty to end the thirty years' war with Egypt.

There is something surrealistic in such thoughts—of human insects and of the redemptive power of the human soul. With Begin in the dark tunnel there also stood 6 million dead. Were it not for them he would not have stood there. To think such thoughts in this dark tunnel, inside this vast pyramid, is to contemplate the more baffling, fantastic aspects of what people call Zionism. It was Kazantzakis' "quixotic despairing campaign of the green leaf." Elsewhere he writes: "The soul of man is the burning, but not the consumed, bush."

A LITTLE WHILE LATER, in the hotel lobby, I run into an acquaintance, Karl Kahana, an Austrian Jewish philanthropist. Kahana has been a supporter of Israel for years, and a chairman of Israel Bonds. He is on friendly terms with President Sadat, as well as many Israeli leaders, and has played a certain role in the past to bring Egyptians and Israelis together.

I tell Kahana of my thoughts in the tunnel of the Great Pyramid, and we speak of the momentous turn of events. Then he shakes his head. "Isn't Begin spoiling it all now?" Kahana dislikes Begin. He is one of those few, but not uninfluential, Jewish community leaders in Europe and America who are no longer ready to endorse the official Israeli policy line as unquestioningly as in the past. He thinks that Begin, with his settlement policy on the West Bank, is undermining this unique opportunity for peace. He says darkly, "Israel has been given a last chance. There is not going to be another on⁄ ." What are they doing with it? We argue. Israel is afraid of the Palestinians and of the Syrians, I say, and it is not unreasonable, this fear. Kahana thinks it is.

He says bitterly, "The Jews are so afraid of death they are ready to commit suicide."

THE NEWSPAPERS REPORT the arrival of a new British ambassador to Cairo, Michael Weir. Weir is an old friend. I ring the embassy and ask to speak to the ambassador. He comes on the line sounding a bit flustered. He is very reserved. He cannot see me, he says, but not because he is too busy. Not right now, anyway.

"You see," he says with a little stammer, "Camp David notwithstanding, eh, it is a bit tough for me at this moment to meet in Cairo with an Israeli." I am amused by this evasion and at the same time grateful to an old friend for his frankness. He could have given me a polite excuse. Instead he exposed an important truth. The British, like the other European countries, are acting cagey and standoffish toward the Egyptian-Israeli peace treaty, since it has been rejected by the other Arab states. The French have even publicly criticized it. The Europeans do not have a *foreign* policy any longer, they have a *trade* policy, and the rejectionist Arab states have the oil. In the early days of the United Nations, making war was regarded as the great transgression against international civility, but nowadays the making of peace is so regarded.

No such problems with Ambassador and Mrs. Mahmoud Hassan. They are the parents of Sana Hassan, my collaborator on *Between Enemies,* whom I mentioned earlier. Sana is still in America. I am invited to tea in her parents' apartment on Gezira Island, overlooking the Nile. Furnished in fine period pieces and the me-

mentos of a long diplomatic career, the apartment is one of those fantasy settings one reads about in old memoirs or sees in certain movies. On the river below, the feluccas sail by; on the Chippendale table in the drawing room stands a framed picture of Franklin Delano Roosevelt chatting with my host in the Oval Room of the White House. In this formal setting there is a warm feeling of family and easy hospitality. The Hassans welcome me almost like a son. I realize that behind Sana's compassionate sense of reconciliation, so sensational at the time, there was a family history.

Tahsin Bashir, Sana's former husband, is also here. Although he is now divorced from their daughter, he still calls Ambassador and Mrs. Hassan Papa and Mama. Ambassador Hassan is a man of the old regime, a pasha, very slim, very gentle, very refined; his face is vaguely reminiscent of Proust's, and likewise, in his calm reflective manner, he is *à la recherche du temps perdu*. He is retired from the Egyptian Foreign Service. He was ambassador to the United States and his country's delegate to the United Nations in 1947, when the United Nations established the state of Israel. Like Ismail Zidky Pasha and others, Ambassador Hassan wanted his government at least not to oppose the resolution. His advice was rejected.

His Israeli counterpart at the United Nations in 1947 was Abba Eban. Ambassador Hassan recalls his acute embarrassment when he one day had to reject a private communication from Eban suggesting an informal talk. He could not even shake Eban's hand. Such civilities were forbidden in the new era. Hassan was of a different age.

Ambassador and Mrs. Hassan are very proud of their daughter. They admire the single-minded courage that led her, earlier than most Egyptians, to stand up publicly for peace. Tahsin sits in his armchair, smilingly puckishly.

"Sana was the pioneer," exclaims Mrs. Hassan. "It took more courage for her to visit Israel than for Sadat! She deserved the Nobel Prize!" she adds extravagantly. "How they all maligned my daughter at the time. The slanders they printed about her in the newspapers! Of course people immediately said she must be your mistress! That's the way people here react to a woman of courage. They said you had seduced her! *Moi, monsieur, je me suis foutue de cela,*" she adds grandly; "*après tout vous êtes assez charmant. . . . Vous prenez une autre tasse du thé?*"

Sana's sister, Nawal, is pouring tea. She has soft features, a round, lovely face, is wearing large horn-rimmed glasses. Nawal's voice, like Sana's, is gentle and soft. She exudes a great calm. As with her sister, behind that gentleness is an iron will. Nawal is a director of the Center of Egyptian Civilization, an institution that she has built up almost single-handedly during the past five years. Its library and collections are used by Egyptian and visiting scholars. Like Sana, Nawal is a fighter; her battle is the preservation of the old Mameluke architecture in central Cairo. She is also one of Egypt's more active ecologists. Her center is located in an old Mameluke building —Nawal had it partially restored to its ancient glory—behind the Khan el Khalili bazaar. She promises to take me there on a tour.

Tahsin and Nawal have a little argument over Nawal's latest crusade: to block the projected demolition of an old section of central Cairo in order to make room for modern hotels and apartment houses. "But it's run-down," says Tahsin, "and not particularly beautiful. Full of dirty workshops and warehouses."

Nawal thinks that it should be restored for its present inhabitants, who mustn't be thrown into some dismal, impersonal public housing scheme, she says, that will break up the social fabric and breed crime and alienation. It is the usual argument, to which no one has yet found a conclusive answer. We are all engaged in it. In Cairo, as elsewhere, the bulldozers make a greater noise and are winning. Nawal, with her soft voice, is not giving up, though.

Tahsin has a car and chauffeur waiting for him downstairs on the embankment. He drives me home through the darkened streets. We speak of Sana, who is now following an academic career in America, like so many gifted young Egyptians, and may not come back in the near future. "Nawal, on the other hand, has decided to remain in Egypt," Tahsin says with approval. "Do you know how many Egyptian academics there are in America today?" I do not know. "Guess!" Maybe three hundred, I say. "No. Almost three thousand."

He tells me a typical Cairo anecdote. A man asks another if he is emigrating. "No," he answers. "In that case you are not an intellectual."

We pass the high stone walls of the British embassy. I don't tell Tahsin of that morning's conversation with the ambassador. The embassy windows are lit up. Tahsin points at them and says, "Egypt used to be governed from in there. Even though it was only the residence of a consul general.

"They ruled like viceroys," Tahsin adds, but not bitterly. Few are bitter anymore. Time is still the great healer. The great lords of humankind—Cromer, Gorst, Kitchener—are anecdotes and footnotes today in the history books. My friend Michael Weir, by contrast, is a civil servant. Lord Kitchener's great ballroom in the residence is now the visa section.

SOMEONE ASKED ME THE other day if I wanted to meet Anis Mansur, editor of *October* magazine. Mansur is said to be a personal friend of President Sadat. Not particularly, I answered. What's the point? Mansur's articles have been filled for years with crudities and references to the international Jewish conspiracy of dope smugglers and whorehouse owners. Think it over, I was told; Mansur has lately come out very strongly in favor of the peace. No one in the Egyptian press has been supporting the treaty as firmly as Mansur. In a recent issue of *October* he even wrote warmly about Sana Hassan, whom he had attacked in 1975. This made me pause. Mansur now praises Sana for being a kind of torchbearer. Her great dream of reconciliation has come true. I am intrigued by this change—it does not appear to be merely on the surface—and decide to go to see him after all. Mansur receives me at short notice in his office on the Corniche al-Nil. He is standing in the far corner of a large, elongated room with his back to the door, gazing at his books. Many of them seem to be about Jews. Jews are a favorite subject of his, as are ghosts and unidentified flying objects, and men in outer space and quack religions, all of which he has written about profusely in the past.

He begins to turn only when I am about halfway to his desk. Then he looks up abruptly and examines me with a penetrating look. I do likewise. The scene, I fear, is a bit theatrical. Mansur is wearing a well-tailored safari suit. A head of soft curly hair over a round, good-looking face. With a little flourish he offers me a seat. I ask him to tell me about his work. He likes to talk about himself, for as he puts it, he is a much misunderstood man. He would like to be thought of as an artist. He has written sixty-three books, he says, proudly; eleven original plays and television dramas. His last book was published a month ago. The next is due in six weeks, a comparative history of religion. He writes every day from 5 A.M. until 10.

Mansur has also translated into Arabic the works of Friedrich Dürrenmatt, Eugène Ionesco, and Samuel Beckett and the short stories of Alberto Moravia. From the English? "Oh no, from the original. German, French, Italian." He is fluent in these languages. We continue our conversation in German. His German is perfect. His grandmother was German, he says. We pass to Italian, which he speaks with equal facility, and furthermore with a remarkable histrionic gift of clowning in several regional accents. He opens with the heavy dialect of the Venetians, then passes to the guttural vernacular of the South, finally to the soft nasal sounds of the Milanese. He waves the vowels like flags. He is now studying Hebrew, he says, using the "original" twelfth-century text of *The Guide for the Perplexed* by Maimonides.

"Even though," he hastens to add, "Maimonides first wrote that book in Arabic." Mansur has been a journalist since 1947. Nasser had him fired from *Al Akhbar* because of some political article that displeased him. So he became a professor of philosophy at Cairo University. His thesis was on Nietzsche. His special field is contemporary philosophy, he says. Which philosophers in particular?

"Oh, Kierkegaard, Heidegger, Sartre, Unamuno, and Martin Buber." Yet his great love is literature. Do you like Dürrenmatt? "I love Dürrenmatt." Max Frisch? "A marvelous writer." How do you feel about *Andorra* (Max Frisch's attack on anti-Semitism)? Mansur thinks it is a great work of art. We go on in this manner, speaking

alternately in four languages about art and poetry and Sartre's debt to
Heidegger and Kierkegaard. He sounds perfectly sensible on these
subjects and is clearly a very erudite, even charming man, with a
vigorous, perhaps too vigorous, sense of humor.

Finally I throw up my hands and say, I just cannot understand it!

"Understand what?"

I can't understand how a civilized man like you, a lover of Sartre
and Max Frisch, could write such . . .

"Such what?"

Such downright shit, Mr. Mansur.

He is not taken aback. On the contrary, he is enjoying himself.
What could I possibly mean by such an accusation, he demands. I
have brought with me a little list of quotes. On August 19 . . . , I
begin.

"Ah, that's my birthday!" he exclaims.

On August 19, 1973, I repeat, to give you one example, you wrote
that the Jews were the enemies of mankind . . . the crimes they
commit in the occupied territories, not even Hitler could have committed. . . . it is a good thing Hitler slaughtered six million of them,
people all over the world have come to regret that Hitler had not
burned the rest in the gas furnaces. Jews by nature are traitors. Jews
sold Hitler and Germany to Russia and America. Jews are blood-
suckers. People all over the world have become convinced that Hitler
had been right, et cetera.

Mansur calmly listens to my list of quotes. Then he says, "Oh,
that! I see!" Do you? "Well, there was a war on when I wrote
all that. In times of war a writer's tongue must be his cannon! Today
I would not write that stuff, of course. No! In times of war I tell
people that their enemies are terrible. In times of peace I say that
they are humans like ourselves." No, he reassures me, he does not
detest Jews. On the contrary, he admires Jews. He is speaking very
quickly now. "I used to have many Jewish friends in the old days,"
he says effusively. He wants me to understand his position. His task,
as he sees it, to be guardian of the people. In this part of the world,
people tend to be sentimental. He, Mansur, must at times warn them

of the great dangers they face, and at other times soothe the pains and heal the wounds.

Even now, he thinks, there is a danger that Egyptians may embrace Israelis too warmly, simply because there is peace. He has heard that Israelis have been kissed in the streets of Cairo. There is a hell of a lot of money in the Arab world. In the new era of peace the Jews could get their hands on it. What?! "Oh, don't be so sensitive," he cries. "Why are you so sensitive? You shouldn't . . ." It trails off. He smiles. Don't the Jews love money? So what if they do? Everybody loves money. He, Anis Mansur, also loves money, and he is in favor of extending cultural relations with Israel as soon as possible. Arrange dialogues, exchange books, and exhibits, and symphony orchestras. We must do all we can to consolidate this peace. We must help one another, and, to begin with, as we walk toward the elevator, Anis Mansur offers me his car and chauffeur to take me back to the hotel. I thank him and say I prefer to walk a little. Mansur shrugs his shoulders. "It's a free country."

THE EDITORS AND ANNOUNCERS OF the Hebrew-language section of Radio Cairo come out from behind their little desks in the crowded newsroom. The air is thick with cordiality and curiosity. They speak a bookish Hebrew, fluent but archaic. "Verily we say unto you, shalom, shalom, from the fountains of our hearts."

". . . And it came to pass that when Sadat was returned from Jerusalem, he said in a press interview . . ."

I am asked many questions, urgently, in this strange amalgam of flowery biblical phrases and current vernacular that they have picked up from Israel Radio broadcasts. ". . . Pray explain to me the true policy of Israel's nuclear research program. . . ." They read the Israeli newspapers regularly, after a two- or three-week delay. The newspapers arrive via Paris.

"What are thy impressions of Cairo, our beloved capital city . . . ?" ". . . Where is thy habitation in Jerusalem . . . ?" Please, have a coffee. Have a drink. Look at our program of daily broadcasts. Have a cigar. Stay a little longer. For so many years they have spoken the language only into empty air that now, a live listener in the room, they can't let go of him.

Samir Farahat, chief political commentator of the station, is a Hebrew poet. Every week he reads a new poem on the air. Copies of his most recent ones are folded into his breast pocket. The fine calligraphy in black is adorned with little flowers drawn in red between the stanzas:

> A moment of safety is a rosy dream
> In the life of a man who has made a covenant with anxiety,
> A moment of safety sprouts white roses
> In the desert heart of a man
> Where until now grew only thistles and thorns.

> God's gift to a mother whose tears have whitened her eyes
> For her beloved, her one and only son
> Torn from her bosom by the ravages of war,
> Now peace, peace unto all men.

Over the years a lot of nasty words have poured forth from the Hebrew section of Radio Cairo, including some written by Anis Mansur. The old program has been changed completely, says Farahat. It has also been renamed. It used to be the "Voice of War." Now it is the "Voice of Peace from Cairo." The latest innovation is a daily radio show on cooking, "Zahawa's Kitchen."

Farahat comes from a little hamlet, Sarsalian, not far from Cairo. "The true Egyptian is a villager with an open heart," he says. "There is a sacred greenness in his heart forever and ever. He sees a child of God in every man. He feels bound to honor and love him."

In 1975 Farahat was still rhyming holy revenge. The windows in the newsroom are flyspecked and look out over the Nile. The building is reflected in the pale green water. Samir Farahat, poet, commentator, propagandist, gazes at the river. Pensively he says, "This, this is my inspiration."

ANOTHER AFTERNOON IN THE country in the house of the architect, Ismail. This is the fourth time we have met. The first few times were exploratory, so to speak, set pieces dictated by courtesy and the peculiar circumstances of our past lives, which by chance unfolded on opposite sides of a chasm. Ismail's brother, I learned on our second meeting, had been wounded in the 1970 "War of Attrition." It came out casually in a chance remark about something else. He has not mentioned it since. But we've been like two dogs sniffing one another. I have a feeling that he has played a certain set record for me, as I have played one for him. We have gotten closer since our last meeting. I can tell he is more relaxed. I am still a bit tense, as I always am in Egypt, but pleased to be away from the dusty city in the quiet teeming green with Ismail.

We do not discuss politics. The air is hot but not heavy. We walk through the fields. The clover smells fresh; it has just been watered. We pick berries from a bush and talk about Italy. There we have something in common that we both cherish. This is always the beginning of something like friendship. We speak of a Romanesque façade in Lucca, the miraculous beauty and sadness of a Donatello head in the Bargello in Florence. His sullen David always reminds me of the strangely mature faces of certain young people I have known who have gone to one war and to another with no hatred or despair, but with no hope either. A sense of the transience, the hapless precariousness of life and happiness is written in these faces.

We cross a canal. An arrowhead of ducks rises from the reeds. The color of the land here is a swollen bruised gray. Ismail loves the soft light of the Tuscan countryside, the chiaroscuro in the hills at dawn, or under a lightly overcast sky. In Egypt the light is harsh, the sky a distant blaze of sand. The nearly treeless landscape resembles a hard face, lacking in pity. Through the dry blades a distant gabble of birds. This is "new land," reclaimed from the sands in the 1950s by the digging of a canal. We come to a pasture; the ground is dusty as though it suffered from dandruff. There is a village ahead, a cluster of eucalyptus trees and mud houses.

Ismail's girl friend is walking with us. She is a tall, olive-skinned young woman. An open face, broad, cordial. Very clear, very brilliant hazelnut-colored eyes. A firm, flat nose: the dark features, the high cheekbones suggest a distant Nubian ancestry; she is a native of Upper Egypt, the graduate of a French university. She interrogates me about my wife. My wife is American. Why hasn't she come too? She couldn't, we have a young daughter in school. I must promise to bring my wife to see them on my next visit to Egypt. She makes me feel it is more than courtesy. I would like that very much, in fact. We must all go to the beach in the summer. Are the beaches in Israel polluted? Rather. Ismail takes her arm and mine. We walk through a small grove of mangoes and palm trees. The palms are thin, like feather dusters. The mangoes are overgrown and glow like lanterns among the leafy branches. I hardly notice the heat among the steamy foliage, as though it were the odor of some unburied spring.

We reach the outskirts of the village. A boy is walking by the roadside with an open book in his hand. He is learning by rote. This is a common practice, Ismail says. It loads the memory without exercising the mind. The village is built entirely of mud houses. Straw is stored on every roof and is a constant fire hazard; the village, fortunately, has a communal water faucet; the peasants no longer drink the disease-infested water from the canals. We enter a two-room shack occupied by a family of eleven and an old cow. In the courtyard is a spiked pigeon house, pointed at its top. The peasant is a small, swarthy man about forty-five years old. His youngest child has recently been killed by a hit-and-run driver; a new child, the tenth, is on the way. The peasant supports his large family on slightly more than one hectare (about two and a half acres) of land. *Al hamdulillah,* thanks to God, he says, though it is difficult to see what cause he has to be grateful. A few children are crouched around a television set in the second room. An Egyptian film is broadcast, an upper-middle-class melodrama of love and money and fine cars, set in a white Regency-style villa with marble statues and delicately gowned and bejeweled ladies fainting on the raked gravel paths by the lawns of a great private park. The theme seems strange in these surroundings.

"The people who make these films and broadcast them," says Ismail, "think that because the peasants are poor and squalid, they need a dream."

Later that evening, we attend a small social gathering in a house not too dissimilar to that shown on the television in the afternoon. An elegant supper is served. The wide, pillared terrace is overgrown with exotic plants. The house, the lawns, the swimming pool, the old furniture of indeterminate European provenance, the priceless Persian carpets in the salon, the servants—three Sudanese in heavily embroidered gowns—are clearly not of this era.

The guests include two businessmen from Alexandria, a bank director from Cairo, the executive of a hotel chain, a transport contractor, and their wives and grown children. Our host is the retired director of a nationalized company. One of the guests says, "They've ruined this land. Everything for the Arabs. But we are Egyptians! Nasser only made the rich poor and the poor poorer." His son's wife is a practicing pediatrician educated in England. She went on a pilgrimage to Mecca a year ago. Since then, he says, she has been wearing a loose veil, not the strictly traditional one, but it partly covers her face. She thinks it has "value," it is important to her.

The conversation is relaxed. The main themes are family matters, trips abroad, cars, houses. Ismail is building a new villa for one of the guests. Someone mentions Lawrence Durrell's *Alexandria Quartet*. One of the women comments on it rather angrily. An absurd plot, she says. No Copt millionaire, or even pauper, would be a Zionist spy. His Jewish wife, maybe, yes; a Nessim Hosnani, never.

The house and terrace are brilliantly illuminated. From farther away, outside in the Egyptian darkness between the bushes and the canals, come the sounds of a million crickets and frogs.

IN TEWFIK AL-HAKIM's book *The Soul Regained* (1927), there is a brief exchange* that perhaps explains why the book helped turn Nasser into a revolutionary:

* Quoted in Harry Hopkins' *Egypt the Crucible* (London: Secker & Warburg, 1969).

"Believe me, Mr. Black, don't underestimate these poor people. There is a hidden power in them. They lack only one thing."

"What's that?"

"An idol—a man who personifies their character and their aspirations and who is for them the symbol of an ideal."

The late Gamal Abdel Nasser, for all his half-baked notions of Caesarism, xenophobia, and "Arab socialism," certainly personified an idea that had inspired Egyptian patriots since the emergence of modern Egypt in the nineteenth century. He breathed a fiery nationalism, which, in the eyes of a downtrodden people, demoralized by colonial rule and the whims of a corrupt upper class, appeared as the very realization of the idea of independence. He ruled dictatorially over Egypt for eighteen years, in the name of a pedantic nationalist-socialist ideology, which, for all its eclectic dilettantism, obscured for a while the basic fact that he was governed by no principle save that of personal opportunism. When Nasser died, in 1970, the heritage he left behind was singularly disastrous. "There is a role wandering about aimlessly [in the Arab world] in search of a hero," he had written in 1954. Whatever that role was, he had played it badly.

A large part of Egypt, including some valuable oil fields, was under occupation, seemingly permanent, by an enemy he had rashly, stupidly, needlessly provoked three years earlier into a war that resulted in the virtual destruction of his vaunted Army and Air Force. The Suez Canal, an important source of revenue, was blocked. He had failed dismally to realize his greatest dream: the unification, under Egypt's aegis, of the Arab world, as the German states had been united in 1871 under Prussia. At the time of Nasser's death, the Arab states were more divided, more hostile to one another, than ever before. In Egypt itself, what progress had been achieved by the "saintly revolution of the armed forces" had fallen victim to what Sadat later called the golem of socialism, bureaucracy, irresponsible planning, and the brutal excesses of police surveillance.

Despite the agrarian reforms, the high dam at Aswan, the new resources of electric power, and the enormous effort at modernization and industrialization, the rate of economic growth, in real terms, had dropped precipitously to less than half what it had been under Farouk's corrupt *ancien régime*. Shimon Shamir, in *The Decline of Nasserist Messianism,* says that Nasser's great charismatic appeal was the result of his ability to project a new collective identity. He heralded the rise of a great Arab nation, from Morocco to Iraq, a "New Man" to challenge the West politically, militarily, and culturally. *Nasserism* was not originally an Egyptian term. It came from the Arab world beyond Egypt, just as in the nineteenth century pan-Germanism was often more ardently endorsed in Austria and in the German principalities than in Prussia itself. For better or for worse, few men in the postwar world have succeeded in attaching their name to an ideology: Stalin, De Gaulle, Mao, and Nasser.

Sadat is hailed today as the "soldier of peace" and sometimes of "peace and war," but there is no Sadatism, he does not represent an "ideology." Nasser represented an ideology because, as Shamir says, he was the first modern Arab leader who was "authentic": i.e., genuinely Egyptian or Arab, rather than another Europeanized oriental, bourgeois, liberal, communist, or fascist politician. In an era of disorientation Nasser was able to pose as the man of destiny, the savior, or guide, or Mahdi or Führer, who would lead the Arabs out of darkness into light. Shamir cites a poem by Nazar Kabani:

> Our cup filleth for you
> Our love for you
> Intoxicates us
> As the Sufi is drunk with the spirit of God.

Since 1974 many revisionist tracts have been published in Egypt and Lebanon that attack Nasser personally as a corrupt man, who, even as he pretended to be the frugal puritan, lived in indecent luxury. The critics bemoan his legacy of duplicity and mistrust, and decry his reign as the "age of terror," "the hated years," in the "taped republic" where everyone was listening in on everybody else, and speculating with the record—using it for personal profit and intrigue. There have been several personal memoirs full of sordid revelations—such as *The Silent Speak* and *Nasser's Secret Life*— telling us how the courts were put under pressure and the judges threatened with reprisal if their verdicts did not fit the government line; how the journalists and writers were manipulated and the trade unions stripped of their right to defend the workers' interests. But above all, the memoirs decry the terror, the concentration camps, the torture chambers of Nasser's political police.

In the prisons "Israeli spies were treated as gentlemen and Egyptian political prisoners as slaves. This was so because the Israeli spies were guilty of an affront against the state, whereas the political prisoners were guilty of an affront against the tyrant." (Mustapha Amin, a leading journalist and former editor of *Al Akhbar,* imprisoned by Nasser on the charge of maintaining contact with a foreign diplomat; in the second volume of his memoirs.)

The publication of revisionist exposés on the Nasser era reached a crescendo in 1975. It has since abated, if not ceased altogether, apparently on order. Sadat may have felt that such freedom of expression could threaten the safety of his own regime. While it lasted, it was reminiscent of the guarded spelling out of the deadly sins of Stalin in the days of Khrushchev.

And yet Nasser undoubtedly touched such deep nerves in the consciousness of modern Egypt that there remains, not surprisingly, a certain amount of ambivalence and occasional nostalgia. Nostalgia is, of course, the hallmark—or fig leaf—of all criticism of Sadat by Nasser's former colleagues. They had hoped to control Sadat after Nasser's death but were instead stripped of all their excessive powers. Nasser's name is similarly evoked in a nostalgic vein by the communist—as well as the noncommunist—Left. The communists have also suffered under Nasser; but they resent Sadat's Western orientation and deplore the gradual reintroduction of a free economy, the rise of a new class of capitalist entrepreneur, and the partial dismantlement of Nasser's state controls over industry, banking, and business.

The ambivalence remains also a characteristic of others who look back wistfully on the "Age of Giants" that is no more. Mohammed

Heykal, in his book on Nasser, approvingly quotes André Malraux—no mean exponent, himself, of nationalist obscurantism in our day.

"Regardless of everything, regardless of success or failure, victory or defeat," Malraux told Heykal, "Nasser will go down in history as the embodiment of Egypt, just as Napoleon became the embodiment of France." It is harder for a foreigner to understand why the French should be so grateful to Napoleon than it is to understand the abundance of sympathy for Nasser that remained behind among the ruins.

It is not their revolution that the French admire when they profess a love for Napoleon. But in Nasser many Egyptians still love what Tewfik al-Hakim has called an "eternal," perhaps naïve, "hope." A children's crusade. Napoleon was not untutored or ingenuous. Nasser's revolution was naïve. It was strangely innocent at least at its outset; the Free Officers wanted to wipe clean the slate in order that national politicians better fitted to do so would govern. Only afterward did they go shopping for ideas.

"We went to men of ideas for counsel and we went to men of experience for guidance," Nasser wrote in *The Philosophy of the Revolution* (published in English in 1956). "Unfortunately we did not find much of either. . . . Every man we asked had nothing to recommend except to kill someone else. Every idea we listened to was nothing but an attack on some other idea. . . . We were deluged with petitions and complaints . . . but most were no more, no less, than demands for revenge, as though a revolution had taken place in order to become a weapon in the hand of hatred and vindictiveness."

In the end the revolution became just that in the hands of Nasser, an avid regime of hatred and vindictiveness, as Tewfik al-Hakim would complain. But even Tewfik al-Hakim, as he published his scathing attack on Nasser's coup d'etat, and on Nasser's tyranny and dishonesty, admitted that "in my heart, I love him." He blamed only himself for that. Even if history absolved Nasser, which it might, Hakim wrote, "I don't expect history to absolve a man like myself, a thinking man who yet allowed sentiment to blind his eye and *lose his awareness* to what was happening around him."

Shamir cites Louis Awad, who said the responsibility of intellectuals for Nasser's sins was greater than that of the technocrats. They should have known better.

I am reading Mohammed Heykal's book on Nasser, *The Cairo Documents*. Although Heykal is an unrepenting admirer, I find he offers important insights into Nasser's personality. The main impression I receive of Nasser is one of childish innocence. Upon meeting success, this innocence turns into megalomania, and upon failure, into self-destructive ire and disgust. Like other "Messianic" figures, Nasser seems to have been a manic-depressive. Events initiated by him always precipitated the "unforeseen," which even the hagiographer finds difficult to condone. The key expression that recurs in Heykal's book is that for Nasser events were forever getting out of control. Many of the major initiatives that he undertook seem to have been inspired by irritation, anger, or vindictiveness: the Egyptian-Soviet arms pact of 1955, the nationalization of the Suez Canal, the recognition of East Germany, the Six-Day War of 1967. According to Heykal, Nasser did not usually act; he rather reacted.

From a certain moment, Heykal claims, events simply took an inevitable course. He rarely says why. If Nasser had not so often been so impetuous, perhaps events would not have been so inevitable. Heykal says, for example, that when Nasser invited the East German dictator, Walter Ulbricht, to Cairo, he did not mean this as an affront to West Germany. Heykal would like us to believe that Nasser simply could not refuse a "sick" man who wished to recuperate in the sun. This is difficult to accept, yet from then on, events again took their inevitable course.

Nasser hated war, says Heykal, and perhaps he did. Moreover, according to Heykal, Nasser even foresaw the defeat of 1967! If he provoked that war, it was because he saw himself constrained to act on behalf of the Arab nation, says Heykal. He would like us to believe that it had been a case of suicide for patriotic reasons.

Worse things follow. Heykal claims that Nasser had warned the Egyptian Air Force of the possibility of an Israeli preemptive strike. When that strike came, it was just as Nasser had "foretold." One would think that Nasser was nothing more than a commentator, another Heykal who merited praise for his foresight, while others were guilty for not having heeded his prophetic warning. The generals, Heykal says, decided to evacuate Sinai, without consulting Nasser. When he heard this, Nasser wept "for the first time since his childhood." He went back to general headquarters (shouldn't he have been there in the first place?) but "it was too late." The Army had already been beaten.

This impression of wily naïveté is not necessarily borne out by Nasser's own book, published shortly after the coup d'etat, under the pretentious title *The Philosophy of the Revolution.* The memoirs of dictators, even when written by themselves, are not commonly the most reliable source of information. In this case the memoirs were ghost-written by the same Mohammed Heykal, Nasser's chief scribe.

In *The Philosophy,* Nasser develops his celebrated theory of the "role in search of a hero." He speaks of three great "circles" waiting to be delivered by a savior, an Egyptian savior, presumably himself: 55 million Arabs, 224 million Africans, and 400 million Moslems (the figures are those of 1954; they may have doubled since) would be joined together in "interaction." The pilgrimage to Mecca would "become an institution of great political power." That power must be wisely wielded but also *"without limit."* It was probably an exaggeration to see *The Philosophy,* as Guy Mollet and Selwyn Lloyd saw it in 1956, and later Dulles and Eisenhower, as a new *Mein Kampf* in which an oriental Hitler lays bare his boldest dreams of empire and conquest. Yet Nasser was not altogether the holy innocent in this book that Heykal in later years tried to portray him. The dream of empire might have worked if Nasser had been a more prudent man. Recklessness is not innocence. Bismarck was prudent. Nasser was merely defiant, careless, and rash.

Sadat, in his memoirs, says that Nasser was plagued by terrible "complexes" since childhood. In *The Philosophy,* Nasser displaced those complexes into the public realm, as many politicians had done before him and since. The public paid the price, and in the end so did Nasser. Heykal claims that Nasser really died in 1967.

My own, rather worn-out, copy of Nasser's book was given me in

1956 by the information department of the Israeli embassy in Washington. They had bought up—and distributed—nearly the entire American edition, to ensure that the book reached every congressman and senator and every editorial writer in the United States. No more effective form of anti-Egyptian propaganda was conceivable at the time.

A TOUCH OF BURLESQUE last night as I walked in Midan al-Tahrir, the great square behind the Hilton Hotel on the bank of the Nile. I had spent the evening with a "leftist" intellectual who assured me that Sadat would be toppled quite soon, and that there was in reality much less popular support for this peace treaty than there would seem to be. He did not convince me or any of the others at the small gathering at a lawyer's apartment overlooking the Nile. But I came away depressed at what quite clearly appeared a deep reluctance on the part of a certain class of Egyptian intellectuals to endorse the peace treaty with Israel.

As I crossed Midan al-Tahrir on my way home, a nice-looking young man came up and asked me the time. Then, conversationally, he asked where I was from. When I said I came from Jerusalem, he flung his arms around my neck and kissed me on both cheeks. "Welcome, welcome," he cried, with great feeling. "Sir, we have been praying for years for this day to come. War is very, very bad. Peace is very good. Israel is very good." He went on talking in this vein, pumping my hand, patting my shoulder, and it seemed to me that he almost had tears in his eyes. The depression in which I had left the lawyer's home lifted like a fog. I shook his hand and thanked him.

Then he leaned forward and said, "Listen. I have four girls. Very pretty. Very young. Two Italian, two Greek. You like one?"

ECHOES OF THE PROVERBIAL "affability" of the Egyptians, remarked on by many observers from Edward Lane down to the present. There is a movement afoot among "leftists" and other opponents of President Sadat to demonstrate their opposition to this "American-inspired" peace treaty with Israel. They have decided to boycott Israelis visiting Egypt; they will not meet or talk to any Israelis. S.H. is one of the instigators of the proposed boycott, but since he is a polite man of considerable erudition and charm, when I call him on the telephone he invites me to lunch at his club to explain why he must boycott me.

"It is nothing personal," he explains over grilled shrimp and a bottle of white wine, "it is a matter of principle. We must protest the betrayal by Sadat of the Arab cause."

Then we talk about his close friends and acquaintances in Israel —leftists mostly. He has often met with them in the past, in Italy and France, at a time when such meetings were almost tantamount to treason. He asks me to call and give them his best regards. He is very sorry, should they come to Egypt he would be unable to meet with them again. "It's not personal," he repeats, "it's a matter of principle." He is sure that the first Israeli ambassador to Egypt will be socially "ostracized."

"We must make a stand," he says.

VIII

THE RELATIVE EASE WITH which Egypt is making the psychological transition from war to peace still baffles me. On the surface it would seem that a switch has been thrown, sending the train off on a different track. The emotions that have run one way for so long are now running in another way, smoothly, efficiently. There are very few apparent symptoms of withdrawal or adjustment.

In Israel, government and popular opinion have always clamored for peace. There has been but little manifestation of "hatred" for the enemy, or of overt war propaganda in the media or in the school curriculum, as in Egypt. Yet the psychological transition from war to peace seems more difficult in Israel than in Egypt. It is not merely a question of faith or lack of faith in a piece of paper, duly signed and called a peace treaty, but a problem of mental readjustment. The new situation is one that few Israelis believed they would see in their lifetime. The same applies to most Egyptians I have met. Many confess they were "startled" or "surprised" by President Sadat's peace initiative, and yet they quickly adjusted themselves to it. There was war. Now there is peace.

Experts of the vaunted old school of orientalism may explain away this apparent contradiction with the usual generalizations about the Arab "character." Dissect it, take it apart, put it together again in many learned words that resound with the same hollow rhetoric they impute to the subjects of the treatises. The often quoted peroration in T. E. Lawrence's *Seven Pillars of Wisdom* immediately comes to mind:

> This people was black and white, not only in vision but by inmost furnishing: black and white not merely in clarity but in apposition. Their thoughts were at ease only in extremes. They inhabited superlatives by choice . . . they oscillated from asymptote to asymptote . . . a people of spasms, of upheavals . . . color blind. . . .

A few lines later, Lawrence says that, since the dawn of life, Arabs "had been dashing themselves against the coasts of flesh," in successive waves, whatever that means. Arabs were a "limited, narrow-minded people whose inert intellect lay fallow in a curious resignation." And then, this sudden thrust: "Arabs could be swung on an idea as on a cord."

If there was a "cord" somewhere, I suspect it was being pulled from both ends. Could it be that popular hatred of Israel had in reality never been as deep as Nasser's propaganda had pretended? Conversations with all manner of Egyptians—as well as a certain amount of documented evidence—suggest that in seeking peace Sadat was not leading but following the Egyptian people. He was accommodating the common man, weary of war and sacrifice, and the leading intellectuals and literary figures who had formed something like a peace movement. Professor Bernard Lewis, the Princeton Arabist, writes that Sadat "gave expression to a desire which had existed and had been gaining in strength for a long time. To this policy he himself was a comparatively late convert."

How this desire developed in spite of thirty years of intensive indoctrination is a question that should fascinate Arabists as well as students of propaganda; while those of us who complain of this or that aspect in our schools' syllabuses may ponder with anguish or relief the possibility that the impact of teachers upon young people is not, perhaps, as great as we thought.

An American professor at an Egyptian university says that a few years ago he asked a student to state his opinion of the Arab-Israeli conflict. The student said, "By God, we shall destroy them." A few weeks later the American scholar held a seminar on "Egypt in the Year 1990." The question he put to his students was: "What would be the relations between Egypt and Israel in the year 1990?"

The same student replied, "Well, somehow we will have to find a modus vivendi with them." This is called by social scientists a case of *anticipatory dissonance,* says the American scholar.

I HAVE BEEN VISITING several schools this past week in Cairo and in the provinces. The main impression I come away with is that there is little if any discernible trace left of the massive war propaganda and race hatred that for so many years were inculcated into Egyptian children's minds. Some of the more blatant instances of this racism are common knowledge. The Egyptians themselves never made any secret of it. It has been documented by serious scholars. Several theses based on selections from Egyptian school textbooks have been published.

The best-known—probably the most extreme—examples came to light in 1967, when the Israeli army occupied Gaza. A large amount of material was found in the Egyptian state-run schools: official guidelines issued by the Egyptian Ministry of Education, textbooks, and children's drawings and compositions. One primer in Arab grammar purported to teach the definite article *al* (the) by examples such as "*The* Jews are the Arabs' deadliest enemy." In an arithmetic exercise, pupils were asked to apply themselves to the following problem: "If six fedayeen heroes kill four out of twelve Jewish soldiers, how many Jews remain alive?"

Another grammar exercise required such phrases as "The enemy was defeated," "The enemy was humiliated," "The enemy is bloodthirsty" to be put into the future and past tenses. In one elementary school, a composition by a fourth grader, marked "Excellent" by the teacher, was found. It said: "I am thirsty. The sun is beating down on my head. Only a cup of Jewish blood can quench my thirst."

Several childrens' drawings were discovered that depicted Egyptian tanks squashing frightened Israelis under their chains, and soldiers marked with stars of David wielding huge kitchen knives to slaughter Arab women and children.

I find no traces of all that in the schools I have visited. I have been to six schools so far, two by prearrangement with the Ministry of Education. And I have walked unannounced into four other schools in Cairo and the nearby provinces. I was allowed to chat, more or less freely, with teachers and pupils. I find no noticeable differences among the various schools. In every school I have found walls covered with drawings by the children that hail the advent of peace, and inscriptions in Hebrew: *Shalom,* שלום. The ubiquity of these drawings and slogans may well be the result of a ministerial directive. The drawings obviously reflect the children's exposure to state television, and yet at the same time a remarkable degree of spontaneity in texture and composition is evident. The media undoubtedly inspire the children to glorify President Sadat's efforts to establish peace as heroic, historic, benevolent, and so forth. Sadat makes many television appearances, and each of his frequent speeches is broadcast in its entirety, and then rebroadcast three or four times.

But in many of the drawings almost equal space is given to Begin, Moshe Dayan, and other Israeli leaders. There are many doves flying about, of course, and almost as many flags and portraits of Sadat triumphantly driving into Cairo upon his return from the peace conference, being greeted by the multitudes. On a number of drawings, peace is graphically translated into naïve—i.e., genuine— images of a nonpolitical nature. Peace is being at home, happily playing with a great many wonderful toys, going to a swimming pool. Peace is being a well-dressed child in Western-style clothes nestling in the broad bosom of a mother, vaguely pyramid-shaped. Peace is picking flowers or licking a huge cone of red and yellow ice cream. Tanks have become toys at playgrounds; one is harnessed to a plow and pulls it across a green field in long dark-brown furrows. The colors are extraordinarily vivid. This, I am told, is a characteristic of Egyptian children's drawings, as it is of Haitian. Strong reds, blues, greens, and yellows dominate.

In every school I visited I was led into several classrooms and told that I could converse with the pupils for as long as I wished. Egyptian school discipline is relatively rigid. Relations between pupils and teachers are rather formal. Under the circumstances, conversations with pupils, though friendly, tend to be a little stiff and perhaps constrained by the forbidding presence of the teacher. But in each class I visited I also asked the pupils to write a short composition on the subject of peace and what they thought it meant to both Egypt and Israel. The compositions were written spontaneously, without guidance, and were given to me as I left without being read by the teachers. A few excerpts:

The Jewish people was dispersed, a people that knew untold suffering. Moses took them out of Egypt, after Pharaoh was so mean to them. . . . Afterward they suffered badly. The worst suffering was inflicted upon them by the Germans, who burned them. In modern times they have been granted a homeland of their own . . . they deserve that and Israel deserves to live in peace if its troops withdraw from the occupied territories of Sinai and the West Bank. . . .   —A ninth grader

I support this treaty also because I have been personally affected by the October War. One of my relatives fell in that war. . . . We have an opportunity for peace and I call upon all Arabs to seize it.

Peace is the most beautiful thing in life. God enjoined us in his sacred books to seek peace. War causes only sorrow and destruction for all. I believe that peace will bring permanent prosperity to both Egypt and Israel . . . we must cooperate. . . .

—A tenth grader

Those [in the rejectionist Arab states] who oppose this treaty between Egypt and Israel cannot in all truth live without war, as they are the only ones who profit from it. But nations who fight one another, whether they win or lose, both end up as losers . . . in lives and property.

[For us] this peace means an end to poverty, backwardness,

disease, ignorance. We cannot deal with these difficulties as long as all the resources are diverted to the waging of endless war. . . .

With the signing of this treaty every Egyptian reaffirms his Egyptian identity and looks proudly down on the rejectionists and purveyors of hostility [to Egypt].　　　　　—An eighth grader

Now if we could get rid of the Arabs' states we might call on all peace-loving states to help us—since we have fruitlessly collaborated until now with those who oppose peace. They themselves never participated in any war and did not suffer its hardships. The [Arab] rejectionists live in [oil-derived] plenty. . . .

Peace is the supreme commandment of the Torah, the New Testament, and the Koran. The prophets preached peace. Even in the days of the Prophet Mohammed an armistice was signed with the Jews and they lived in peace thereafter.　　　—An eighth grader

Our religion is the religion of peace. It would not have been called *Islam* if that word were not derived from the root *s-l-m* (same as *salaam,* peace). O Ye Sons of the beloved Fatherland, bless our president Mohammed Anwar al-Sadat for being a pious Moslem who believes in peace.　　　　　—An eighth grader

Israel wants peace—but is afraid of us. The truth must be said, even if in the past we have tried to deny it. Israel as a state exists. Therefore, it is better to make peace in justice and negotiation than wage unprofitable war. The blood that was shed on the battlefield, let it flow through the veins of humans engaged in building and reconstructing our peoples.

The price of oil went sky-high. Was Egypt the beneficiary? No. We only suffered losses in wars for the Arabs, wars which they themselves were unwilling to fight.　　　　　—A ninth grader

We forgot, or perhaps only chose to ignore, that Abraham had been the common father of both peoples.　　　—A tenth grader

IN SEVERAL CLASSES I would pose this question: Which of you has a father or close relative who participated in one of the wars? By their ages (twelve to seventeen), all might have fathers or uncles who had served in the Army.

There was silence when I put this question to a class of eleventh graders at one high school attended by upper-middle-class children in Cairo. The school is well equipped with laboratories, a good library, and spacious playing fields. Most of the pupils came from relatively well-to-do families. Some are sons of the present political and administrative elite. It transpired that none of them had a father, or close relative, who had seen active service.

It was a totally different response in the seventh and ninth grades of a school in the lower-middle-class section of Bulaq, in the heart of Cairo. The ninth grade was crowded into a small classroom overlooking an adjacent junkyard. There is no fine auditorium here, no school bus, no laboratory, no library, no playing field. Instruction is given in three crowded shifts, from 8 A.M. to noon, noon to 4 P.M., and 4 to 7 P.M.

Of forty-two boys, thirty-one said they had had a close relative in the war. I asked them a second question. How many had lost a close relative? Twenty-six boys raised their hands. None spoke before given permission by the teacher. Then, like gunshots, their answers resounded in the room:

"I lost one."

"My father . . ."

"Two uncles . . ."

"One."

"My father . . ."

"My cousin . . ."

"My cousin . . ."

I suddenly understood that in these parts, as in Exodus 12:30, "there was a great cry in Egypt, for there was not a house where there was not one dead."

I was quite shaken and probably somewhat pale, for when we left the classroom the principal sensed my embarrassment and, taking my arm in his, said, "I am sure it is the same in Israeli schools. That is why it is so good that Begin and Sadat have found a way out of this awful mess."

While he was speaking, in earnest tones, the gymnastics teacher came down the corridor toward us. He was a sturdy man of about thirty, wearing his blue tricot shirt and white sneakers. The principal said, "Let me introduce you to our great sportsman, Mr. Jabbar. He was a captain in the Army during the October War." Then, perhaps to lighten the atmosphere, perhaps with a touch of black humor, said to be widespread in Egypt, he added, "It's a pity you didn't kill *him*."

MR. HALIM GEREISS BEGAN HIS career is 1942 as an elementary school teacher. A little while later he entered a teachers' college and completed his studies at the University of Birmingham, in England. Today he is undersecretary in charge of syllabuses and examinations in the Egyptian Ministry of Education—like many senior civil servants, a Copt. In his large office—in the former residence of a prince—the wall is hung with prints depicting the glories of pharaonic Egypt.

He is a solid man of medium height; the warm, intelligent eyes contrast oddly but not unpleasantly with the apparent hardness of his slim face; the lines of his mouth are softly drawn, under the bristle of a gray mustache. Mr. Gereiss smiles broadly. When he smiles, his face changes, as though he switched veils; the stern civil servant becomes a friendly country doctor inquiring after the children and dogs. He and his colleagues, he says, have been preparing for peace since 1974. How? *By rewriting history.*

All history books have been thoroughly revised, he says, by several special commissions. The old versions have been withdrawn. New books, based on a revised syllabus, have been issued to all schools, in geography and civics (the term used here is "national education"). All negative references to Israel, all denunciations of Jews, all cries for revenge have been deleted. Peace is the message now. The smile disappears. Mr. Gereiss leans forward and says, "But are *you* ready for peace?"

Do you doubt it?

"Well, you are such energetic people. . . ."

I assure Mr. Gereiss that most Israelis do want peace, truly and honestly. Mr. Gereiss implies that he still has some doubts. But he would like to believe. Everyone in his ministry would, he says.

There is a new integrated syllabus for "social and environmental studies" intended for fourth to sixth grades. The new syllabus begins by acquainting children with their local province. It continues with the history and geography of Egypt from ancient times to the present. The emphasis is on *Egypt,* says Mr. Gereiss. "We are first and foremost Egyptians. We are also Arabs, of course, but not, I repeat, not Syrians, not Iraqis, not Palestinians." Much has changed from the days of Nasser, says Mr. Gereiss. He should know, for he also participated in the preparation of the old syllabus under Nasser. The old syllabus emphasized Arab studies, Arab history, Arab destiny. "I knew even then that this was not enough. But Nasserism was a necessary stage in Egypt's maturation," he says. "For two thousand years we had been dependent on others. Nasser was the first man who gave us independence. But his philosophy was born on the battlefields of Palestine. He was too fixated on that. Sadat is different. He is an Egyptian fellah."

The new textbooks, says Mr. Gereiss, are based on the most recent techniques of environmental education. So thoroughly has the syllabus been purged that Mr. Gereiss can no longer furnish me with examples of the old textbooks. They have been recycled to produce paper, he says. Paper is expensive and must be paid for in foreign currency. Today's Egyptian schoolchild hears the word *Israel* in class for the first time when he is eleven years old. But there are no denunciations anymore. "Just facts."

The outline of study is given in a copy of the new syllabus, which Mr. Gereiss leaves with me. Eight chapters cover Egypt's "struggle for independence." The seventh chapter deals with Israel. It appears factual and offers what seems at least an objective framework of studies. At least on the surface it seems free of denunciations, though not free of some of the value judgments of the past:

1. The Establishment of the State of Israel.
2. The War of 1948.

3. Israel's Territorial Expansion.
4. The Tripartite Agression of 1956.
5. The 1967 War.
6. The Glorious War of 1973: Arab solidarity and the oil weapon.
7. Sadat's Peace Initiative: the peace treaty with Israel.

"We no longer teach anyone to hate," says Mr. Gereiss. The children are taught that Egypt's defeat in 1967 was caused by the irresponsibility of "the politicians around Nasser." Yet Israel is not blamed for taking advantage. "In geography we teach global geography. The planet earth."

Before I take my leave, Mr. Gereiss returns to what he calls the spirit of Egyptian history. His basic tenet is similar to that of Kamal al-Malakh, the archaeologist. "Under Sadat," he says, "we have become Egyptians again. Remember, much of Egypt's history can be summed up in one sentence: 'Pharaoh sent troops to secure the eastern border.' That is our present border with Israel. As long as we feel secure in the east we can dedicate ourselves to what ever Egyptian wants: peace and quiet and the good things of life."

Mr. Gereiss is very much in favor of cultural exchanges with Israel—"as soon as possible, tomorrow!"—even joint summer camps for children. There is a proposal to attempt the writing of a *joint* history book on the events of the past forty years, for use in selected high schools. If that should happen, I reflect, it would be the beginning of "The wolf also shall dwell with the lamb." Yet so much would have to be excised from a joint book that in the end we might all "eat straw like the ox." Mr. Gereiss, however, is hopeful.

There is much less optimism to encounter upstairs in the same building, in the rarefied air of Dr. Ismail Hassan's office. Dr. Hassan is Minister of Education, Culture, and Scientific Research in President Sadat's Cabinet. He is a former president of Cairo University. In the outer office hang the pictures of Dr. Hassan's predecessors in this office. Since 1836 there have been seventy-one Egyptian Ministers of Education, which would make a rather short average term of only two years. It is clearly one of the most difficult public posts in Egypt. Each year almost a million children enter—or are supposed to enter—first grade. The continuing expansion of school facilities, though very great, does not catch up with the unchecked growth of population. Close to 8 million students are enrolled in the schools. But the effective rate of illiteracy appears to be higher today than fifteen years ago.

On the primary level, the expenditure in 1978 per pupil was only thirty dollars, a third of the average spent in other developing countries. Two shifts are common, three are no rarity. On the other hand, the Egyptian school system is singularly top-heavy. Half a million students were enrolled in the universities in 1979. The universities have so expanded in the past fifteen years that many graduates no longer find adequate work in Egypt and are forced to emigrate.

These problems, and many others, weigh heavily on Dr. Hassan. He looks harassed. There is little wonder that he has not yet found time to contemplate the educational and cultural consequences of this unexpected peace treaty. He appears to be in no great hurry. His manner is cool. He is very reserved, very careful, with none of Mr. Gereiss's fervor and enthusiasm for Egyptianism. The main difficulty posed by the peace treaty, he says, is how to explain to the pupils Egypt's present relations with the Arab countries. The crisis with the Arabs, not the peace itself—everyone is for that—creates a main difficulty for teachers.

Cultural exchanges? Youth camps? "We must not hurry with these things. *Not at this delicate stage.*" He repeats this last phrase several times. "Everything is still very delicate, complicated, charged with conflicting emotions." A considerable amount of time must pass, he thinks, until relations can be "normal." After the Palestinian problem is solved, Egypt will deal with Israel "as with any other nation in Europe." (He does not say in the Middle East.) Then, perhaps, the time will also come for an exchange of students, maybe even summer camps for Israeli children in Egypt.

Will Egyptian children also come to Israel? Egyptian children are too poor, he says. Only a few would be able to afford such a trip.

Would it not be worth while to bring youngsters of both countries together at an earlier stage? Perhaps it could help to improve the atmosphere, and dismantle prejudices. After all, it is only a few hours' bus ride from Cairo to Tel Aviv. "No," says Dr. Hassan. The conditions are not ripe. "And in our country," he adds, "the people like to follow the leaders, not the other way around."

DR. HASSAN'S RETICENCE is still on my mind when I notice an interesting series of interviews in *Al Akhbar* with the writers I have met, Tewfik al-Hakim, Naguib Mahfouz, Hussein Fawzy, and Yussef Idris. They respond to an inquiry by a reporter: Why do you think your works are taught and read in Israel?

The question is not entirely an innocent one. In the past, several Egyptian writers—not those interviewed—have complained that the interest shown by Israeli scholars in Egyptian literature is a form of "psychological warfare," an attempt to "spy" on the Arabs through analyzing their poems and novels. There was, of course, a certain amount of justice in this complaint. This makes the interviews even more interesting.

Tewfik al-Hakim again speaks nostalgically of his personal relationship with Abba Eban, who translated one of Hakim's earlier books (*Diary of a Country Deputy*) into English forty years ago. Hakim says that he has agreed to write the introduction to a forthcoming *Festschrift* entitled *Abba Eban's Friends*. Who would have thought that possible less than a year ago?

Naguib Mahfouz does not seem perturbed by the fact that two major Israeli studies of his works were written by former high-ranking Israeli army officers. He says that the great interest in his work of Israeli readers stems from the very commendable desire of civilized people to know the culture of their neighbors.

Yussef Idris says that behind any political reasons lie emotional ones. Israelis study Egypt as a culture. They read Egyptian novels because they want to live in this area with Egypt. They want to integrate into this part of the world and absorb its heritage.

Hussein Fawzy says, "They read our books because they want to live with us." Egyptians should do the same. He is the only one who mentions a *two-way* exchange.

ONE OF THEIR GREAT phrases is "integrate into the area." I am constantly hearing it. What does it mean? In many cases, I assume it means that we should "assimilate," as the Jews of Egypt had done before they were thrown out, or as the Copts are assimilated in Egypt, and the Christians of Lebanon in Arab culture I find this rather hard to take. It is a form of extreme cultural narcissism. Perhaps they mean a *mutual* symbiosis, as between Arabs and Jews in medieval Spain, though none of the integrationists say so explicitly. Few seem to have thought these injunctions through to the end; the general expectation so far seems to be, simply, that Israelis should become Arabs.

I often wonder how seriously this is intended. Some of those who urge Israelis to "integrate"—i.e., assimilate—within the predominant culture of the area simultaneously call for the "Westernization" of Arab thought, or deplore the fact that the Middle East has not had an eighteenth-century Age of Reason. I am not equating the brisk radicalism of Israeli culture and technology with "reason." I would only say that Israel is "different," though perhaps much less so than many Egyptians think, or fear. And even the Arab world will probably remain a cloth of many colors. Cairo is still undoubtedly the main cultural center of the Arab world, as Paris at the turn of the century was of Europe, and its only authentic capital city. But what "integration" is there between Egypt and Iraq, save by a common religion and a common classical but not spoken tongue? Or between Lebanon and Saudi Arabia? There is a common heritage, of course, as in the former European provinces of the Carolingian empire. And yet as the European states move toward unity there is no urging the Dutch or the Danes to become French or German simply because they are minority cultures.

"But Jewish society is exclusive, while Moslem society has always been inclusive and open." This is another favorite argument. It does not become true simply because so many romantic Arabists in the West have endorsed it in the past. The truth is that both societies are "exclusive" because they have enclosed themselves for too long behind curtains of faith that preserved them through the ages. To amalgamate in any way the destinies of Israelis and Egyptians, both countries would first have to abandon this exclusivity and become secular. Both would have to separate religion from state, and from nationhood. Both are equally conservative in this respect, and have been growing increasingly so in the past decade.

A SPOKESMAN FOR THE OPPOSITION to the peace: Kamal ed-Din Hussein was Vice-President of Egypt under Nasser and one of the Free Officers who staged the 1952 coup d'etat. In *The Philosophy of the Revolution,* Nasser describes the scene in the besieged Egyptian positions in Palestine in 1948. Major Kamal ed-Din Hussein was sitting near him in the trench, looking distracted, with nervous, darting eyes.

"Do you know what Abdul Aziz [a fellow officer] said to me before he was killed?"

"What did he say?" Nasser asked.

Kamal ed-Din Hussein, Nasser reports, replied with a sob in his voice and a deep look in his eyes. "He said to me, 'Remember, the biggest battlefield is in Egypt' "—not in these foreign parts.

This is still Hussein's view today. He speaks bitterly of the corruption he considers rampant in Egypt as a direct result of Sadat's policy of economic liberalization. A gang of crooks has taken over the economy. The crooks are getting rich at public expense. Sadat's own hands—and those of his wife, Jihan—are not clean.

Kamal ed-Din Hussein is one of the four original Free Officers who continue to firmly oppose the peace treaty. Former Major Khaled Mohiedin, a communist, is another. Kamal ed-Din Hussein is at the other extreme: he is a former member of the semiclandestine Moslem Brotherhood. Hussein is not strictly speaking a Nasserist, for he fell out with Nasser in the 1960s and in 1967 accused Nasser of having "destroyed" the very people whose dignity as free humans he had hoped to restore. Hussein had a similar falling out with Sadat soon after he took over. He says that Sadat is a ruthless dictator. Sadat concluded this peace with Israel against the wishes of the Egyptian and Arab peoples.

How can that be? Is not popular opinion in Egypt clearly in favor of peace? Hussein sees no contradiction. Hitler and Göring also knew how to fabricate public opinion.

There is, he claims, a difference between an honorable peace and a shameful peace. This is peace through capitulation. Egypt has signed her sovereignty away to the Jews. The Jews will come in and take over. Egypt will be the springboard for a Jewish empire, the cornerstone in a devious design to control the entire East, from the Nile to the Euphrates.

How could Israel possibly seize the entire East from the Nile to the Euphrates when it has such a difficult time holding on the tiny West Bank and Gaza Strip? No problem, according to Kamal ed-Din Hussein. The Russians send them fifty thousand Jews a year, superb manpower, mathematicians, engineers, and nuclear physicists. The Americans send money. Coexistence is impossible between Egypt and Israel.

Why is coexistence impossible? Isn't Israel withdrawing from the Egyptian territories it had occupied and giving back the oil wells it so badly needs? Nonsense! Egypt is not regaining full sovereignty over Sinai and the oil wells. Sadat has agreed to demilitarize the area. The true masters of Sinai will be the Americans. This treaty is bad, bad, bad. And what about the status of Jerusalem? Nothing is assured. It is a real disaster.

A VISITING DUTCH JOURNALIST told me of M——, another prominent opposition figure whom he interviewed a few days ago. M—— had been a powerful man under Nasser, but was accused of plotting against Sadat and removed—with a state pension—from the various offices he held. When the Dutch visitor asked him why he was so opposed to Sadat personally, to Sadat's regime, to his economic policy and his peace, M—— blew up in rage. He seemed to have been drinking heavily. He is also said to be a compulsive womanizer. The Dutch newspaperman suggested this may be another reason for his growing political isolation. (Robespierre said of Danton, "One cannot conspire and fuck at the same time.") M—— offered the Dutch journalist another drink, but he would not stay for more than half an hour.

"It wasn't interesting," he said. There was a time when a visiting newspaperman would have walked five miles in the heat for a ten-minute private briefing with this man. Newspapermen are a merciless race. When they are bored they either mock you or just go away.

HOW POWERFUL IS THE opposition to Sadat? Most "knowledgeable" people I have spoken to believe the opposition is marginal and disorganized. Kamal ed-Din Hussein's fearlessly outspoken frankness is surprising. Unlike other figures in the opposition, he does not mind being quoted. He is frequently sought out by foreign correspondents in search of divergent views. He lives in a luxurious apartment and receives a high state pension. Hussein's apparent immunity probably stems from his position as one of the original Free Officers. Another explanation one hears is that the "outs" have traditionally been treated gently here; it is the civilized Egyptian way of doing things. Nasser was the exception, according to this theory. Under Nasser, Hussein kept silent, or he would have ended in a concentration camp or at least under strict house arrest.

The Army so far has been loyal to Sadat. The present opposition is an odd assortment of Marxists and communist sympathizers on the left, Moslem fanatics on the right, and former Nasser satraps—or "neo-Nasserists"—in the middle. The chances of overthrowing the regime are said to be slight, except on the crest of a sudden popular revolt, à la Khomeini, by Islamic fundamentalists.

THE GREAT MOSQUES ARE not crowded. Even on Friday, surprisingly, they seem only partly filled. Great voids of space gape at you through the pointed arches and graceful lacework of arabesque. In the nineteenth century, Edward Lane attributed this phenomenon to the great number of Cairene mosques, and their size. But the population of Cairo has since grown from 250,000 to almost 10 million.

The older mosques—Ahmad ibn Tulun, Qalawun, Sultan Hassan, and Al Azhar—are of breathtaking beauty, surpassing, in the marvelous simplicity of their lines, even those of Spain and North Africa. The color tones are ash and gold. Such places are unassailable expressions of human passion and faith, collective works of art like the great cathedrals of Europe. Like the latter, they fill one with awe and wonder at the paradox of bestiality that in humans comes coupled with marvelous dreams and a gorgeous genuis for hope.

The ninth-century mosque of Ahmad ibn Tulun is a cloistered court, well proportioned, as clear as the finest Romanesque. It stands in the shade of a massive watchtower. The form is based on a walled, fortified enclosure. Elegant arches surround a well: the driving force behind Islam was the nomad. This is oasis architecture at its best but in the heart of a great city which, in the fourteenth century, ibn-Khaldun, the Arab historian, had called "the metropolis of the universe, the garden of the world, the anthill of the human species, the gateway to Islam, the throne of kings."

There are beautiful wood carvings in the mosque of the Mameluke sultan Qalawun: its cruciform plan was introduced by Saladin. The four arms were related to the four rites of orthodox Islam. Today the dark caverns, as in so many other Cairo mosques, are occupied by homeless squatters, who put up tin partitions and tents in the shadow and dust of the magnificent cloister. The gold is fading under the ash. Inside and outside of Qalawun are the crumbling hovels of the poor, children in rags and men smoking nargilehs. The world cannot feed them but offers them enough intoxicants of various kinds to sustain their dreams.

The sun beats down on the great stone rectangle of Al Azhar, with its fine arches and pointed, slightly spiraled pear-shaped domes of delicately laced stone. Built and rebuilt again and again over the centuries, enlarged with additional sanctuaries, study rooms, and dormitories for Koranic students from all over the Moslem world, the University of Al Azhar has always been the most prestigious center of Islamic studies. Today, medicine, agriculture, and engineering are also taught; but Al Azhar's main function is to train ulemas. It is a hotbed of religious puritans, who protest—and occasionally demonstrate—against the debauchery and corruption of modern life.

By the main gate a large sign heralds the forthcoming World Conference of Ulemas. "We enunciate our hope of working out a renewed life under the banner of Islam." A primary purpose of this conference—the eighth in recent years—will be to redefine the character of "Islam as a religion of peace." The fourth conference, in September 1968, was—according to the published protocol—dedicated to war. Its pressing theme had been the waging of jihad, holy war, against the Jewish "enemies of God and human life . . . as is evident from their holy book."

Israel (in 1968 still referred to by insinuation, rarely by name) was a land of evil deviates, riffraff and human refuse that did not constitute a nation; the superiority of Islam over all other religions would guarantee the ultimate triumph of the Believer against the nonbeliever through the destruction of the "Jewish state."

The participants in the 1968 conference invoked just about every authority conceivable to justify the doing away of the Jew; even the stones say, "O Moslem, this is a Jew! Come along, pick me up and smite him down!" The complete proceedings of that conference were made public and followed up by an English translation of almost one thousand pages, issued in 1970 by the Egyptian government printing office.

The opening remarks were by the Vice-President of Egypt, Hussein al-Shafe'i. He called upon the ulemas to prepare themselves to strike terror in the "holy war against our enemies and the enemies of God, and others besides since there is no call today more articulate, nor an appeal more sacred than that of the oncoming struggle." The then Rector of Al Azhar, His Eminence the Grand Sheikh Hassan Mamoun, also spoke at the inaugural session. He chastised the Jews who "had been destined to dispersion by the Deity," and were now again "a spearhead . . . against Arabs and Moslems . . . the enemies of humanity . . . the lingering spirit of the Crusades, that had been utterly routed by the feats of valor and heroic resistance of our forefathers."

The present Director of Al Azhar Institutes, Sheikh Ragab al-Abidy, is said to have been chosen by Sadat for the position. His office is in a high vaulted room in one of the labyrinthine annexes to the mosque. He speaks in a low resonant voice, through an interpreter. He does not wish to discuss the proceedings of the conference of 1968, which he had not attended, he says. But the war was a very bitter one, he explains. It required the mobilization of spirit as well as body. Now peace has been signed. But sacred Jerusalem (Al-Quds, the Holy) is still in alien hands! He says alien, not enemy, hands. The ulemas and imams of Egypt support Sadat's peace initiative to a man. There is a historical precedent for what Sadat has done. The Koran permits treaties with infidels if they are concluded from a position of strength. Mohammed made an armistice with the Jews of Medina; a peace treaty was concluded even with the Crusaders, for Islam is not a religion of war. Islam preaches peace to all men of goodwill. President Sadat has given the Israelis every opportunity to show they are men of goodwill. They must now prove that Sadat's faith has not been misplaced.

How shall they do that? By evacuating the holy city of Jerusalem, says the Sheikh. By returning Jerusalem to its lawful owners, the Moslems. By ending the wanton desecration of Jerusalem, and of Hebron where the shrine of Abraham, Isaac, Jacob, and their saintly wives has been profaned through conversion into a Jewish synagogue. The struggle for Jerusalem and the Shrine of Ibrahim will continue, he says; if necessary, it will last centuries. But is not Jerusalem at least as holy for the Jews as for the Moslems, who also have Mecca and Medina? No, Jerusalem is the third after the two noble sanctuaries of Mecca and Medina, but not the least important. It is the place associated with the *mirag,* the heavenly ascent of the Prophet, peace be upon his name. Jerusalem was and will be Arab again.

Could not Jews and Moslems share their holy sites? Never. Jerusalem is the burial ground of the saintly martyrs, from among the companions of Mohammed. Their very bones. Believers cannot condone sovereignty there by nonbelievers. Nor at Al Aqsa and the Mosque of Omar. It is not men who postulate this rule. God saith the truth and it is He who guideth us to the path of rectitude.

BEYOND THIS QUARREL over what Gibbon would have called "the stately monuments of superstition" remains the larger issue of religious fundamentalism versus modernism. It has plagued Egypt since the first quarter of this century. It is perhaps no accident that the infamous Moslem Brotherhood, known for its terror and assassinations, was founded in 1928 in Ismailia, the headquarters of the Suez Canal Company, the heartland of Egyptian technology. The Brotherhood derived its power from the social and psychological crisis caused by modernization, technology, and Westernization, of which the Canal and all its works were among the first great examples. The Moslem Brotherhood maintained its strength over the years and subsequently posed what seemed at the time the only serious threat to Nasser's rule, not out of love of liberty but out of fear of the new and the unknown. The Moslem Brotherhood is today outlawed in Egypt, but the sentiments that inspired it are still alive. Sadat's regime is only just beginning to cope with them. The daily signals from Iran are clearly audible. In the new multi-party system promised by Sadat, the Moslem Brotherhood will undoubtedly redouble its efforts to be recognized legally as a party.

Meanwhile various splinter groups and offshoots operate clandestinely, under such names as Allah's Army, Front of the Jihad, Troops of the Hegira, or Party of Islamic Liberation. They claim that Egyptian society, under Sadat's more liberal economic policy, is debauched and corrupt, a huge whorehouse. Its public institutions are paralyzed by embezzlers, bribery, and nepotism. There is only one cure for these ills: a return to the pristine purity of Islam, a halt to industrialization, Westernization, and modern education with all its dangerous by-products of moral lassitude and permissiveness.

President Sadat, himself a demonstratively devout Moslem, seems to have done little to defuse these pressures. His life-style of conspicuous consumption—even more than that of Nasser—and his company of luxury-loving rich men are the epitome of what the fundamentalists—and the Marxists—are complaining about. The slogan of the fundamentalists is "For every shah there is an ayatollah." But who would that ayatollah be?

Unlike the situation in Iran, no ayatollah has as yet appeared. The present clergy in Egypt is not a semi-independent body, as it is in Iran. It is an arm of the state today even as it once was under the pharaohs. The nonestablishment fundamentalists are especially strong among university students, a phenomenon not too difficult to understand. The effort and expense of attending the overcrowded universities no longer guarantees a peasant boy the same social advancement it once did. The result is demoralization and distrust. At several universities the militants have succeeded in segregating women students and have forced them to wear the veil. Nor have women students—including some studying medicine and science—been unwilling converts to the new puritanism. There is a pious hope that behind the veil they may yet fathom spiritual depths and certainties that are deemed lost in a secular world, vulgar, materialist, morally disintegrating, nervous, and afraid.

I have seen several veiled women on the campuses; and curiously even in some Cairo discothèques, which suggests the prevalence also of a kind of religious chic. Yet fundamentalism is by no means a mere fashion. There are acts of sabotage and violence, and clashes between the police and the fundamentalists, especially in the provinces. In Al-Minya, a town in Upper Egypt, a clash took place outside a main mosque while I was in Cairo. The event was not reported in the newspapers. One policeman was killed, twenty rioters were seriously wounded. A foreign observer who was there tells me that fundamentalist students from the local university placed themselves at the head of a crowd of devout Moslems coming out of the mosque after Friday prayers. The crowd then rioted in the streets, chanting, "Moslem power!" "Death to the Zionists and the Americans!" "The peace treaty is treason!" "Sadat is the Enemy of Allah!"

Sadat ridicules the fundamentalists as a gang of fools and attacks them, as well, as a seditious minority of communists masking their true faces under pious beards. He derides his other foes with equal disdain: men like Heykal, the brilliant journalist who was Nasser's chief propagandist; Khaled Mohiedin, leader of the crypto-communist Progressive Union; and Kamal ed-Din Hussein. Mohiedin clashed with Nasser in his lifetime, but is now posing as guardian of the Nasser heritage, which, he claims, Sadat has betrayed. In his autobiography, *In Search of Identity,* Sadat dismisses the neo-Nasserists as empty shells and shipwrecks, driven only by envy and hatred. Sadat's book was partly dictated by him, and partly ghostwritten. It is a fascinating book in many ways, not necessarily for its historical accuracy, which may leave something to be desired, but as a rich source of clues to the character and self-image of this extraordinary man.

I had read *In Search of Identity* before coming to Egypt. In Cairo, in my room over the Nile, I often leaf through it again, especially in the early morning hours when the traffic below rouses me from my sleep. Reading such a book in its proper ambience, an ambience, moreover, that the author has succeeded in changing so thoroughly, lends it a certain poignancy. The point should not be pressed to absurd lengths of pedantry, in the manner of those who would inspect an author's bathroom in order to understand his work better. But Sadat's is a political book. Its subject is both Sadat himself and the country in which he grew up and matured, and which he is now ruling as a more or less benevolent dictator. Once one has seen the Egyptian landscape and has become more familiar with the society and the people described in Sadat's book, the image it projects upon rereading, in Egypt, is imprinted on one's mind with added plasticity and perhaps with better understanding.

There are two versions of the book. A first version—in Arabic only—appeared in installments in Anis Mansur's *October* magazine. The erudite, multilingual Mansur is said to have been one of the ghost writers. In the first version there is an anti-Semitic remark (excised in the second, which appeared some years later, after Sadat's pilgrimage to Jerusalem). In the first version, peace is not the dramatic climax, or even a major theme, as it is in the second, which was considerably edited by Sadat's American publishers, and rewritten.

In the original Arabic version, for example, Sadat muses about his mind. He compares it to a Swiss clock mechanism. He sometimes takes out his watch and looks at it admiringly, thinking that this is how his own mind works. All of this—and much else besides—is missing in the second version. Yet there is enough left to lay bare curious, often charming, occasionally baffling aspects of the personality of this man.

His sense of theater: as when he reveals that before embarking for Jerusalem he planned to summon the leaders of China, the United

States, the Soviet Union, Great Britain, and France to meet with him in Jerusalem and lay together the cornerstone of peace. (Later he would propose staging the signing of the peace treaty on Mount Sinai, where he would also be buried in the ashes, as it were, of the burning bush.) As a boy, Sadat wanted to be first an actor, then a lawyer. "I am an artist," he says. He lists the great inspirational moments of his life, as a child and as a prisoner in jail, and the great books that influenced him: the Koran, H. C. Armstrong's biography of Atatürk (*Grey Wolf*), and *Reader's Digest*. His favorite author is Lloyd Douglas, the American inspirational writer.

When he was secretary of the World Islamic Union in the 1960s, he informed a visiting American clergyman that he had just made an earthshaking discovery: Christianity, Judaism, and Islam were one and the same. The clergyman asked him to explain; Sadat brushed him aside with the remark that the theologians would have to work out the details.

He is at once gregarious and a loner: outgoing, warm, affable, practical, and at the same time, moody, brooding, even sullen, to a point where he appears to be almost a mystic, or a holy fool. Above all, however, a shrewd peasant. A master in the art of survival, in some ways an Egyptian Schweik. Yet unlike Schweik—the symbol of another downtrodden, long-oppressed people—never without a grand stratagem in the back of his mind—and a dream.

He is the man whom no one took seriously for almost twenty years of public life as Nasser's faithful shadow; the man nicknamed "Colonel Yes Sir," or "Colonel Sakhsakh" (Colonel That's Right), who, when he was called Nasser's "pet dog," only smiled. He was founder and first leader of the clandestine organization of Free Officers. Only after his arrest in 1942 was he succeeded by his close friend Nasser. Yet even Sadat's vaunted role as one of the leading conspirators in the 1952 coup d'etat appears in this book in an unexpected, rather charming light.

On the eve of the uprising he happened to be far away from Cairo, in the Sinai desert. Nasser signaled him to come back immediately; the revolution was about to begin. Sadat rushed back to Cairo. But since Nasser was not at the railroad station, as he usually was, Sadat decided that the revolution had been postponed; he went home and took his wife to a movie.

Meanwhile the rebels take over the army command headquarters. Sadat comes home from the cinema and finds a message waiting for him there, a summons from Nasser. He rushes to the Al Abbassia barracks, but since he does not know the secret password, he is stopped by the sentry. He protests, saying that he is Colonel Sadat. Upon learning his high rank, the guard places him under house arrest; those were the rebels' orders for all senior officers. . . .

In 1970 he becomes Nasser's successor on an interim basis, while the serious contenders for the office shuffle for position. He himself is not considered significant. The American envoy in Cairo reports to Washington that Sadat cannot last more than four weeks. This view is shared by senior Israeli army intelligence experts; they pass the word that Sadat is in all likelihood a dope addict. And yet this seemingly insignificant stopgap is more lucid, and stronger, than anyone had thought. On his first day in office he throws out Nasser's chief aide, who had come to him with transcripts of telephone conversations taped by the secret services. Take this rubbish away, he says.

Within half a year he dismantles Nasser's old "power centers" in the public administration and in the secret police. This was to be known later as the second "corrective" revolution of May 1971. It was the beginning of the end of the Nasser police state. And he launches his first peace initiative; he utters the tabu word *salaam*— and behold, he is *not* assassinated as Nasser often privately said he himself would be if he did.

The rest is well known. The Israelis misread Sadat's early peace signals. Seven years later, in Jerusalem, Sadat asked Dayan why. Dayan admitted that they had not believed in Sadat's sincerity. If he had only flown to Jerusalem in 1971 to break down the psychological barrier . . . Instead Sadat had gone on talking about peace *and* war as two equally possible options. The Israelis were vain and intoxicated with the triumph of 1967; few things can be as debilitating as a great victory. Dayan was saying openly he preferred continuing the occupation of Sinai without peace to peace without Sinai.

Sadat clearly underestimated the psychological dimensions of a conflict that had lasted for decades and could not be ended simply by uttering a forbidden word: *Salaam.* The specialists in Israel came up with fine points in Arab linguistics and claimed that if Sadat really wanted peace he would not have said *salaam* (peace), but rather *sulch:* reconciliation, fraternization between enemies. Many a hair was split over this issue; in the end the *sulch* party won. It was also better suited to current Israeli government policy. Dayan considered Sadat politically too weak to survive, and the Egyptian Army absolutely incapable of resorting again to war in his lifetime.

Sadat was to prove him wrong on both counts. In his book he broods about this, but with no malice. Rereading the book, one is struck once again by the odd contrast between the obfuscations he professes ("Politics is the art of building a society wherein the will of God is enacted") and the rational goals he sets up for Egypt in his policies. The great difference between Sadat and Nasser comes clearly into view. Nasser pursued impossible tasks with pitifully limited means. Sadat pursues limited tasks but is ready to go to great lengths to achieve them. For the first time since the revolution, writes Sadat, Egypt knows exactly what it wants.

He is, naturally, very full of himself and of Egypt as an Idea. They are one and the same to him, History and the Self, as burden and as fate. "I Anwar al-Sadat, a farmer born on the banks of the Nile—where man first saw the dawn of time—submit this book . . . this is the story of my life which at the same time is the story of Egypt since 1918—for so destiny has decreed."

Since his early childhood he has had a certain "image" of himself and of Egypt, much as De Gaulle had when in the opening lines of his memoirs he writes: *"Toute ma vie je me suis fait une certaine idée de la France."* Sadat resembles De Gaulle in more ways than one. He loves Egypt, but not necessarily those who inhabit it. It would appear from this book that until his rise to power Sadat's life among his fellow Egyptians had been a nightmare of indolence and intrigue, chaos, egotism, and rancor. What had sustained him in their slothful company for so many years, he says, was the "power of love." He discovered its mystic dimensions in prison, where the

Creator Himself "became my friend," and he, in a series of mesmerizing revelations "established conscious communion with all existence . . . my soul took off like a bird soaring into space . . . into infinity."

Sadat had been imprisoned by the British during World War II, as a suspected collaborator with the Germans, and again in 1946 as an accomplice in the murder of the pro-British Egyptian politician Amin Osman: like Begin, Sadat is a former political terrorist. He dismisses this dark affair in a short paragraph; there was certainly more to it than would appear from his description. Amin Osman's crime had been to state that Egypt must never sever its links with Britain. This, Sadat writes, was "tantamount to a self-imposed death sentence." Sadat and his friends made haste to execute it, although during the actual killing Sadat was waiting in a nearby café. All were arrested, however.

In Cell 54 of the Cairo Central Prison, Sadat writes, he learned "to conquer time and space"; gradually "love became the fountainhead of all my actions and feelings." The implications of the term *love* that Sadat uses so often are worth pondering. As he is a politician, one's first reaction is to suspect rhetoric, conscious or unconscious. But politicians, if they believe in anything, believe in themselves and in their words; a word, through repetition, becomes something like an article of faith. If it is no mere rhetoric, is it something ephemeral, outside of the physical, as Sadat claims, a religious feeling? In his book he speaks of an "inner light," in words reminiscent of the American inspirational writer Lloyd Douglas. What is one to do with such words in the realm of practical politics? It will not do to dismiss them as ornament. When Queen Isabella of Spain was presented with a copy of Elio Antonio Nebrija's *Gramática* (one of the first grammars written about a modern language), she asked bluntly, "What is it for?"

The Bishop of Ávila replied, "Your Majesty, language is the perfect instrument of empire."

What Sadat calls "love" by his own confession is also a very shrewd, realistic estimate of the self, of one's real goals, and a chameleon-like ability to weather storms by keeping his mouth closed and waiting patiently for the main chance. Nothing but "love," as he puts it, enabled him to stay in office under Nasser, as "the only man among the 1952 revolution leaders [Nasser had] not harmed." Shortly before his death Nasser looked around him, writes Sadat, and realized that "there was indeed one man with whom he never quarreled," Sadat. He "loved" Nasser dearly, Sadat writes, although it is difficult to see why. Perhaps he did. Tewfik al-Hakim had even less reason (unlike Sadat he had not been Nasser's crony in the Army); he also says he loved Nasser. Sadat and Nasser had originally been obsessed by the same ideas, many of which were to prove disastrous for Egypt. Sadat, by his own admission, was occasionally more foolhardy than Nasser.

Yet, unlike Nasser, Sadat seems to have learned that a man who cannot change his mind will never change reality; perhaps he learned this in the isolation of Cell 54. He describes his period in jail as the formative period of his adult life. Statesmanship is often little more than a holding operation, the craft of presiding over some status quo imposed by past wars, present fears, and the realization, often belated, partial, and disappointing, of the dreams of former generations. How many statesmen today are able to overcome an entrenched policy? A status quo? When they do, as Sadat did, it seems almost like changing one life form into another.

How exactly he came to it, and *why*, remains unclear in both versions of Sadat's book. Perhaps he deludes himself as well as his readers when he suggests that he waged the 1973 war only to restore Egypt's self-confidence and break the diplomatic deadlock—to attain peace. If the Israeli forces had crumbled, as they almost did, would he not have pushed ahead to "liberate" Tel Aviv? Or, when he writes that he was forced "with a heart that bled," to agree to a cease-fire. He did so, he says, not because the Israelis had recrossed the Canal and advanced to within sixty miles of Cairo, nor because in the end it was clear that neither side could win, but because he had discovered, he says, that he was really fighting the United States of America. . . . He hints that the United States might have dropped an atom bomb on Cairo, as it had on Hiroshima.

Sadat quotes Henry Kissinger as having threatened him, "The

Pentagon will strike at you." In the Arabic version these arguments were more strongly articulated than in the English. Perhaps they were intended for domestic or intra-Arab consumption. Sadat is a politician, not a historian. The lacunae remain. They puzzle a reader, especially if he be in Cairo, alone with Sadat's book in a room over the Nile, trying to surmise the real sequence of events and to reconstruct the true motive.

When Sadat went off on his pilgrimage to Jerusalem he was widely acclaimed for his courage. There were also, quite naturally, those who begrudged him all that fame and glory. One, I remember, was my good friend the late Ze'ev Shek, at that time Israeli ambassador to Italy and a very hearty man. He had grown impatient with all the clamor and finally brought his annoyance to an undiplomatic climax when, at a state function in Rome, President Leone of Italy complimented *him* on Sadat's saintliness and courage.

Shek, who was a survivor of a Nazi concentration camp, responded by telling Leone a story. Shortly after World War II a Russian officer was explaining to a Czech peasant the rich array of medals that adorned his uniform. "This one I got for fighting at Stalingrad," he said. That one for Leningrad, for Kharkov, Berlin, Prague, and so forth. "And this one," he added, pointing to the last, "I got for saving a nice Czech girl from rape." The peasant naturally wanted to hear more. How had this last act of heroism come about?

"Very simply," said the officer. "I changed my mind."

Others still wonder whether Sadat himself fully "knew" what he was doing. It appeared at the time that his decision to fly to Jerusalem had come to him almost overnight. He seemed to have given his aides—and the Israelis—barely seventy-two hours to reflect on what they might say to one another. This has led some people to assume that he acted on an impulse and without fully calculating where this impulse would lead him; or else that he calculated on achieving one end and achieved another. Much of what we know of history as it was really made, as against what politicians pretend it is, tempts one to endorse this view. As a supporting argument, there are two great tomes of Tolstoy's *War and Peace* and, with more cynicism than tragic despair, A. J. P. Taylor's well-known remark that the greatest masters of statecraft are those who do not know what they are doing.

But if I attempt to sum up, as I must, what we know so far as "fact," I am led to believe that Sadat knew very well what he was doing. I have spoken to enough Egyptians to know that in making peace Sadat was following the Egyptian people, not leading them. The first vague signals he sent out in 1971 and 1972 were misunderstood and he must have wondered why. In flying to Jerusalem, Sadat correctly assessed the magnitude of the psychological problem which Arab hatred had built up over the years in Israeli minds, and which he had ignored until then. He could have chosen to negotiate secretly with Israel, or through intermediaries. But he seems to have understood the prior need to "legitimize" Israel in Arab as well as in Israeli eyes by a flamboyant, personal gesture. Nasser wished to lead the Arab world by making war on Israel; Sadat wishes to be its leader by making peace with Israel.

I am led to believe that if the present treaty, for whatever reason, should break down, the situation can never revert to the old status quo. The total hostility that had marked this conflict for almost fifty years was broken by President Sadat. Even for many Palestinians, I think, Sadat has changed the nature of the conflict from total war over sacred principle to one—more common in history—over this or that piece of real estate. With one dramatic gesture, he brought Egypt—and many Arabs—back "into history" from a nether world of deadly abstractions that allowed for no compromise. He has made both Israelis and Arabs, in a sense, "normal" again.

I tell this to my friends Joe Kraft and Tahsin Bashir one evening, over drinks, in Kraft's room. Kraft is not usually given to superlatives. He says he thinks that Sadat is truly a great man, we must all hope he lasts. Bashir thinks that this depends to a certain extent on Israel, too. So the circle closes.

THE PRESIDENT RECEIVES ME at his country house, by the river, some twenty miles north of Cairo. A splendid park. Old trees, freshly cut lawns. Rose bushes and sweet peas. A gatehouse in mock-Gothic manned by uniformed guards, but there are surprisingly few of them. The main house is surrounded by wide arched verandas. It stands in the shade of a huge sycamore tree, carefully manicured even on the top, which is five stories high; it seems to have been clipped from a helicopter.

President Sadat is in his sitting room. He is a lean man of medium stature, perfectly built, perfectly poised, so perfectly dressed in striped gray flannels and exquisitely matched shirt and tie that one suspects he keeps a fine English tailor in his closet. His face is dark, almost black. Under the low, receding forehead, a pair of sparkling warm eyes; a broad nose, soft fleshy lips, a hard chin. He is puffing his pipe. On the wall, a large map of the Middle East on which Israel is still blacked out. His back is turned to it, though. He has been briefed on my collaboration with Sana Hassan. "Really, I could have hanged her," he says harshly.

Why? I ask. Because he is not a young man, he says, and like most Egyptians he has been mobilized in the national cause all his adult life. This Sana Hassan broke ranks. "Really, I was very furious with her. Very furious."

But didn't she merely say in 1974 what he himself would be saying three years later in the Knesset?

Well, yes, that is true. He is no longer angry with her. I should tell her that. "For sure, we are free of all complexes now." There is peace. Soon there will be free travel, trade. A new era is beginning, he says, clutching his pipe in one hand, gesticulating with the other. There is a slightly rough edge to his deep voice. When I ask him if trade and tourism and the other forms of normalization between Egypt and Israel will be stopped or curtailed in the event that no satisfactory solution is found to the Palestinian problem, he raises his voice and cries, "Shame on you! Shame! This is the language of conflict! We are finished with that. Peace is a fact. Normalization is a fact." Whatever the difficulties that remain, there is peace and "there is no going back on that."

I ask Sadat why it had taken so long. Why hadn't he gone sooner on his peace mission to Jerusalem? Four wars. Hundred thousands dead.

"Well," he begins, "you see . . ." He does not answer immediately. He leans back in his Chippendale chair and fingers his pipe. The agonies of peoples ultimately become the exercises of schools, but first politicians converse about them casually. Why not sooner? There were many reasons, says Sadat. Historical reasons, personal and political. In any event, it could not have happened before the 1973 war. In that war Egypt was able to regain her dignity and pride. It freed her from the complexes caused by almost a decade of most terrible humiliations. "We were humiliated," he says again. "For that reason I refused the offer of Kosygin to meet with Golda Meir in 1972."

On the other hand, he thinks that Israel twice prevented possibilities of making peace. The first opportunity came immediately after the Six-Day War; another, in 1971. If Moshe Dayan, in 1967, had only had a better understanding of the "Arab's psychology," if, instead of saying, "I am waiting for them to ring me up," he had taken a plane and gone straight to Cairo (as Sadat himself flew to Jerusalem in 1977) with a gallant offer, "believe me, ninety-nine percent of the Egyptians would have hailed him as a hero." Really, he is surprised, he says. Dayan was born in this region, he ought to have known us better. He should have realized that after humilating us so terribly he could not expect us to come and beg Israel to dictate the terms.

In 1971, he says, another possibility was missed. That February, soon after he had come to power, he declared that he was ready to make peace, the first Arab leader who had ever said so publicly, in a speech to Parliament. Golda Meir, he says, ignored him. "She had no guts," he complains. Or else she must have thought that Egypt was a dead horse.

I interrupt to say that, as far as I can remember, as late as 1975 he was offering only the vaguest deal in return for complete Israeli withdrawal: no demilitarized zones, and no diplomatic relations or trade, which, as he put it, must wait for "future generations."

That's true, he says. But he changed his mind in the summer of 1977. "I realized that your side was ready to continue indefinitely with the state of no war, no peace. For me that was not enough." The situation on the Arab side that summer was "even worse," he says. He realized that the other Arabs were simply incapable of making real peace, "because of ignorance, backwardness, inferiority complexes, and corrupt leaders." The Arabs wanted to persist in their "total rejectionism," even as they do today. That was even worse, he says, than what Israel was doing. "When I realized this, I decided. I was sure of myself. The October War had freed us of all complexes. I decided that I had only one alternative, to go and challenge you in your Knesset. Now that we have peace, I hope that as many Israelis as possible will come here and discover for themselves that we mean it with all our heart."

BETWEEN TWO ARGUMENTS on current affairs the President muses about distant history. Everything sounds so neat in the rarefied air of this elegant, well-appointed room. Delicious coffee is served in tiny cups of thinnest china. Historically, he says, Israel was associated in Egyptian minds with British colonialism and oppression. "My first political lesson, as a boy, was the outrage at Denshawai. I grew up hating the British."

As a young man he had read that, in the Balfour Declaration, the British had promised Palestine to the Jews as a national home. "In other words, you were the ally of my main enemy." But this was long ago. As he speaks, I cannot be sure how long. Perhaps he senses the perplexity. "I grew up hating the British," he adds. And, with a sly smile, "It is ironical—I didn't know at the time that my wife would be half-English."

He seems a man of deep emotions, a virtuoso in self-control. But when he talks about the other Arab leaders, the "rejectionists," his voice rises in anger. The terms he uses most frequently are psychological. They are "lunatics"; if he cannot prevent them from running mad he will lure them, at least, into a straitjacket that will not work loose for as long as he is around. King Hussein of Jordan has not joined his peace initiative because he is a "schizophrenic." Does he mind being quoted? Not at all; "everybody knows Hussein is a schizophrenic; his father was also schizophrenic." Sadat does not think much of ideas, although he wins success by using them, nor of interests or fears, even when legitimate. Whatever trouble there still is, its roots are "psychological"; only Egypt has freed itself completely from all "complexes." The Israelis' refusal so far to grant self-determination to the Palestinians—he thinks it is temporary—merely proves that they have not yet overcome the "psychological block," which constitutes 80 percent of the problem. He sounds as though his main task, as he sees it, is to open a huge psychiatric clinic for Syrians, Jordanians, Palestinians, and Israelis alike.

AN ARMY HELICOPTER lands on the narrow strip of concrete between the river Nile and the President's town house in Cairo. It is totally dark. There is a heavy scent of jasmine in the air. Just after 4 A.M. I follow Mrs. Jihan Sadat into the narrow cabin. The helicopter rises and flies over the rooftops toward Cairo International Airport. Below, the city lights glimmer in the dark. "A beautiful city," says the President's wife. "Gorgeous. Like a very old lady in jewels."

At the airport a few minutes later, there are banners and a small guard of honor stands at attention in the dark. In Egypt the President's wife is accorded royal treatment at all hours. A red carpet has been laid. She walks the short distance to a waiting executive jet. Mrs. Sadat is on her way to attend a ceremony in Aswan. We take off and the plane flies south. The Nile Valley is still black, but in the east glow the first pinks and reds of a magnificent desert dawn.

Through the roar of the jet engines, Mrs. Sadat speaks about peace. Her face is soft and pale. Her smile, when it comes, is almost shy. Peace is here, at long last, she says. It should have come sooner! But it's done. This is what we have dreamed about all these years. You'll see, everything will fall into place now. Quite naturally, you'll see, with fewer difficulties, probably, than one thinks. Of course every beginning is hard. Many people are worried, or astonished, and some are shocked. But they are a tiny minority.

Below, the desert turns gray, then a pale gold, and from one end of the horizon to the other there is nothing but sand. She continues to receive many letters from Israelis, says Mrs. Sadat, some very moving, they are mostly from mothers and schoolchildren. She answers every single one. Certainly, she says, there are some people in Egypt who complain that "Begin is very difficult." The others—they are a majority, she and her husband among them—consider Begin a very hard man to negotiate with, but he is honest and he keeps his word. Above all, he seems a strong man. It's better to deal with a strong man rather than with a weak one, even if the dealing is tough. Begin is a "fanatic," of course, she says. It is difficult for one who has been a fanatic all his life to change overnight. She once told her husband, she says, laughing, that Begin must be a Soviet agent. But she is convinced, she says, that in the end everything will turn out for the best. There will be peace with the other Arab states as well. She feels sure about that. "They are our brothers, but we are more developed and advanced. Some of them are still in the tribal stage. They will follow us, you'll see. Their peoples want peace very badly."

Suddenly she inquires, "Have you seen Abu Simbel?" I say no. "But you must see it!" she cries. "It is the most beautiful spot in Egypt." She orders the pilot to change course and go first to Abu Simbel. There is a great deal to be said for travel on presidential jets, even at such an early hour. After a while, we circle low around the vast statues of Ramses II. They were cut out from the rocks a few years ago and lifted to a higher spot above the new Lake Nasser.

She very much favors cultural exchanges, says Mrs. Sadat. Let them be frequent and intensive. Above all, she favors visits by young people. "The children must get to know one another. Everything is always easier with children." But the grown-ups, too, already get along with one another, much better than a few months ago. "Between women," she insists, it will be the easiest to make peace. "Women forgive and forget sooner than men!" She seems convinced of that. What she says sounds a bit sentimental. But it is pleasant to hear. Below, the desert is ablaze in the morning heat.

A MEETING OF THE LOCAL Rotary Club in a provincial hotel in the Nile Delta. The hotel is still under construction; it has been for the past six years, with long, unaccountable interruptions. But the public rooms and kitchens are operating. A fleet of cars is parked in the dust between the cranes and cement mixers. The Rotarians dine on lentil soup, fish and macaroni, roast, and a dessert made of sesame seeds, which is a specialty of this region. Among those present are senior officials in the provincial government, directors of nationalized firms, doctors, lawyers, engineers, and businessmen in the private sector, which has flourished here, as elsewhere in Egypt, since Sadat's liberalization measures.

After dinner they listen to a lecture. The guest speaker is an Egyptian scholar, a specialist in international affairs. His theme is the Middle East after the peace treaty. He covers the whole scene, from Morocco to Iran. He praises Sadat's courage and imagination and goes on to refute the arguments of the rejectionists in the Arab states. Their accusations are groundless, he says; Egypt has not turned its back on the Arab world. On the contrary, it remains the vanguard of the Arab world and will continue the struggle for Palestinian rights. Israel will be forced to withdraw from the occupied territories.

A discussion follows. No one protests the peace treaty. No one says anything about the Palestinians. The questions put to the speaker touch upon the current disconcerting situation in Iran. The real fear in this room, filled with serious men and women, is the rise of Khoumeinism. The mood harks back to the beginnings of Egyptian nationalism early in this century, at once bourgeois-liberal and anticlerical. It is not Israel, or Zionism, that worries these people, but rather the sudden politization of Islam.

The discussion then turns to domestic problems. There are the usual questions, rhetorical ones, really, about the bureaucracy: the difficulty of making things move, the endless gantlet run for permissions, funds allocated but not spent, plans approved but not carried out. Every year, a million new mouths to feed. The guest speaker agrees that these are crucial problems. He reminds his listeners that for the first time in modern history international interest is "focused" on Egypt's domestic problems. Many people in the West realize that the domestic stability of Egypt is a main guarantee of the new peace. The guest speaker says this with more hope, probably, than certainty. There is no such certainty. The West doesn't want war, of course. But it needs oil very badly. Oil is, as they say, the opium of the West; in various forms all are hooked on it, housewives and children and pacifist preachers, and there is no telling yet where the trip may be taking them, and us.

THERE IS A YOUNG WOMAN in the audience. She says, "Everybody is fed up and tired, they feel they have done enough for the Arabs. They want to be let alone and be Egyptians again."

Her remark ties in well with the general mood of this Rotarian meeting. I am hearing similar remarks all the time. In the streets of Cairo the words *Palestinian* and *Arab* are frequently invectives. The sentiment is by no means restricted to the uneducated. A European businessman who is staying in my hotel says that he asked a prominent minister in Sadat's Cabinet where he might spend an evening out in Cairo. The minister said, "Don't let them take you to the Sahara Club. It's not pleasant there. Too many Arabs!"

There is prejudice, of course, in every country, in Britain against American tourists, in France against Germans, in Denmark against Swedes, and so forth. But bigotry apart, I am continually struck by the tendency of Egyptian intellectuals and politicians, in conversation or writing, to refer to *"the* Arabs" rather than *"the other* Arabs." Sadat changed the official name of the country from Nasser's United Arab Republic to Arab Republic of Egypt. Almost everybody calls it just Egypt. The newspapers do not use the official name, and one does not always find it even on postage stamps or official stationery.

The young woman in the audience says the name Arab Republic of Egypt is "absurd." She feels very strongly about this. Under Nasser, she says, "Egypt's true identity was denied. Schoolchildren were made to recite endlessly, 'I am an Arab, my father was an Arab, etc.'" She thinks the trouble with the Free Officers was that they had come from a petit-bourgeois provincial milieu, with few links to the intellectual elite of either Cairo or Alexandria. Nasser suppressed the "Egyptian character" of the country under an avalanche of pan-Arab rhetoric. The reasons for this were political, but even politically pan-Arabism ended in dismal failure. Under Nasser, Egypt was not the Queen of the Arab world, but its prisoner. "When Egyptians claimed that they were Egyptians, the Arabs trusted them. When they said that they were Arabs, the Arabs suspected Egypt of foul play."

This sentiment, so different from the whipped-up verbiage of pan-Arabism in Nasser's days, is everywhere apparent. It is spelled out rather forcefully in a book published recently by the Egyptian historian Professor Nimat Fuad, *A Plea for a Rewriting of History*. Professor Fuad calls for the liberation of Egypt from the yoke of fear, dictatorship, and cultural illusion through a rediscovery of the main phases of Egyptian history, the classic pharaonic, the Christian, and the Islamic. Fuad's book, says the young woman, could not have appeared before 1973. Even people who disagree with its more far-reaching conclusions consider it an important contribution to the continuing debate on Egypt's future role in the area. The general emphasis on Egypt as a unique entity is further enhanced by the acerbity of recent Arab attacks on Egypt, the "traitor" to the cause. There is in fact so much talk that one is tempted to believe in the powerful resurgence of a new local patriotism, with possibly far-reaching results for Egypt and its neighbors, until one remembers that the debate over Egypt's identity is not a new one. It has been plaguing Egypt for years. It first arose in the nineteenth century when the traditional base of Egyptian society was upset by colonial rule and modernization, precipitating a crisis of identity that has never truly been resolved. It has troubled every important writer from Taha Hussein, early in this century, to Tewfik al-Hakim, Naguib Mahfouz, and the younger poets and novelists of today.

Egyptian nationalism began with the apposition of "Egypt" to the Ottoman Empire, and originally regarded Islam and Arabism as merely complementary factors. Mustafa Kamel, the Western-oriented founder of the nationalist movement in Egypt, dismissed Arabism as an illusion. Nasser, with more military heaviness than exactitude, said of his *Philosophy of the Revolution* that it was a "reconnaissance patrol to discover who we are." Sadat finally called his book in English *In Search of Identity,* and in Arabic *In Search of Self*.

Taha Hussein, the famous blind novelist, was a student at Al Azhar and later a convert to outright anticlericalism in the name of science. At a time when Egyptian nationalism was still focused on gaining independence from British rule or on union with the Sudan rather than on Arabism or war against Israel, Hussein wrote a celebrated book, *The Future of Culture in Egypt,* in which he urged Egypt to be a Mediterranean country, a part of Europe, not of Africa or Asia. But in his later years Taha Hussein returned to Arabism and Islam and announced that he would like to combine in himself two personalities, one critical and inquisitive, the other irrational, even mystic.

The perennial nature of this argument, with its ups and downs, never conclusive, naturally coincided in this century with the shifting tides of Egypt's political fortunes. *Höchstes Glück der Erdenkinder sei nur die Persönlichkeit* (Man's highest fulfillment is to become aware of his true identity): when Goethe made this famous proclamation on the eve of the age of nationalism, he posed a problem to which successive generations rarely found a satisfactory answer. Like other nations, the Egyptians have never been able to agree what their collective personality was. As in other countries, the conflict has traditionally defied easy resolutions; the most shallow answers were generated by the complexities of the times. The argument is not likely to be resolved any more quickly in Egypt than the perennial quarrel in Israel over "Who is a Jew?"

This crisis of identity is not, when one comes to think of it, the only parallel between the two countries. Both profess an ardent nationalism, based on religion as well as on ethnicity. Both nationalisms, at least at the outset, were a revolt against religious obscurantism. Both nationalisms at the outset were seized by Messianic strivings to create a new human being, and at the same time by a naïve faith in science.

Nasser and Ben-Gurion equally believed—wrongly, as it turned out—that "faith unites us but science makes us free," a line first written by Theodor Herzl, the founder of modern Zionism. Both peoples were pariahs, who came to look upon themselves as chosen. Both peoples were ready to believe in spirits even when they no longer believed in God, and postulated a secular role for religion as a social and national force. Both subscribed to a peculiar form of nationalist socialism, which is now regarded in both countries as hopelessly utopian. Both peoples strained to set up exclusivist nation states, yet regarded themselves as part of a larger ethnic whole. Both were future-oriented but often found it cheaper to live in the past. However remote that past was, both were obsessed by it; both made desperate attempts to discover continuity where there had been so much change. The Jews had at least preserved a script and a language and a faith; but in Egypt all three had changed at least three times through pharaonic, Hellenistic, Christian, and Islamic eras.

Both peoples were stamped, as it were, by geography: Egyptians by the Nile, Jews by the dispersion. Both have found it difficult to define their exact geographical limits, and as a consequence both suffered. Both developed through the wars an equal obsession with the "mentality" of the other. Each used its view of the other society and culture to sanctify its own culture and political aggressions. Both pretended to have a monopoly on suffering. Both were obsessed with formalistic legal definitions of what was essentially a political problem. Who was the aggressor in 1948? In 1956? In 1967 and 1973? And who the attacked? Jews always had a penchant for Talmudic hairsplitting. The Egyptians first emerged into national life under the strong influence of the Napoleonic Code; Egypt's struggle against Britain was always described as "Egypt's *case*," as was Israel's.

Both countries, indeed, seem tired now. "This is no longer a legal question," my friend Tahsin Bashir said the other day with a casualness that surprised me. "It's a political one. You get yourself a lawyer, we get ourselves one—we waste time."

THE YOUNG WOMAN AT THE Rotary Club meeting is amused by all these parallels and comparisons. She takes them less seriously than I. Her quick mind lends a jewel point to her plump prettiness. She laughs. When she laughs she has a rare beauty. She tells me the story of K——, an ardent Israeli "peacenik" who came to Cairo. There was a great deal he wanted to discuss, and to compare, as I have done. On his first night in Cairo, she took him to a restaurant with a few others she wanted him to meet. But he was so happy finally to be here that he got drunk and fell asleep in his chair. They tried to awaken him. He fell asleep again. They had to carry him home, feeling rather sorry. It reminded her, she says, of an old tale. A man had just been given a beautiful bride and vowed to kill her with his passion. He took her once and fell asleep. She shook him after a while, and said, "Wake up, killer!" But he went back to sleep.

IX

ALEXANDRIA AT HIGH NOON. A few missile boats are moored in the old port. The new harbor is hidden behind the domes and minarets on the promontory. A wide esplanade curves around the sun-drenched bay. In the hot air, dazzled pigeons, dusty palms, and spectacular views of the sea and the city: Durrell's "capital of memory." For one who has never been here before—hardly dreamed he ever would be—Alexandria is a bookish experience, books remembered, books loved: Lawrence Durrell, E. M. Forster, C. P. Cavafy.

Books lend the city an added quality, more manifest here, for some reason, than in Cairo. Certain characters, phrases, scenes, snatches of dialogue and verse, vaguely imprinted in the mind, come back in the disorderly fashion of incompletely remembered dreams. Colors and smells. Anecdotes, certain figures, perhaps fabled, but like fables, strongly evocative. Captain Jorge y Nelken Waldberg, mentioned in so many memoirs of the turn of the century, a Romanian with a commission in the Argentine Army, a Swedish name, United States citizenship, editor of the local French newspaper, who, a Jew, was a dignitary of the Greek Orthodox Church.

On the sea esplanade a beggar leans against the crumbling balustrade, motionless as a crouching sphinx. On the sidewalk, the smell of salt air and strong black coffee. There is the clank of feet and wheels on the nearby road. Voices in the wind. Plutarch says that when Antony heard strings of a mystic company in the streets of Alexandria, he knew that the gods had abandoned him and he said farewell to the Alexandria he was leaving. The site of the ancient Serapeum. Pompey's Pillar, the red granite came from Aswan: Forster thought it an "imposing and ungraceful object." The modern lighthouse; the better-known ancient one, the Pharos, was almost twice as high.

The old Cecil Hotel, the Ramle railroad station. When the long train pulls away it reverberates with echoes of literary scenes. Durrell's Irish schoolmaster saying good-bye to the Greek cabaret dancer Melissa: "The long pull of the train into the silver light reminds me of the sudden long pull of the vertebrae of her white back turning in bed . . . the crunch of rifle butts and the clicking of Bengali. A detail of Indian troops . . ."

Vanished Irishmen, Greeks, Italians, Jews, Englishmen, and Bengalis. Breaking statues and turning the gods out of the temples, as Cavafy wrote, does not mean they are dead. But there is King Farouk's old palace at Ras-al-Tin, with its unsurpassed collection of kitsch, furniture, paintings, and chandeliers, kitsch gothic and marble and ebony cigar holders studded with diamonds, and pornographic neckties. The Turkish sea citadel is built on the ruins of the ancient lighthouse tower. There are no traces of the Academy where the legend of Egypt was recast eclectically in a fusion of Eastern mysticism with the clear, cold reason of Hellas, and Jerusalem with Athens. Nor of the seventy Jewish sages of Alexandria simultaneously at work translating the Old Testament into Greek, each secluded in his cell, but all seventy versions miraculously identical, so that they were said to have been inspired by God.

The great Jewish synagogue, Prophet Elijah, is still there, however, on Nebi Daniel Street, closed and shuttered except on Fridays and the High Holy Days, when it opens for a congregation of some dozen old men and women.

Close by is the former palatial mansion where Cavafy lay dying and wrote "Waiting for the Barbarians," who yet do not arrive "and now what will become of us without Barbarians? Those people were some sort of a solution." The sly, coquettish poet's study is preserved within the building of the Greek consulate.

The images that rummage through one's mind on a short visit here. It is philistine for a bookish fellow to be in such a hurry at a place like this. Unlike Cairo, this city follows you. The past is palpable not in statuary and painted walls but in so much compelling literature. It is a rather selective past.

An Englishman I know who was here a few years ago and then visited me in Jerusalem spoke wistfully, I remember, of the drastic changes in Alexandria during the twenty-five years following the officers' revolution. "The city lost its soul," he said. The Greeks, the Italians, Jews, and Armenians had left, or were chased out. "The magic city of Cavafy, Forster, and Durrell is gone," he said. At the time I did not notice, but now that I am here I wonder about these possessives. It suddenly occurs to me that Cavafy wrote mostly about ancient Greeks and Hellenes, and Durrell's *Alexandria Quartet* is populated almost totally by Englishmen, Frenchmen, Greeks, Armenians, and Jews, a surfeit of exotic expatriates headed by that classical "Jewess of neurology," Justine. Very baroque, and a bit satiating. Even in Proust, not every main character is a duchess. Nessim, of course, is a Copt; no one can be more "Egyptian" than a Copt, but wasn't he a Zionist spy? The only Egyptian Arab that I can remember in the *Quartet* is the corrupt pasha who takes Nessim's money to close the untidy treasonable affair. "Man is only an extension of the spirit of place." Where are all the other Egyptians? There must have been a million in Durrell's time. Today there are two million.

"The Orient has almost always been a European invention," Edward Said, an American-Palestinian scholar writes in *The Orientalists*, a remarkable book I had been reading with great fascination before coming to Egypt. Said's field is comparative literature. His book is a critique, often quite devastating, of Western novelists and Orientalists who have written about the East, from Chateaubriand and Nerval to my friend Yehoshafat Harkabi in Jerusalem. The "Orient" of so many Western writers never existed; or it has changed beyond recognition with the emigration from Alexandria of the Greeks and other "foreigners," Italians, Englishmen, French, and Jews. The Jews, like the Greeks, had been here almost since time began. Egyptian-Jewish culture, Egyptian-Greek culture, now belong to the archaeology of knowledge. Can they ever be resurrected?

Here, under the tall palm trees that throw long thin shadows on the Mediterranean, between these pseudo-European palaces crumbling from neglect, and the pillars of the old Cotton Exchange, here is a natural place to ponder this question with as much realism as one can marshal. Here Nasser went to school; his father had been a mailman in Alexandria. Here, after the attempt on his life, Nasser whipped up the crowd to a frenzy, saying that he, himself, was replaceable, each one of them was Gamal Abdel Nasser. Here, during the Suez crisis of 1956, he told the West to go and drown itself in the sea, if it wished.

Between 1956 and 1962 Alexandria suddenly ceased to be a Mediterranean city that had looked out on the sea just as Venice had looked out more on the Adriatic than to Italy behind the lagoon. A sad kind of beauty lingers in its streets that look more like those of a city in Italy or the Dodecanese, but are populated today only by Egyptians. Some of the old street signs remain: Rue des Soeurs, Rue Champollion. The great sea esplanade has been renamed Road of July 26, 1952; Mohammed Ali Square is now Midan al-Tahrir (Independence), but the founder of modern Egypt still looks down on it from his bronze horse.

This was once the "summer capital" of Egypt. The King and his entire Cabinet, the senior administration, would move to Alexandria with the diplomatic corps and "society." The revolution put a dramatic end to all that and hastened the departure—or expulsion—of the "foreign" community. Today even the governor of Alexandria, a pleasant rotund man with a white mustache and thin combed-back hair, reeking of eau de cologne, admits that it was a great pity, a great pity, dear sir, that so many foreigners left. Their contribution had been so great, so great. Ah, the Jews especially, he says. Everybody always got on more or less amicably, until relations became complicated by politics and poisoned by the aggression of 1956. Yes, and everybody wishes so much to renew contact.

My friend Shalom Cohen spent his childhood in Alexandria. He attended Victoria College, a large forbidding-looking quadrangle of stone and well-tended lawns, which in both architecture and curriculum was fashioned after a British public school. As a boy he was simultaneously an Egyptian nationalist and a Zionist. As he marched in anti-British demonstrations, so he joined a Zionist youth organization and trained to become a pioneer in Israel.

As an Israeli soldier in the War of 1956, he felt some anguish at having to fight against Egyptians, and was much relieved when, on the fourth day of that war, he was able to induce the Egyptian garrison at Sharm al-Sheikh to surrender without bloodshed. The outflanked Egyptian commanding officer apparently could not resist Cohen's excellent Alexandrian dialect. Cohen still has relatives in a Jewish old-age home in Cairo. He told me this little story: he had gone back to the building of the Zionist youth club to which he had belonged as a boy in the 1940s. It is a vocational training center now. The caretaker, he discovered, was still the same man. He shook Cohen's hand and said, "You got what you wanted! You and all the other young gentlemen who filled this house! You wanted a state of your own, didn't you? Now you have it. And *inshallah,* there will be peace. We will be brothers again, as in the old days." Brothers? Friends? Perhaps. But most likely from afar.

FRIENDS AND COLLEAGUES, or almost, cooperating with one another from afar, is the logic behind *al infitah,* the Opening, Sadat's decision in 1974 to attract foreign businessmen as well as Egyptian flight capital back to Egypt with offers of a tax haven and promises of immunity from confiscation and the stranglehold of state bureaucracy.

The new policy began early in 1974. It was a direct result of the self-confidence regained in the October War. Sadat, in his so-called *October Paper,* spelled out the principles of this new policy, which was soon after made into law by national referendum. In the *Octo-*

ber Paper, Sadat sought to reformulate once again the national goals and overcome the heritage of Nasserism. Its language marked a radical departure from the usual revolutionary rhetoric. In terminology more Western than Third World, the revolutions postulated in the *October Paper* were the "technological revolution" and the revolution in science, communications, and transport. In the *October Paper,* Sadat looked forward to the "Year 2000" and to an "Open Society."

Nasser's ideological manifestos held up the dream of United Araby; Sadat's *October Paper* stressed the country's unique "Egyptian" identity. In practice it promised to let in "fresh air," in three important fields:

In foreign relations: a greater opening to the West.

In domestic affairs: a greater measure of "democracy," "rule of law," and "civil rights."

In business: the reintroduction of a private sector to function alongside the socialist economy.

In foreign affairs the opening to the West has since led to the signing of a peace treaty with Israel. In domestic and economic affairs there is still a long way to go in this authoritarian state before there will be democracy or any measure of free enterprise unfettered by rigorous state controls. There is a beginning of change, however; the future will show where it leads. There has been a certain restoration of the rule of law in Egypt; the courts are certainly more independent now than in the past thirty years. There is still no freedom of the press, but there is less thought control than before, and individuals are no longer at the mercy of a brutal political police.

In domestic politics there is the recent permission to form new, but officially "approved," parties; in business there is the policy of *al infitah,* the Opening. Free zones have been established for local and foreign investors, in Cairo, Port Said, Port Taufiq, and in this former stronghold of enterprising foreigners and Egyptians, Alexandria.

Joseph Kraft and I are taken to see the Free Zone of Alexandria. It is located a few miles west of the city on the old road to El Alamein. It is designed to serve as a tax haven for industrialists who employ local labor, import their machines and raw materials duty-free, and ostensibly export the finished products. We drive along a new four-lane highway, past formerly wild and isolated beaches, where Justine swam with her Irish schoolmaster. Here Nessim made love to Melissa where Antony and Cleopatra may have before them, and E. M. Forster rhapsodized about the wild life, the shy gazelles, the birds, and the white sands.

But Alexandria has since crowded to the west. The pristine beaches are dotted with new houses and slums, factories, army camps, and restaurants. A wide asphalt road leads down to Justine's secret coves. The wandering dunes surround the barbed-wire fence of the Free Zone.

Kraft and I are welcomed by the director of the zone. He greets us with enthusiasm and obeisance due more to the representatives of Morgan & Company than to two skeptical reporters who moreover have heard that some of the Free Zones are a paradise for black marketeers. Cars and other consumer goods are unloaded duty-free, and smuggled past corruptible customs officials to Cairo and Alexandria. "In vain may heroes fight and patriots rave if secret gold creeps on from knave to knave." One outraged Egyptian official told Kraft that in Port Said alone less than $30 million was collected in custom duties, although taxable goods worth $0.5 billion had been unloaded there.

The director is the son of a prominent Alexandrian family. He is a former customs official himself. He waves these rumors aside, saying, "That cannot happen here! Maybe in Port Said, but not here!" He wears a fine English tweed jacket, gray wool tie, and silk shirt. "The cost of the entire infrastructure is carried by the government," he says. The investors build their own plants and pay an annual fee of one dollar per square meter. Fifty-five industrial projects have already been approved. Twenty are owned by European, American, Kuwaiti, or Libyan businessmen; the rest are owned by Egyptians who hold foreign capital.

"We do not ask too many questions," he adds with a knowledgeable smile. "Everybody is welcome. Everyone!"

Kraft asks, "Israeli investors too?"

"Three weeks ago I would have had to answer you with a regret-

ful no," says the director. "Today I am pleased to be able to say yes.
Let them come. *Ahlan wasahlan*. As long as they invest money, they
are welcome."

"It won't disturb your Libyan and Saudi investors who have
opened factories here?"

"No problem! They don't come here for politics. They come to
make money. Money is the only language here. So what if an Israeli
plant finds itself next to the Kuwait carpet factory!"

The real problems, meanwhile, are of a different nature. Although
the Free Zone was opened in 1975, there are still frequent breakdowns in electricity and no reliable telephone links with Alexandria
or any other place. The telex, however, functions.

Awni J. Sarraj is general manager of the Kuwaiti-owned Middle
East Carpet Company, which opened in 1976. Mr. Sarraj is an elegant young man in his early thirties. His office is air-conditioned, a
rarity here. The fine furniture in teak and leather is Italian. Seven
million dollars have been invested in this plant. Two hundred and
fifty workers are bused in daily from Alexandria and earn an average monthly wage of one hundred dollars, he says. The main inves-
tor is Emir Sheikh Jabir, the ruler of Kuwait. His portrait, framed in
gold, hangs on the wall next to Sadat's. The carpets produced here
under a Belgian license are exported to Saudi Arabia.

"No one has stopped ordering carpets from us. Even after the
boycott was imposed on Egypt. This boycott is like a soap bubble,"
says Mr. Sarraj. "It will pop in no time."

We have been introduced by name only. I followed Mr. Sarraj
through the production lines. I ask: You are Kuwaiti?

"I am Jordanian," he says. "And you? Are you English, or American?"

Israeli.

"Ah," says Mr. Sarraj. He smiles broadly. *"Shalom u'bracha,"*
and he continues in Hebrew. "Actually I am Palestinian. Born in
Jaffa. I have been to several carpet factories in Israel. I visited there
three years ago. Let us hope things will be all right from now on."

Inshallah.

"Yes. And convey my regards to Mr. C—— of Nazareth. The carpet company."

A little while later, the director drives us to lunch at an opulent private club in the heart of the old European quarter of Alexandria. The former Syrian Club, it has recently been renamed the Alexandria Club. The furniture is *fin-de-siècle* French. The waiters are Sudanese giants wearing dark embroidered robes and white turbans. Shrimp and grilled lobsters are offered from huge silver platters; then there is English roast, with a good local wine.

The director is a perfect host. Coffee? Brandy? A cigar? Outside, it is hot and humid. Inside, it is cool. Through the closed shutters comes the strong scent of jasmine and roses in full bloom. Nero imported roses from Alexandria for his great banquets, according to Suetonius. Petronius reports the presence of Alexandrian singing boys at the gargantuan parties given by rich freedmen of Rome. In the dim light it is not Romans who look down upon us from the walls but long-departed Syrian and Lebanese traders; the portraits are framed in heavy, dark carved wood.

The host refills our glasses. We are all feeling fine, and quite sated. The host speaks of nothing but friendship and cooperation. The Psalmist said, "Behold, how good and how pleasant it is for brethren to dwell together in unity!" Brethren? Yes, but from afar.

The host offers another toast. "I am extremely pleased to welcome you here. We shall be happy to see you return. With pleasure we welcome investments in our Free Zone, from America, and from Israel." He had been pleased to hear that Prime Minister Begin, in a speech in New York, had urged American businessmen to invest in Egypt. An investment in Egypt is an investment in peace. "Investors from all the world, we say, 'Welcome to you!' *Mabrouk, mabrouk.*"

BEFORE I CAME TO Egypt I did not properly appreciate the extraordinary psychological impact on so many Egyptians of the October 1973 war. I knew what it had wrought in Israel: general depression, the final demise of the political old guard, an improved sense of reality.

Surely it is a mistake, I rashly told an Egyptian acquaintance a few days after my arrival, to name so many bridges and squares, and even a new city in the desert, after the October War. We were walking along the Corniche al-Nil. Ahead of us was the new October 6 Bridge, spanning the river to Gezira, and continuing on this side over the roofs of the city as far as the Ramses railroad station.

"Why?" said the Egyptian, looking surprised.

We all know, I continued, that the October War ended in total stalemate. Moreover, an entire Egyptian army corps was surrounded. And the Israelis almost reached Cairo.

The remark precipitated a long response, and I have since been careful not to repeat it. I should have known better. Although the 1973 war ended in a military draw, it broke the political stalemate. It opened the road to peace (as we now know but did not realize at the time), a peace "between equals," as many Egyptians say.

The key word is *equals*. It is not easy for Israelis, who for years have been terrorized by the Arabs, to fathom the full meaning of this term *equals*—until one hears, again and again, that rightly or wrongly a similar—perhaps worse—terror had reigned on the other side as well. Some Egyptians seem to have been so convinced of Israel's "qualitative superiority" in military strategy, science, diplomacy, finance, technology, and propaganda as to believe in the "invincibility" of 3½ million Israelis—apparently Supermen—over 80 million Arabs. The psychological consequence was a towering inferiority complex, almost a self-hatred and a gnawing fear that they might somehow be an "inferior" breed. We forget that the same world press that now trumpets the resurgence of Arab and Islamic power suggested in 1967 that there was something genetically wrong with the Arabs. Although the Arabs had provoked the long series of wars, Israel's recurrent successes instilled a fear of Israel as a mysterious cancer, an octopus that would in the end swallow them. The syndrome was not eased by the traditional contempt Arabs had held for Jews throughout the generations, as a cowardly race whose blood would only defile a man's sword. The awful humiliation of 1967 turned fear into an uncontrollable, agonizing rage. Sadat, in his memoirs, says that he closeted himself at home, near the pyramids, for three weeks. Overwhelmed by the agony, he brooded over the consequences of the "denigration." He feared it might herald an end for the Arabs similar to that of the "Red Indians of America. . . . That Egypt should survive became my dominant passion."

It does not matter that the Arabs had started the ruinous cycle of wars; it does not matter that if Egypt had not assaulted the nascent Jewish state in 1948, Israelis might never have taken on the image of fantasy figures, buccaneers, pitiless fighters, "blond" Jews, Jews as goyim, with the Bible in one hand and a missile thrower in the other. It does not even matter that Egypt might have had her territories and oil back in 1967 in return for peace, and instead resolved with the other Arabs, *no peace, no negotiations, no recognition of Israel.* The more solidly a neurosis is ingrained in the mind, the less it can be imagined that things might have developed differently. Or that events might yet change in the future, for by now—as Heykal and the other apologists for Nasser often point out—"events take on their inevitable course."

What this neurotic attitude to one's leaders and to oneself must have meant in the years after 1967 can even today be sensed in the tortured atmosphere and story plots of Mahfouz, Idris, or the young Suleiman Fuad, the author of a hallucinatory short story, "June Blues." Their half-crazed protagonists, crippled and perverted, stammer inchoate protests out of Arabian Nightmares.

Or, conversely, one realizes what it must have been like from the way Egyptians now talk of the 1973 war. The term most often used —the "crossing over"—almost suggests a rite of passage. The actual feat, in terms of military engineering, the fording of a ditch of water a mere hundred yards wide, is of little significance; what matters is the renewed self-confidence it gave people who almost came to believe in their own inferiority. Paradoxically, as it proved that Israel was not a country of "invincible" devils and monsters, it demythologized the entire conflict and became a catalyst for peace. When the fighting was over, Sadat says in his memoirs, "we harbored nothing but respect for one another." Such a sentence could not be uttered after 1967. Sadat had lost a younger brother "who was like a son to me," in the 1973 war, five minutes after it began.

"We are no longer motivated by complexes," Sadat writes, "whether those of defeatist inferiority or those born of suspicion and hate." By a curious, perhaps unconscious, slip, in describing his arrival in Israel on his peace mission he ignores Begin, who waited for him at the bottom of the stairway, and mentions only those he had fought in 1973. "The minute I stepped out of the plane I found myself face to face with Golda Meir, who had cut short her visit to the United States to greet me on arrival. We exchanged greetings." He next mentions Moshe Dayan, Abba Eban, and General Ariel Sharon, "who had led the famous counterattack." Then "President Ephraim Katzir (a university professor, an excellent man) and myself were driven to Jerusalem." Begin had also been there, but he does not mention him. It is as though he had not seen Begin. He had come to salute the men (and the woman) he had fought and be saluted by those upon whom he had "inflicted unprecedented losses."

Why did they salute him? "Because they respect men who fight" (i.e., don't run away, as in 1967) and, even more important, because they respect a man who "after his victory can stand up and say: Right. Let the October War put an end to all wars." Let us sit down and talk together like civilized men, "to discuss what you want: security, instead of resorting to force."

What a happy change from the violent rhetoric of days past. Yet why did it have to be achieved through so much unnecessary bloodshed? Psychologists, rather than lawyers and missile technicians, should be put in charge of foreign ministries and high army commands. Israelis, too, had been prisoners of their psychology for too long and probably contributed unconsciously to the long delay of peace. I remember an Israeli general telling me on the fifth day of the Six-Day War, as we sat on the banks of the Suez Canal, "We'll be here for the next hundred years. These people are not made for war," he added, pointing to the shacks on the other side and the lean cow that was going around in a circle pumping up water, as in the days of Thutmose.

Another general, in the exaltation of that flash victory, cabled his son, "Finished the job for you too. From now on there won't be any more wars." And a few days later in Jerusalem a young politician (today Begin's Minister of Justice) coined what would soon be a popular rhyme, although poetically, and otherwise, rather faulty:

> *Shetach meshuchrar/Lo yuchsar.*
> (Liberated land/Stays in our hand.)

The "fogs of war" that the strategists always complain about were followed, after the victory, by fogs in the minds of politicians, who came to believe that the balance of power was tilted in favor of Israel for all time. It was a mistake for which a very high price would be paid in 1973. The Egyptian Army performed so much better in 1973 precisely because it was not on a foreign expedition, as in 1967 and 1948, but was fighting a war of liberation on its own soil.

I remember the tremendous fuss, not without reason, we always made in the years before 1967 over the refusal of certain Arabs to shake hands with an Israeli, even at a convention or some innocuous cocktail party. A French diplomat once asked me why we cared so much. "What's so important about a handshake?" he said. But it *was* important. The refusal showed they were not treating us as human beings. At an infinitely higher cost to all, the Egyptians had to regain their own bruised pride before they could meet us as humans. The tragedy is not made lighter by the ludicrous, though not entirely illogical, reflection that the same Israeli generals who were ignominiously fired for the "mishap of 1973" ought perhaps to have received medals instead. Had they not been caught napping on Yom Kippur 1973, would there have been peace now?

SAMUEL BECKETT SAID in his study on Proust that the observer infects the observed with his own mobility. I went to see a film at the Metro Cinema in downtown Cairo; in the dark, between two scenes of Technicolor violence, I suddenly remembered that this movie house was a kind of landmark in the short history of Israel. I grew tense and for some moments lost the action on the screen.

In 1954 Israeli intelligence officers, fearing a rapprochement between Nasser and the United States, ordered their Cairo spy ring to place explosive charges in various places, including the USIS library and the Metro and other cinemas in Cairo and Alexandria. The idea was conceived and executed with equal clumsiness, and without the knowledge of the Prime Minister. It gave rise later to the notorious Lavon Affair, which would poison and haunt Israeli public life for almost a decade.

The responsibility for this crazy scheme has never been clearly established. The head of Army Intelligence claimed he was acting with the full knowledge of the Minister of Defense, Pinhas Lavon. Lavon denied this and accused the Army of disobedience and plotting behind his back. Behind the scheme was the childish idea that it might cause a rift between Egypt and the West, and perhaps even keep the British from evacuating the Canal Zone. The childish idea turned out more a murderous college prank. The bombs, hidden in eyeglass cases, did not explode, or caused no damage. The actual perpetrators—idealistic young Egyptian Jews who did not know why they were doing this but believed it must be vital for the security of Israel—were arrested almost immediately. Two were sentenced to death, one committed suicide, seven were condemned to long terms of imprisonment.

A sordid, tragic affair. To complicate matters even further, the Israeli "control" of the Cairo spy group was later exposed as a double agent, simultaneously working for Egypt. He had been given his Cairo assignment to rehabilitate himself after a criminal conviction. The entire affair still leaves many unanswered questions. Could it be that both Israeli and Egyptian schoolboy espionage masters were attempting to complicate the other's relations with the United States? Real life imitated a John Le Carré plot. It reflected the growing pains of a newly born, still-disorganized state. Yet as with some children's diseases, the scars remained well into adult life. Under the impact of the executions, Prime Minister Moshe Sharett, who until then had been secretly negotiating an accommodation with Nasser, broke off contact. ("We shall not meet under the gallows," he wrote in his recently published private diary.)

Marvelous shots of the Nile and of Luxor appear on the screen; the film was shot in Egypt. David Niven, Bette Davis, and Peter Ustinov are in the starring roles. I am glued to my seat wondering what would have happened if the plot had never been hatched, if the culprits had not been hanged, if Sharett had continued the contacts with Nasser that he himself regarded as very important. Another result of the affair was that Ben-Gurion returned to office from retirement. Ben-Gurion believed in a policy of force, unlike Sharett, who preferred quiet diplomacy. Sharett believed that peace with Egypt was possible; Ben-Gurion did not. Ben-Gurion's return to power meant the end of Sharett and his policy of quiet diplomacy and accommodation. It led to Israel's participation with Britain and France in the 1956 war against Egypt, which Sharett bitterly opposed. He saw it as an abortive adventure, in collusion with "two declining empires," which would turn the chances of Israeli-Arab peace "back by ten degrees," he wrote. Who is to say now who was right and who was wrong? No one, really.

But the pretty film I am watching in the Metro Cinema is irreparably spoiled for me. When it is over I walk out into the street. A long line is queuing up at the box office for the late show. The title of the film is *Death on the Nile,* and it is based on the Agatha Christie novel.

MICHAEL WEIR, THE British ambassador, calls to invite me to supper. I am pleased, but somewhat astonished. I hadn't expected him to change his mind and actually see me so soon. In fact, I had been sure he would not call at all. Chastising myself silently for my paranoia, I thank him and ask if a taxi driver will know where the British residency is.

Weir replies with a clipped "He had better." If he doesn't? "In that case Egypt is in worse shape than one thought."

As it turns out, the driver does not know. I decide not to tell Weir; I assume he has heavier problems on his mind. The stately residency is on the bank of the Nile. It is perhaps the most splendid and most cumbersome anywhere, with its enormous rooms and bathtubs built for a master race, large as coffins. The residency is enclosed, fortresslike, behind high walls. The great stone lions on the pillared portico look fierce, but seem French-made. Servants in silver robes shuffle through cavernous, dimly lit halls. This is strictly Agatha Christie country.

Ambassador Weir and his wife are waiting in a small drawing room. He has a new wife since I last saw him a few years ago in New York; otherwise he is much the same: witty, intelligent, well informed, worried about the Arabs and the Jews as he has had to be over the past twenty years, for he is one of Whitehall's leading experts on the Middle East.

We have a few drinks. Is this treaty going to work? "Logic is against it," says Weir. "But then there is Sadat, who is an Egyptian *nationalist.*" The appellation doesn't sound so ominous as it might have in this room, only a few decades ago, when it was thought, in Lord Cromer's words, that nationalism was too dangerous a toy for a "subject race" to play with, especially one so "unalterably, eternally, abnormal" as Egypt (Lord Milner). We joke about this.

Then we move to the adjacent dining room, where Anthony Eden amazed Nasser by speaking Arabic, quoting Arabic poetry rather condescendingly, according to Heykal, much "like a duke dismissing a vagabond." We dine agreeably on overdone meat and good French wine. The plates are crested. The food is not what it may have been under some of Weir's predecessors who lived surrounded by servants, as though they were well-kept domestic gods. Sir John Eldon Gorst, according to Peter Mansfield,* "employed seventy European and Egyptian servants, including the former chef to Baron Rothschild who also played the violin brilliantly and was paid five hundred pounds a year." Lord Kitchener, though he rode about Cairo on a donkey, constructed the vast ballroom that is now the visa section, where some forty thousand Egyptians are annually given a fairly rough time.

The Weirs complain about the high cost of keeping up the place. It was built for a viceroy, not for the ambassador of an offshore island. They also complain about the walls in the huge rooms, which,

---

* *The British in Egypt* (New York: Holt, Rinehart & Winston, 1972).

apart from a few official portraits, are empty. Who owns enough pictures nowadays to decorate so much empty wall space? Or, for that matter, books? Weir had expected to find many. When he arrived he was surprised to see not a single volume in this vast mausoleum of power.

After dinner we go on a little tour of the house. This is Weir's first major ambassadorship; serving it out under the dark portraits of Cromer, Gorst, Kitchener, and Allenby that hang on the walls of his ghostly study appeals to his sense of history, and humor. Lord Cromer, with his ruddy face and short-trimmed white mustache, looks rather like a country surgeon. Weir shows me the study with a certain pride, also with some irony, which I find very appealing.

In this large, dark, headmasterly-looking room, so many decisions were taken, at a time, not so distantly past, when "God was in heaven and England ruled on land." So much that was once Egypt was made or marred here. Echoes of Zaghlul Pasha and Mustafa Kamel, fathers of modern Egypt, told by Lord Cromer that Britain's task was to give Egypt "good, not free, government."

In addition to the many Egyptians who passed through this room, hat in hand, to make their pleas for independence, the founder of modern Zionism, Theodor Herzl, had also been here in 1902, and in a foul mood, for he found Cromer the "most disagreeable Englishman" he had ever met, full of "tropical madness" and "unlimited vice-regalism." Herzl had come to negotiate with Cromer the lease of the Sinai peninsula for the homeless Jews. The British Government in London had offered him those arid sands for his proposed "Judean Province of Egypt." Herzl saw it as a stepping-stone to Palestine, then still under Ottoman rule. The great question, on which everything depended, was the acquisition of water. Herzl proposed to build a pipeline from the Nile to the Sinai. It was one of the reasons why Cromer vetoed the scheme; he thought that the construction of siphons under the Suez Canal might cause unnecessary interruption to the shipping traffic. He also considered Herzl a "wild enthusiast."

While talking about this incident, we stop under the portrait of

Lord Milner, who had considered Egyptian nationalists "savage Red Indians." Herzl, incidently, foresaw the power of Egyptian nationalism. "They are the coming masters," he wrote in his diary after his interview with Cromer. "It is a wonder that the English do not see this. They think they will be dealing with *fellahin* forever." It is always easier to see through another man's blind spot than through one's own. When the same Herzl visited Palestine he did not even see the fellahin there. From the record he has left, it would seem that the Arab population of Palestine had simply vanished before his eyes, as in their Thousand and One Nights.

We look into the spacious garden where Mountolive, Weir's fictional predecessor in Durrell's *Quartet*—and like Weir, moody and ironic—took off his shoes and walked barefoot down to the river, "feeling the brilliant grass spiky under his bare feet," for it was of a "coarse, African variety." It still is, but at the bottom of the garden no longer is there the Nile. The bottom was sliced off in the 1950s to make way for a public esplanade. The Egyptians had wanted to do this for a long time but could never get the British to agree. Weir says that it took a special clause in the Anglo-Egyptian Canal Zone Evacuation Treaty of 1954 to ensure that the Nile esplanade could finally be built.

Late that evening Weir walks me out through the massive iron gates. One of the servants—Weir calls them *wahibs*—runs off to find a taxi. We walk to the near corner, where the American embassy is located. It is surrounded by searchlights and armed guards. "The American ambassador has four bodyguards!" Weir says. He at least can move freely about. We shake hands. I get into the taxi. Through the rear window I watch his receding figure walking back slowly through the dark toward his gate, with his hands in his pockets.

A TOUR OF THE CANAL ZONE: the shore of the lake is planted with eucalyptus trees and lawns. Holidaymakers are lying on deck chairs in the sun. The air smells of jasmine and lotions, ice cream and cakes. The wind is drawing circles on the lake. Children are splashing water. It is hard to imagine that this placid resort spot, a few miles outside of Ismailia, was the site of one of the bloodiest battles in the 1973 war. At this northern corner, Lake Timsah meets the northern section of the Suez Canal. A few hundred yards from here the Egyptian Army crossed the Canal and stormed the heavily fortified Israeli positions on the East Bank. A young woman roars by on water skis. One sees no trace of the Bar Lev Line, which was considered impenetrable at the time. I remember it in 1973 as a row of steel and concrete bunkers, narrowing at the top, surrounded by minefields, sand walls, and barbed wire. From a distance the fortifications looks like Aztec pyramids or burial grounds of some prehistoric race. Everything has disappeared. The Canal has been widened at this spot. The Egyptians have been in a great rush to erase the last traces of the line. They are buried in sand, or submerged in the water, and repressed, as it were, like sex in a Victorian novel.

In the past year another channel has been dug here, one of three new bypasses, to enable two-way traffic in the Canal. Between the two channels a flat sandbank has remained, commonly called Tourism Island. Plans have been drawn to build a hotel there. It is strewn with scraps of old metal and a few dry thistles and shrubs. The scraps will probably be buried soon, or used to line the sides of the Canal. Over this barren heap of sand the two armies had bled one another in the 1969 War of Attrition. This had been the dead point from which none could go farther. Here they stopped. From here they shelled the other side of the Canal; and from there, this side. Here a fatal legend was born. Here glimmered a fata morgana that stupefied an entire people. The impenetrable Bar Lev Line, with its underground vaults, infirmaries, ammunition stores, sophisticated electronic gear, cinemas and well-equipped kitchens and observation posts, dug-in tanks, and artillery. Here, finally, everything collapsed on a hot afternoon like a house of cards: military concepts, a policy, the whole life philosophy of a small beleaguered nation that had somehow lost its sense of proportion and reality. The sandbank absorbed the cries, the groans, and the blood.

Nothing can be seen now. Instead, convoys of ships pass in the

Canal, an average of seventy each day. In the morning the convoys go south; in the early afternoon they move in the opposite direction. Shortly after two—desserts are just being served at the little tables on the lawn (*omali,* a typical Egyptian sweet based on milk and nuts)—the first ships in the afternoon convoy come into view. A Russian tanker is followed by Saudi and Panamanian freighters. And Sakharia abu Hamat, a public relations man for the Suez Canal Authority, says, "Soon an Israeli ship will pass through. We shall give it a little celebration."

Abu Hamat is a young man, tall and muscular, in gray flannel trousers and a light jacket. He has brought a young woman with him, who has just been hired by the Authority because of her fluency in Hebrew. He smokes English cigarettes in an uninterrupted chain. It is not the only thing he has in common with many Israelis: like many Israelis he cannot make a living on one job. He holds two others, at a local travel agency and as deputy manager of a hotel. "We hope to see tens of thousands of Israeli tourists here," he says with the unrestrained warmth and enthusiasm of so many Egyptians outside of Cairo who are not senior government officials. "Look how beautiful everything is!" he exclaims. The thick palm trees are reflected in the water. "Don't you agree? Don't you think that thousands will want to sit here in the sun and watch the ships go by? Upon my life, what a marvelous view! I cannot take my eyes off it."

We lunch in the nearby clubhouse. I sit next to an official of the Canal Authority. The main course is fried brains, an Egyptian favorite. This reminds my neighbor of an anecdote. Egyptian humor is similar to the Jewish and comes with an ironic bite directed against the self. After the 1967 war, my neighbor says with a smile, there were two butcher shops opposite one another on either side of the Canal. One was called "Dayan"; the other, "Nasser." A man in Ismailia came into Nasser's shop one day and demanded his favorite dish of brains. "Here we sell only *tongue,*" said the butcher. "For *brains* you go to Dayan's."

Three brand-new Canal Authority tugboats are tied to a nearby jetty. They are named *Salaam I, Salaam II,* and *Salaam III.* A bulldozer whips up the dust on the opposite shore.

I remember an excursion to that shore in the spring of 1971. The city of Ismailia lay in ruins at the time. General Ariel Sharon, commander of the Israeli Southern Front, drove us south from Al-Qantara to this strip of sand opposite Ismailia. The clubhouse where we now sit was sandbagged and served as a position for Egyptian snipers. The general was entertaining the late Pinhas Sapir, at that time Israel's Minister of Finance. He was eager to show Sapir the extensive road network that army engineers had built between the Bar Lev Line and the rear. He also wanted to impress him with the fact that it had cost 20 percent less per square yard than civilian-built roads in Israel.

The old financier nodded his heavy head. He was half asleep from the heat, or the fatigue. I remember his saying, "Yes, a very good road." And after a short pause, in Yiddish, *"Aber wohin furt man do?"* ("But where does one go on it?") Then he sank back and went to sleep in the corner of the backseat.

In 1971 we were a dissynchronized people. Our ancestors had been the most fanatic civilians on earth, scholars and peddlers, at a time when other peoples, in Europe and elsewhere, were hailing this army or that. In 1971, when most Europeans and Americans did not want to hear of armies, uniforms, or even flags, we were soldiers, reposing in our dusty crumpled uniforms as though they had been the swaddling of our fathers and forefathers.

A SMOOTH HIGHWAY LEADS to a new housing development a few miles north of Ismailia. It was built over the past three years to house evacuees and workers on the Canal. Almost a million inhabitants of the three main cities on the Canal had been evacuated between 1968 and 1975. Most have since returned. There are thirty-four thousand inhabitants in the new suburb, living in eight thousand two- or three-room apartments. It was built in record time—less than eighteen months—and is named after Sheikh Sihad, the ruler of an oil emirate in the Persian Gulf, who has partly financed the project. Mass-produced on a single scale, the houses are faced with slabs of pink stone. In the more recently built sections the money apparently ran out; the bleak concrete façades are bare. Shutters are painted bright red. The rent for a two-room apartment is ten dollars a month. So far, very few trees have been planted, although there is an abundance of water. The surrounding grounds are still bare, sandy, and bleak. But there are six schools, two new mosques, and a small shopping center where a loaf of bread costs less than six cents and beans are thirty cents a pound—food is heavily subsidized.

Later we drive back south, through the streets of old Ismailia. They are lined with trees and flower beds, dark old wooden houses, and, of course, huge portraits of Sadat in all the familiar poses. *Peace— Sadat—Suez Canal. In Peace We Build—with Force We Defend.*

Ismailia is a pretty place. As in other Egyptian cities outside of bursting Cairo, the streets are neat. The parks and boulevards planted in the last century are well tended. The sidewalks are in one piece. Though the streets are filled with traffic, people, and beasts of burden, there is not that feeling of multitudes here as in Cairo. The population has doubled since 1968. On the gingerbread balconies of the wooden villas that once belonged to the French employees of the old Suez Canal Company the matrons of the new administrators are fanning their faces against the heat. The new administration is said to run the Canal with exemplary efficiency. The volume of shipping has more than tripled over the past twenty-three years. How many inflamed Frenchmen during the hectic days of the nationalization crisis of 1956 believed that it would? Ships up to 60,000 tons now pass through the Canal; in 1956 the limit was 30,000. Now in the fall of 1980, ships of 150,000 tons are able to pass through. These estimated annual income will be $1 billion.

Would anyone want to expose the fruits of this tremendous effort to the risk of another war? Certainly not Mashour Ahmed Mashour, the present chairman of the Suez Canal Authority. Not he, nor his chief of research, Dr. Ahmed Amar, who has all the facts and figures in his head and rolls them off in fluent French. Dr. Amar is a tall man, with a calm, professorial manner. He has been working for the Canal for over thirty-five years. His office in the Canal Authority Building (built in 1966) was partially destroyed in the wars. Dr. Amar and his staff spent the war years in the Delta, designing all sorts of waterworks. But the war is forgotten now, he says, as he looks out at the ships below his windows. He also knows the facts and figures of the two main Israeli harbors. "Science is international," he says with a smile.

South of the city center, in a suburb, the road crosses an old railroad track on a wooden bridge and a sweet-water canal. The mud huts on both sides of the canal still lie in ruins. On the last day of the 1973 war, Israeli troops reached as far as these huts in the bridgehead they had established on the West Bank of the Canal. Farther down the road, close to the Bitter Lakes, where the Israelis crossed over to the western side, new earthworks are in progress. A tunnel is being burrowed out under the Canal. It will link Egypt with the Sinai. The deep, dark hole in the sandy ground is teeming with workers and machines. The tunnel has already reached the other shore. Two more tunnels are planned. But an English engineer in charge of works here says he doubts they will be built. "They are not economical," he says. Ferries are much cheaper. The tunnel will cost more than $100 million.

Aren't there military reasons to build them? "You must be joking," he replies. "One blow—and poof." Dr. Amar of the Suez Canal Authority does not think much of the tunnels either. "Too vulnerable," he says. Besides, they might hinder future development of the Canal. Dr. Amar believes in bridges. But President Sadat believes in tunnels. Mashour Ahmed Mashour, chairman of the Canal Authority, says, "However vulnerable or uneconomic, Sadat wants a link *on land*. It is a symbol for him. A kind of umbilical cord between Mother Egypt and the land she lost, which he has restored."

ON THE SHORES OF the Great Bitter Lake there are a few dusty palms and mud houses and plantations. Utensils, water wheels, even facial expressions are reminiscent of pharaonic frescoes. Here and there are tanks encamped in little clusters, and what look like antiaircraft missile launching sites. This was once the heart of the Israeli bridgehead, which changed the course of the entire war. An Egyptian army corps was trapped behind, on the East Bank in Sinai, without water or food.

On December 5, 1973, a twenty-four-year-old Egyptian marine

sergeant named Mohammed Nadda, dazed with hunger and thirst, swam back across the lake to this western shore, which he believed was still in Egyptian hands. As he came ashore in the early morning hours, he was shot dead by an Israeli patrol. Tied to his body was a wet notebook, his diary.

The scenery, as I stand here, takes on special meaning for me, since I have long had a copy of this diary. It opens in Alexandria early in June 1973, four months before the October War. "My God Almighty. My fate is in your hands. In you I trust." The last entry is scribbled in a hurry, a few hours before Nadda's death. It begins with the words "We are on the verge of complete despair."

The diary portrays a withdrawn, nervous, sullen, hypersensitive young man in postrevolutionary Egypt, the son of uprooted peasants from a village near Tanta in the Delta, now living in a slum area of Alexandria. Mohammed Nadda, as the diary opens, is in his fourth and last year of army service. He has made use of his free afternoons to attend a local liberal arts college from which he has recently graduated. He is soon due for discharge but has small hope of finding a job. "I have not been trained by the government [sic] in any civilian profession," he complains.

But as a sergeant in the marine commandos he has been through a course in skin diving, and he wonders whether he might perhaps find work as a frogman in the harbor. "I don't know why I love the sea. The sea is cruel but the sound of its waves fills me with joy, like a great symphony orchestra. . . . My only purpose in serving at this moment [in the Army] is to be posted to the advanced diving course in September" (July 23).

He courts three girls simultaneously, to one of whom "I plan to give my name." But he is tortured by "incapacity to love," as well as by chronic headaches, virulent ulcers, and quarrels with his father, "who asks me all the time how much money I make, for he needs it. What a large family!" (August 27). The family consists of father, a doorman at a cinema, mother, who works in a textile factory, four children, two elderly aunts. They occupy a little hovel about thirteen feet square, sharing a common toilet with six other families. Even so, Nadda hates to sleep in camp and prefers to sneak away in the evenings to spend the night at home.

He smokes a great deal—"it's my only form of entertainment." He tries hashish, wakes up with a pain "pounding in my head like the bells of Notre Dame," and resolves not to do it again, but does. He has a goodly amount of free time; he goes to the cinema three or four times a week. He reads Tewfik al-Hakim's *School of Fools,* and a "forbidden book" by the critic Louis Awad. There is a fatalist despondency throughout—"faith in God is the only way."

Occasionally he envies the rich. "At eight in the evening my cousin and I walked along the sea esplanade and reached Miami Beach, where we saw how the holidaymakers live, and [realized] how we live in poverty without hope. Yes, we look on and are filled with sorrow. For the hand is empty and the pocket is empty too." Everything seems dismal. "Another day has passed. No upheaval. We are mere dogs and slaves."

He suffers from nightmares. When he sees a film he dislikes he must rush out to throw up in the toilet. "I am not crazy, I don't think I have complexes and I am not looking for paradise on earth. All I want is to live." But life is "like a naked woman," always tempting, never requiting.

"I have begun to read the Koran, and pray. Perhaps it will help" (September 7). Then he pretends cynicism. "Money is the only thing I believe in." At the same time he would starve for a week in order to hear a Mozart symphony. He hates authority, but succumbs to it.

"What happened at noon yesterday I will not forget my entire life," he writes on September 2, 1973. "I went to the military hospital because of my ulcer. Then I thought I would visit the family of a friend who works abroad, in England, to get his address and enjoy a civilized and enlightened conversation with his sister, Samia. She opened the door, and was alone. I asked her if she had passed her high school exams; she said yes. We drank tea and talked of socialism and communism. Suddenly the doorbell rang. A man in the uniform of a brigadier of the General Staff came in. I was embarrassed because I was in my sergeant's uniform. I assumed it was not proper to salute, and greeted him in the civilian manner. He began to shout at Samia for receiving me alone in the house, when she should have talked with me through the closed door. I put out my cigarette and stood up to go. Then he began to scold me, for bringing dishonor upon the house. He showed me the door, using his full military authority. I left with my head bowed. I was very hurt. I hate all men in military and police uniforms. Inside them hide such men as he."

A few days later everything suddenly changes. Nadda's unit is transferred to the Suez Canal. "A new page opens. I enter upon a journey whose end I do not know. We go to war." He has eight months of service left. "Perhaps there will be some purpose to my life now . . . the miracle has happened. The walls of boredom are broken" (September 22). A few hundred yards of water are "between us and the Jews. . . . We have forgotten ourselves and our families." Nadda resolves to prove, through his devotion, the "valor and patriotism of the Egyptian soldier, for the whole world to see. . . . Farewell, my dear parents. My brother Magdi, did you ever imagine that I should participate in battle and be a hero? Do not despair, I shall come back . . . the entire Egyptian Army from Port Said to the Red Sea is crossing the Canal to liberate the land and destroy the Jews" (October 4).

It does not turn out as he had hoped. Nadda is in the first wave that crosses the southern end of the Bitter Lakes in the early afternoon of October 6. Though he is a trained frogman, he is assigned to a mechanical maintenance unit. His tank is the first to explode. They storm a fortification on the Bar Lev Line. In the early evening hours their advance is blocked. "We will not die, we will be victorious," he writes at six in the evening on the first day. On the following morning: "Last night was the longest, most difficult, ugliest night of my life. I was torn between the heavy enemy fire and the bitter cold. I began to think again of mother and the family . . . war is dirty, it frightens me. I hate it. At the same time I am ready to sacrifice my life."

In the evening, a note of passivity again: "There is nothing left to do but wait for death to arrive in their Phantoms [jets] and tanks in the morning. The [optimistic] news on the radio makes us laugh." They dig in on the narrow beachhead. Here they would remain surrounded for the next two months.

The rest of the diary reflects the amalgam of fear and boredom that is the hallmark of all trench warfare, and the gradual breakdown of morale. Nadda himself seems to have been disciplined, devoted, courageous, sharing his last biscuit and cigarette with his pals. In his free moments he muses about life and death. He draws up lists of the things he loves:

"Music: Tchaikovsky, *Overture 1812, The Nutcracker, The Sleeping Beauty.* Jean Sibelius. Georges Bizet, *Carmen.* Mozart, Symphonies Numbers 29 and 41.

"The best books: *Play for All Seasons* by Robert Polette. [Robert Bolt's *A Man for All Seasons*? —A.E.] *Book of the People and the War* by Mochsein. The Koran with modern annotations. The plays of Friedrich Dürrenmatt. Ernst Fischer's book on art. Lorca's *Blood Wedding.* A book I will write myself after the war, entitled *The Difficult Crossing,* i.e., letters that will describe the noise of the cursed shrapnel that deafens my ears at this moment.

"The best films [I saw in] 1973: Sean Connery and Claudia Cardinale in *The Red Tent. The Perverts,* alcoholism, the women of the night. *Balkola,* a thriller. *Cabaret,* death comes, the Satanic plot. *Macbeth.* And the film *The Difficult Rescue,* acted by the Egyptian Army. Produced by: ———— On: ————" (October 28).

He dreams of one of his girl friends. "I dream of her every night. I can't pronounce the word *love.* All I can say now is: Do you have a cigarette? Do you have water? When will the U.N. arrive? When will we die? I write in complete honesty. I love my country and am 'ready' to die, but I cannot. . . ."

When he hears on the radio that the first rains have fallen in Alexandria, he weeps. "Alexandria, my beloved city, how I miss you, and your streets washed with the tears of heaven. Your sea, your people, your accent, your safe bosom, my friends, the steps of the university, the lectures, the games. . . . Mother, if I die, I beg you do not . . . she may die, Father may suffer a stroke. . . . I ask that when my brother Haled grows up he should shudder at the thought of war" (November 2).

"The Jews are getting closer. Their nearest observation post is two hundred meters away. God have mercy on us and our shadows. A strange thing is happening to me. I have started to steal biscuits and other foodstuffs from my pals. I don't know how to justify this. Is it the hunger or some aggressive instinct that seizes people in such trouble as ours?" (November 11).

On November 27, because of some misunderstanding, Nadda is stripped of his rank as a sergeant and demoted to private. "The regimental commander insulted us, beat us, and demanded that we shave our heads. This, of course, was a shock to me. Shall I lose all after such a long period of service? Including the salary I rely on to support the family?"

A week later he decides to escape by swimming across the smaller of the two Bitter Lakes. The last entry—December 5—ends with the words: "War has taught me that some of those who fight alongside me deserve death more than the enemy."

Across the cover of his diary Mohammed Nadda had written: "Whoever finds this diary with my body is asked, with thanks, to hand it to Mahmoud Nadda, Latus Quarter, Adel Kheri Street, off Algasir, the shop of Mr. Jaber, the barrel merchant."

My friend Micha Shagrir of Jerusalem was a soldier on the Israeli bridgehead west of Suez, a few hundred yards from where Nadda was killed. He found the diary and has given me a copy. (The original was kept by Israeli Army Intelligence.) Shagrir, an Israeli film producer, was able to go to Alexandria last year. He looked up Nadda's family and gave them photocopies of the diary. They still sleep in one small room: Nadda's parents, four surviving children, and one aunt; the other has since died. Another small room is filled with the dead boy's books. The common toilet is now shared by two additional families. The father is still a doorman at a local cinema. The mother works in a shirt factory. Until 1976 they had received no word of their son, whether he was dead or alive. In the fall of that year, Nadda's brother Magdi traveled to Cairo, where he spent a week running from one office to another in the Egyptian Ministry of War and finally was given a little slip stating that his brother was apparently missing in action. It was the first official word they had received since 1973. Nadda's mother suffered a nervous collapse after Shagrir's visit in 1978. He had shattered her last hope.

NORTH OF THE TOWN OF Kibrit on the southern Bitter Lake is the little palm grove where Nadda had come ashore. The land is flat. The lake is under a cover of gray mist. The last boats in the afternoon convoy are just sailing through. A dozen or so blocked ships were moored here from 1967 until the reopening of the Canal in 1975. For eight years negotiations to secure their release by clearing the blocked Canal had led nowhere. The deadlock was emblematic of the larger whole. Had the Canal been reopened in 1968, there might never have been the re-escalation of violence; the cities of the Canal Zone might not have been destroyed and abandoned by their inhabitants in the long War of Attrition; perhaps even the 1973 war could have been avoided by a gradual process of military disengagement and withdrawal. But the Canal was not even partially reopened in 1968; the ships remained blocked in the Great Bitter Lake. Why did the negotiations fail?

The Egyptians insisted that the ships sail out by the northern exit, toward the Mediterranean. The Israelis insisted they exit to the south, toward the Red Sea. The archives may be opened one day and give ground for bitter smiles on both sides; indeed, diplomats may decide henceforth to argue only by telephone, without leaving any written record behind. The arguments employed at the time seem silly in retrospect and did not reflect the true positions of both sides. Both sides apparently believed they were doing a favor to the superpower that was protecting them. The Egyptians were eager to open the Canal to the Soviet fleet in the Mediterranean, with its bases in Port Said and Alexandria. The Israelis believed they were pleasing Richard Nixon by keeping the Canal closed and forcing Soviet supply ships bound for Vietnam to take the long route around the Cape of Good Hope.

Within a few years the two nations would serve as guinea pigs for those very superpowers, to test the efficacy of their most modern military hardware. Once more, through the heat and mist of a late afternoon, the great melancholy ifs force themselves upon the reluctant mind, with all the gnawing speculation of wisdom after the event. Such speculation is not altogether idle if viewed against the available alternatives.

Farther south the road joins the main Suez–Cairo desert highway. The land is still flat, nothing but sand, hardly an undulation to break the monotony. A few radar dishes revolve slowly in the distance, and here and there a few stationary tanks are scattered. At Kilometer 101, the Israeli point of advance closest to Cairo, a circular depression remains in the sand where the great tent stood that served as the first meeting place for direct negotiations between officers of the two armies. Here, in 1974, the possibility of peace was first mooted—unofficially—in private conversations between the Egyptian general Mohammed al-Gamasy and the Israeli Aharon Yariv. Farther on, a few factories come into view. Then another war monument, a tank said to have been among the first that crossed the Canal in 1973. Was it Nadda's? It has been placed on a raised platform; we race past too quickly to read the inscription. Through the car radio comes the voice of my recent acquaintance the singer Mohammed Nuch, cooing his current hit song about love.

THE CANAL ZONE AND Ismailia are known as Osman country. Osman Akhmed Osman is Sadat's in-law; his son is married to Sadat's daughter. He is deputy for Ismailia in the People's Assembly. As chairman for life of the Arab Contractors—Osman Akhmed Osman & Co., he is deeply involved in most major development projects, from the widening of the Canal and building of the tunnel to the construction of new towns and the industrialization of agriculture. The Arab Contractors is a family enterprise, one of the largest in the Middle East. It first rose to prominence and riches under Nasser, during the construction of the Aswan Dam.

On the following morning, in Cairo, I visit the chairman's nephew,

Ismail Osman, a director of the company, in its headquarters on Adly Street. Like his politician uncle, Ismail Osman believes there can be no economic growth and no mass prosperity except in peace, and through the revival of private enterprise.

Ismail Osman is a young man, very busy. Every few minutes his rapid speech is interrupted by the telephones ringing on his cluttered desk; aides and visitors continuously enter his office on some important errand and linger until the room is so crowded that Osman asks his secretary to block his door. He wears an American-style suit, and his tie is loosened under the unbuttoned collar of his shirt. He has a round face and curly black hair, and when he speaks he has a tendency to drive his points home with a raised finger.

The Osman firm has major interests outside of Egypt as well, in most of the Arab countries, including Libya. But in the past year, says Osman, "we are concentrating on Egyptian agriculture: we grow food in modern agrotechnical production centers. We should have done this a long time ago, rather than all those wars. We have forty million to feed. This is the great challenge of the future. Food production." With his forefinger he points at a pile of blueprints and statistics.

"There was a time when the government thought it could do everything by itself," he says. Production was nationalized. Laws were passed to regulate every activity. Rents were blocked. This put an end to private construction and caused the deterioration of existing buildings. The rents were even cut in half overnight once to celebrate some political occasion. "Halved! Do you understand? Halved!" They had been totally uneconomic even before. Who would invest in houses under those circumstances? In the cities alone there was a shortage of one and one half million flats. All this was beginning to change now. "The government is encouraging cooperation between private and public enterprise."

On the wall behind his desk hangs a sign that says *Salaam* and another one in English: "We the willing, led by the unknowing, are doing the impossible, for the ungrateful. We have done so much for so long with so little we are now qualified to do anything with nothing."

"It is a great pity that peace was not achieved earlier," Osman says. "Both sides made mistakes. But let us forget the past."

He understands the fears expressed abroad that this entire exercise depends upon Sadat and only upon Sadat. Will it survive him? He realizes that many people wonder, "What if Sadat retires? What if he dies?" He sympathizes with these fears but thinks they are not justified. "The peace is as good as built into the economy and into the political class of Egypt." The opposition is very marginal, he says. It does not bother him. It is not even genuine, he says, but rather artificially generated and financed by "foreign elements." Who these foreigners are, he cannot say. It would not be tactful. He is not worried either by the Arab boycott. His company, he says, has not been affected by it, except in Libya. "We are sensitive but not unsensible," Osman says in a statesmanlike manner. "We are an old people, an experienced people, and with a long tradition."

X

FINAL VISITS IN Cairo. At the editorial offices of *Al Ahram*, the semiofficial newspaper, I am exposed to a long harangue by Hamdi Fuad, the chief diplomatic correspondent. His office is off the large newsroom, with its dozens of desks that rarely seem occupied and its batteries of telephones I have never heard ring. The mood here is far less agreeable, less cheerful, than upstairs, where Hakim, Mahfouz, and the other poets and novelists have their offices.

Fuad is not against peace, or so he says. But he lashes out, quite savagely, against almost everything Israel has been doing in the past, and is still doing: the lobbying in the American Congress, the settlements, the continued bombardment of southern Lebanon by the Israeli Air Force, and above all, Begin's personal manner and style. What an unpleasant and ungrateful way he has of requiting Sadat for the welcome he gave him as an official visitor to Cairo! Begin was here but did not send flowers afterward, as he should have! He will just be another one of those men Kipling had in mind when he wrote: "A Fool lies here who tried to hustle the East."

I have heard such complaints before, but never with such bitterness. I am hardly given a chance to say a word. While this harangue goes on and on, I begin to suspect a deeper cause for Hamdi Fuad's bitterness. It cannot be easy for the diplomatic correspondent—if he is honest—of a semiofficial newspaper, after so many years of faithfully toeing one line, to shift suddenly to another. Few things are so painful as a new idea. This is why the great reformers always maintained they were going back to the true source.

When our quarrel is over we part amicably. I marvel again at that ready humanity of Egyptians, which so often enables the generous impulse of effusive friendliness to overcome political disagreement, until I remember that I have had more reason to be upset and angry than he.

A day or two later I come back to *Al Ahram* to lunch with Ezzedin Shaukat and his wife. We go up to the attractive executive dining room on the top floor of the tower. Shaukat is a young scholar, tall, quick-witted, in charge of research at *Al Ahram.* His research specialty is Israel. He is the son of the Egyptian general who commanded the Egyptian expeditionary force that, in 1948, approached to within a few miles of Jerusalem. I was a soldier in Jerusalem at that time. I remember a night in June 1948 when the southern suburb of Ramat Rachel changed hands three or four times until finally General Shaukat's forces were pushed back toward Bethlehem by a hastily drawn-up contingent of university students, armed only with Molotov cocktails and a few antiquated rifles.

"I grew up in a home where the Palestinian campaign was often discussed," Ezzedin Shaukat says. His wife, a news editor on *Al Ahram,* is expecting a baby. "A baby for peace," she says shyly. She is the daughter of Hafez Ismail, the Egyptian ambassador to France, Sadat's former National Security Adviser. Shaukat claims that Sadat sent Hafez Ismail to Washington in 1971 to tell the Americans that he wanted peace with Israel. "No one wanted to listen to him," says Shaukat. "They thought that Egypt was a dead horse."

But he is happy, he says, that there is peace now, even though it could have been achieved earlier. He reads Hebrew. His main task is to prepare global reports on Israel and the Jewish world, which he has been doing since 1968. What had impressed him most during these years?

"The crisis within the Israeli soul."

He is the first Egyptian intellectual I meet who says he hopes to be sent to Israel as soon as possible, and stay there, if he can, for a few months at least. But no, by no means would he go to East Jerusalem or any of the occupied territories. The Palestinians, he fears, are likely to shoot any Egyptian on sight. Yet he is also one of the most optimistic men I have met so far. He is sure the treaty will work if only Israel "learns to be a part of this area."

What does it mean to be a part?

"It means being sensitive to its feelings."

We also have feelings, I say.

"Yes," he says. "But you were the aggressive party. You came here against our will." Shaukat is too polite to say, "like the Crusaders," but I know this is what he means.

Through the large picture windows there is a fine view of Cairo, with Saladin's citadel on the outskirts. The Egyptians always compared us to the Crusaders, and for a long time they regarded Nasser as a modern Saladin who launched a holy war against the Jewish enclave in Palestine, which, like the Latin kingdom of Jerusalem, would finally be wiped out. The comparison was never carried to its logical conclusion: after the defeat of the Crusaders, the Mongols swept over the Middle East and devastated it.

The adjacent tables are filled with several prominent figures. Editors, politicians, university professors, the writers Tewfik al-Hakim, Mahfouz, Fawzy, Idris, and Dr. Awad. The robed waiters come around with platters of broiled seafood, eaten with tahini of the special, slightly vinegary Egyptian flavor. A few tables away, Nasser's daughter, Odda, converses with a well-known Egyptian Marxist.

Shaukat will not introduce me to the late dictator's daughter. She is known for her aversion to Israelis. The other day, says Shaukat, Ms. Nasser knocked on the door of one of Sadat's close aides and presented him with a memorandum against the peace treaty. She was invited to come in. Sadat's aide sat down and read her memorandum. He told Ms. Nasser that he disagreed with its contents but that she had a right to her views. Then he asked if she would remain for lunch, or perhaps go out with him to a nearby restaurant.

A FINAL WALK THROUGH the older quarters of Cairo, at the foot of Saladin's great citadel. The narrow alleys are lined with old palaces and mosques, and hovels of such poverty as I had previously thought impossible. There is no running water in the houses, and the sewers overflow. Nevertheless, there are plans to begin the construction of a subway. Street vendors are selling cooked noodles and sweet potatoes baked in little portable ovens fired with scrap wood gleaned from some building site. I cross a wide highway that runs between Saladin's citadel and the bleak hills of Al Muqattam, from which Napoleon had shelled the city when it revolted after the Battle of the Pyramids. Directly across that highway, behind billboards for American cigarettes and Saudi Airways, one enters the City of the Dead. Scalped and bare, the tombs are walled but not roofed. In the center of the cemetery there are the famous mosques built over the tombs of the Mameluke sultans. They seem to be the only tombs that have escaped the squatters. Tens of thousands of people live in this cemetery. The roofless tombs—some covered with canvas—face each other and form streets, where children wallow in the dirt and women cook a meal of dry beans on little primus stoves. The nightmarish scene stretches out on the plain as far as the eye can see. There are food stores, and even a few small workshops, and cafés in some of the tombs. The more modern sections of the graveyard are a little farther on, and beyond them one enters the Graveyard of the Martyrs of the 1948 Palestine Expedition. The inscription on one of the tombstones reads: "Do not call them dead who fell for Allah; they live even though they are not sensate."

And over the main gate:

In the name of the Most Merciful God, the relics of Palestine war martyrs have been transported to this immaculate part of the land in a national ceremony, witnessed by people of all classes, the representatives of the Arab League and headed by General Mohammad Naguib, Prime Minister and leader of the saintly revolution of the armed forces, on 16 Shaban the 1372 year of the Hegira. 10 May 1953.

ANOTHER FAREWELL LUNCH, with Ambassador and Mrs. Hassan and their daughter Nawal. We meet at the elegant Gezira

Club, the former high citadel of the British social elite. Hassan was the first Egyptian president of the club, of which non-Europeans for decades had been only token members. That was in 1951, after he had come back from Washington. The restaurants, bars, swimming pools, and tennis courts are filled with affluent-looking young people and with masons and carpenters; the club is being renovated and enlarged for the first time in years.

"There is a new class," Nawal says darkly. The parking lot is filled with new expensive-looking cars not commonly seen in the streets of Cairo. There are still separate lounges for men and women. The spacious grounds occupy a large part of the island of Gezira, but a part has been sliced off, as at the British residency, to make way for the great October 6 Freeway named after the 1973 war.

The Hassans have another guest, a Jewish woman, formerly Egyptian, now living in Paris. It is her first visit back in more than twenty years. She and her family were forced to migrate in 1956, leaving most of their possessions behind. Like so many former Egyptian Jews of a certain class, she speaks about Egypt affectionately and without bitterness—she seems to have done quite well in Paris— with an undertone of irony. "The problems of this country will not be solved," she says, "until Egyptians of a certain class learn to iron their shirts themselves."

She remembers a household in Cairo where four servants were employed only to do the ironing. She expounds on the subject for a while. The theory behind it seems a little too facile.

When the meal is over, Ambassador Hassan formally thanks each of the waiters and then goes to the great kitchens to thank the cooks as well. Everybody bows deferentially, as though he were still president, or the owner of thousands of acres and who knows how many peasants—which he never was—while Mrs. Hassan regrets that she cannot even find a cleaning woman these days.

"*Regardez comment les fleurs sont belles,*" she says. "*Vous aimez les roses, n'est-ce pas?*" Her *o*'s are long; only the *r*'s are marked with a foreign accent. I like talking French with Mrs. Hassan. Rimbaud claimed that in French every vowel had a special color. The letter *e* was white; *i* was red, *u* green, *o* blue (as in *mort;* Picasso also painted tragedy in blue) and *a* black, as in *grande dame.* Mrs. Hassan is wearing a dark suit, and as we part she puts a little package into my coat pocket. *"Mais non, c'est rien du tout. Un petit cadeau pour votre femme."*

A bulldozer is coming up the driveway through the lush gardens. The elderly couple walk back into their past, taking a slow route along the riverfront. They have a long walk every afternoon, and at seven every evening they listen to the news from Monte Carlo.

AFTERWARD NAWAL takes me to visit a good friend of hers, the famous architect Hassan Fathy. He lives immured in a lofty apartment on top of an old Mameluke palace. In the large courtyard there are lofty arches and delicately carved wooden grilles, the *meshrabiyeh,* through which women could look out without being seen. Inside, the walls are hung with magnificent objects and carpets. Through the windows there is a spectacular view over the laced dome of a nearby mosque. Yet all around this palace on the Darb al-Labana (Street of the Milkman), there is nothing but dust, dirt, and garages and workshops in the most dismal slum. Nearby, Saladin's citadel hovers over the crumbling roofs in that atmosphere of ruin and adventure which, in the nineteenth century, Westerners came to see as the peculiar mark of the East.

Fathy is a slim, white-haired man in his sixties. We find him in his living room surrounded by admirers, who follow his every word and address him with great deference as Hassan Bey. Fathy is famous for his theories in support of indigenous architecture. His reasoning is both aesthetic and economic. He expounded it a few years ago in his beautiful book *Architecture for the Poor.** In the late 1940s Fathy put his theories into practice at New Gourna, in Upper Egypt, a village he designed and built entirely of mud brick and other local materials, using domes, vaults, arches, and arcaded streets as the most logical and cheapest form of construction. Fathy believes that the great housing shortage in the overpopulated countries of the

* Chicago: University of Chicago Press, 1973.

Third World cannot be solved except by a revival of indigenous techniques that for hundreds of years had been used so successfully in the Mediterranean basin and in the Middle East and are so pleasing to the eye. Most of his followers, however, are not in the countries of the Third World, nor in Egypt, but in the industrialized West. Like Moshe Safdie, his Israeli kinsman in indigenous architecture, Fathy is not a prophet in his own country. Like Safdie, he is hailed more abroad than at home. In Egypt he is regarded as an impractical dreamer. The irony is that, since New Gourna, the few houses he has built were not for the poor, but for the rich and recherché. I can imagine how bitter he must feel about this.

The telephone rings continuously. First it is Munich, then London, then another call from Munich. He has been invited to MIT, together with his master mason, to demonstrate his technique. But damn it, why are they so high-handed at MIT, they expect his mason to spend a month in Cambridge for but a token fee. He has a family to support. In Egypt, after New Gourna was finished, no one wanted to continue the experiment. Instead ghastly concrete and corrugated tin sheets were preferred, he says. Fathy's *Architecture for the Poor* has never been published in Arabic. He also writes plays and illustrates books. Like many great architects, Fathy has an apocalpytic view of a world run by demons and rogues. It is all falling apart, through waste and pollution, in the hands of political cretins in cahoots with greedy contractors and financiers.

At the same time, like so many architects, Fathy has a solution for everything under the sun. Every problem can be solved, "but first we must define it properly"; he repeats that phrase time and again. Architects, we know, love to play God; perhaps this is because they have accustomed themselves to viewing their models from above. They are rarely content to build us good houses, as the old masons once were, but think instead they can rebuild humans by their walls. Moreover, Fathy, I fear, is a romantic. "It is hard to imagine a village in Egypt," he writes in *Architecture for the Poor,* "without its black-robed women erect as queens, each with her water jar on her head, and it will be a pity to lose the sight . . . stooping for the bucket to a tap in the yard may destroy the magnificent carriage for which our women are renowned." Has anyone asked how *they* feel?

Everything can be resolved, Fathy insists, through "love and dialogue." But alas, there is so little of either. At least we have peace now, I say. "Do we? The Soviet Union with its machinations is still around, and the mad Arab leaders. We are not masters of our own fate."

The voice of a muezzin wafts in harshly through the open window. The glass panes vibrate; the voice comes out of a loudspeaker on a nearby mosque. Fathy is not interested in current politics. Have the wars ever affected his life, personally or professionally? "The wars? No. Yes! Not your wars! Other wars! Wars with the bureaucracy! Wars with stupid public administrations! Wars with unimaginative ministers! Ministers who demand baksheesh. Crooks! Building contractors!" Jihan Sadat, the President's wife, admires his work, he says. She asked the Minister of Housing to employ him. The minister said he could not—Fathy insults the bureaucrats. "Well, they ought to be shot, not insulted!" cries Fathy.

His method is the only one feasible in the Third World, he says. Moreover, it creates environments that are human, not innate breeding grounds for crime and alienation. Millions and millions must be housed. New Gourna, built with mud brick, is a suitable prototype for similar construction all over the world. It is no wonder, he says, that the great building contractors don't see it his way. They prefer conventional forms of construction, in steel and reinforced concrete, to Fathy's bricks of unbaked mud and pressed sand that cost only one-tenth as much. Fathy enables the individual to participate in the building of his environment, as peasants have always done in the past in the lovely Mediterranean villages and towns. But the big building contractors are not interested in loveliness or in saving costs, says Fathy. On the contrary, "they work on a percentage."

ON THE FINAL AFTERNOON in Cairo I go over the notes I have been making during my stay. I discard what seemed impressive in the first flush but now seems trivial. I divide the pages into neat little piles and label them. They illustrate the disorderly state of mind into which one is plunged by an experience such as mine. There is no easy clarity in the confusion of so many different, conflicting thoughts and impressions. It happened so quickly and is still so inconclusive. There are, one hopes, a few started friendships. But they are only beginnings, tentative feelers, hardly more than the casual acquaintance struck up by travelers on a fast-moving train. We are prisoners not only of time but of the suspicions built up in too many years of being stranded at some wayside station.

I pack up the books I bought here. They are not many. I have been trying while I was here to buy books, but found surprisingly few. Either little has been written on Egypt in recent years, or little of what has been written is on sale here. I asked the proprietor of an international bookshop downtown why this was so. He said, "Censorship has only recently been lifted." But foreigners also write books, I said. In the last quarter of the nineteenth century more travel books were written about Egypt than about most countries, with the exception of Palestine.

"Ah," he said. "It was a more leisurely age. People had more time." There are of course Jean and Simonne Lacouture's thoughtful *Egypt in Transition* (1958), Nadav Safran's *Egypt in Search of Political Community* (1961), Harry Hopkins' excellent *Egypt the Crucible* (*The Unfinished Revolution*) (1969). They are not available here. Moreover, all three deal with the background and peak period of the Nasser regime. The West lost patience, or interest, in Egypt after the demise of Nasser, whom many had thought of as a new Atatürk. Sadat's Egypt, so far, has inspired surprisingly few books. In Hebrew, of course, there are Professor Shamir's excellent *Egypt Under Sadat* and Shmuel Segev's *Sadat*. Besides those, very little. There is a long series of mimeographed studies on this or that detailed aspect, prepared by official Israeli research bodies, that read like the records of groping blind men, or of eavesdroppers listening through a thick wall: brute data mostly, and shorn of what is probably the most important thing—a quality of experience. Their main weakness, like that of the Kremlinologists, is their alienation from their subject.

Later, Tahsin Bashir comes to say good-bye. We sit by the large window in my room and once again talk about the future. Bashir hopes that one stage of normalization will lead into and be followed by another, reinforcing it. The process will not be easy, he says, and probably quite drawn out. Let's not forget how long it took the Germans and the French after the Second World War—almost a generation! Prejudice remains. In Israel, insensitivity to the plight of the Palestinians; in Egypt, the rancor at what still seems a foreign intrusion, a new Crusader state, the prevailing myth of the "too clever" and therefore "dangerous" Jew. I ask Tahsin why his friend Louis Awad—certainly no bigot—is so reluctant to visit Israel, even though he welcomes the peace.

"He is an Arabic-speaking Egyptian," says Tahsin. "He is in favor of Arabic culture, but against Arab nationalism, and for this reason he also dislikes Jewish nationalism!"

Tahsin looks tired and a bit harassed. He is, of course, in an especially difficult position as the Egyptian ambassador to the Arab League. But I am pleased to see that despite the strains he appears quite cheerful. He jokes. Give me an inch of luck instead of a mile of industry, says an Egyptian proverb. He does not treat the difficulties lightly. His stoicism is both a strength and a weakness, a very Egyptian way of defeating adversity by ignoring it. Aren't you worried, I finally ask.

Tahsin gets up from his chair and looks out on the river below. It is gray, with streaks of green and pink. "No," he says slowly from the window. "You see, my dear Amos, when the chips are down, there is only one *real* place in this entire area. Egypt. All the rest—forgive me—are tribes with flags."

The idea that Egypt can be isolated seems absurd to this brilliant man. It cannot be. It recalls the proverbial headline many years ago in one of the London newspapers: "Fog in Channel, Europe Isolated."

I was supposed to have dinner with Nawal Hassan. We arranged to call one another at seven. I dial her number, but her telephone is out of order again. I hail a taxi and drive to the house. But she has already left for the hotel. Since the telephones do not work I cannot immediately call another taxi. The resourceful Mrs. Hassan will not be so easily defeated. She commandeers a neighbor—an English banker—to drive me back to the hotel. When I arrive I learn that Nawal has come and has left, assuming a misunderstanding. There is a sweet farewell note, however. Much of the pleasure of Egypt is marred or made by such incidents. The architect Ismail's telephone, fortunately, is in order. He comes over after a short while. In a nearby restaurant we spoon up our *ful* (fava beans)—*ful* in butter, *ful* in egg, *ful* with onion, *ful* with sesame, *ful* with *basturma,* or mashed with cream. *Ful* is one of the glories of Egyptian peasant cuisine, but should best be eaten in the morning, on a strong stomach. We drink a little too much wine.

After midnight Ismail confronts me with the inevitable question. "So you are leaving tomorrow," he says. "Tell me the truth. Did you like Egypt?" I nod, the alcohol rises in my head. "Not really Egypt," I say, unconsciously borrowing on the professor in Cesare Pavese's *La Casa in Collina.* "The Egyptians!"

It is before dawn. I was told to be at the airport at six in the morning. The airport is an hour away by car. I gather my things and ride down in the elevator. I am leaving Egypt as I came, with a terrific headache. Between the ninth and the eighth floors the elevator breaks down. It is pitch dark. I cannot see the button to sound the alarm. If I miss my flight, I reflect, not without some pleasure, I might have to wait, perhaps a week. Flights out of Egypt are overbooked at this season. No human voice is heard through the tightly shut doors. There is another tourist in the elevator. He becomes a bit frantic and pounds on the door with balled fists. Nothing. This exodus from Egypt is a far cry from that other, when seas parted and various other laws of nature were suspended for the benefit of the departing Hebrews. A few minutes later we hear a faint noise, like a file grating on a piece of iron. A dim bulb lights up. Then the elevator begins moving again, by gravity, and very slowly. The emergency generator has started to work. The other tourist has an even earlier plane to catch. He perspires and curses profusely. The concierge is as affable as usual. The other tourist is crying, Taxi, taxi!

On the way out he stumbles on the steps. I get into a brief panic, for I don't seem to be able to find my passport. We are travelers in a foreign country. The very word *travel,* I remember reading some-where, comes from *travail.* This in turn is derived from the Latin *tripalium,* a torture instrument consisting of three hooks that rack the body and tear it apart. The worse the trip, one hopes, the better the reading, which is why Graham Greene's novels are so fascinating.

The ride to the airport takes barely fifteen minutes instead of the prescribed hour. The taxi races out by a tricky route through narrow streets and alleys in the center of town. The driver says it can be used only at this early hour. He points at an open lot filled with parked trucks. This is where the famous Cairo Opera House stood before it burned down. It was made entirely of gingerbread wood and plaster, but said by Coquelin to yield the best acoustics in the entire world. For its opening in 1869, Verdi had been commissioned by the Khedive to write the opera *Aida.* The maestro's work, how-ever, was delayed, Italy being a country as human as Egypt; no damaging inconveniences that I know of are reported, and the pre-miere of *Aida* duly took place with two years' delay. The famous march inspired the tune of Egypt's first national anthem. The driver says, "You did not have an opera house in Israel in 1869?" No. An-other comparison. Is this détente?

The airport is crowded with migrant workers flying to Arabia or the Gulf States in search of work. As I enter the departure lounge I already feel as though I have left Egypt. Airports are non-places. Even the Nile Hilton seemed "real" in comparison to this vapid con-veyor belt that moves people and suitcases from one non-place to the next. The policeman at the counter goes through my passport slowly, with genuine curiosity, it seems, and with a certain bemused incredulity. Based on what I expected, I go away more optimistic than I came; and I fly home, via Athens, to try and sort it all out.

XI

IN THE FLUSH OF DEPARTURE I had hardly imagined how difficult this would be. *"On the one hand,"* and *"On the other"*—the many-handed monster sees you home from such a trip as this. It sits next to you on the plane, grabbing and nagging with questions and concerns. You try to push it aside, but it will not let go. Finally, impatient with the endless balancing of a hundred "on the one hands" with a hundred "on the others," I kick myself and say, Don't fight the problem. Decide it! How easy to say but how difficult to carry out! How does one "sort out" a situation still so raw, so encumbered on both sides by arguments that go around in circles and still look in vain for a moral? The hopes and fears on both sides are real as well as cynically manipulated by state power and propaganda. To be sure, this new peace treaty seems logical. It serves the interests of both parties and of the superpower that is protecting them. But the Arab-Israeli conflict has never been some abstract dichotomy, equitable as in mathematics, but a clash between humans who in their fear and fury irrevocably resorted to tragic choices. The mixture of error and violence does not lend itself to neat conclusions. At the root was a disastrous struggle between two rights, two notions of justice, the very essence of high tragedy—the right of the Jews to a homeland of their own, and the right of the Arabs who also inhabited that land. Egypt had always claimed it was defending the rights of those Arabs. It still makes that claim, although, for the time being, renouncing the use of force. The Palestinians—at least, many of those who speak on their behalf—are not yet ready for such compromise.

For all its pomp and drama, the great breakthrough I have tried to describe in these pages is still overshadowed by too many contradictory truths and smooth diplomatic vagaries and circumlocutions. It is not that I have been listening to lies, I tell myself as I fly home over the eastern Mediterranean, but rather, perhaps, half-truths. It is always more difficult to unravel a half-truth than to spot a falsehood. Only fools tell complete lies. I don't think I met any downright fools during my stay in Egypt.

Then I am back in Israel, in the helter-skelter of Tel Aviv, with its maddening sameness and rectangularity, and its squat four-story houses, salubrious and uninspiring. Tel Aviv is not "Americanized," as is often said; it is not another Miami but a mixture of Warsaw and Baghdad thrown haphazardly together and planted along the Mediterranean shore, a Middle Eastern Lithuania-by-the-sea. It is a city of little dignity, even less style; a hothouse of passion and argument and people overly effusive, boastful, exhortative, expostulative, and didactic. An Englishman I know once took Tel Aviv as a tribute to the Jacobin strain in Zionism. The prevailing tendency to prophesy darkly has become almost second nature here through the melancholy haphazardness and frightening arbitrariness of life in the past three or four decades.

Being back here does not make it any easier to "sort out" the problems. On the contrary, as I look at them from Tel Aviv, in the company of dubious and excitable friends and colleagues, rather than from Cairo where most people seem calm and assured, I suddenly feel as though I have moved a painting from one room to another, viewing it in a strangely different light. One of the first things I see in the newspapers after I land in Tel Aviv is a statement by the trainer of the national football team.

"From now on," he has just told an audience, "let's have less Zionism here and more football." For this sentiment he is severely taken to task by an editorial writer. I also see an announcement of a forthcoming academic conference in Jerusalem on the theme "What if the peace treaty with Egypt fails . . ." The ink has hardly dried on the signatures and already they are expostulating upon the military and economic ramifications of failure! Why wonder about such nervousness? If the peace treaty failed, it would be unfortunate for Egypt, perhaps very unfortunate, but for Israel it would be downright disastrous.

Most of my friends in Tel Aviv seem imbued with a mixture of incredulity and tired hope. Some tell me outright that they think I have been brainwashed in Cairo. Many others very much want to believe that it really is all over, but are too embittered by past experience to put any trust in what they hear.

I tell them what I heard and saw in Egypt. But they want *certainty,* not information. There is no certainty. To seek it is all too human. In this society of refugees and children of refugees, the bloody conflict with the Arabs has been the central experience of the past thirty years. It cannot easily be shaken off. My sister Haya is a case in point. She has always regarded me as a bit wild and extravagant, a younger brother. She welcomes me with a dubious eye.

"Do they really want peace?" she asks, skeptically.

I think they do, I say. Most Egyptians I talked to certainly want peace, I am sure of that.

Haya says sharply: "Naturally you didn't talk to all of them."

Of course not. But most of those I met want it very much. I am sure of that. And Sadat wants it.

"What if Sadat dies?"

There are others, I say. When Sadat made peace, he was following the Egyptian people, not leading them.

"Are you sure?"

I think so, yes. It's not that they love us all of a sudden. But they are fed up. They are tired. Their economic situation is difficult.

"You mean they can't make ends meet?"

It's worse than that, I say, warming up. The economic and social problems of Egypt are almost beyond control. Permanent crisis!

"You see!" she cries. "How can we trust them? So I ask you. Are we doing the right thing? How can we give them back all that territory and oil? Isn't it too great a risk?"

Yes, I say, a great risk. But isn't it worthwhile to take it? Every other alternative implies even greater risks. My sister does not agree. A typical family discussion ensues, which drags on tediously and leads nowhere. And I do not press my point too firmly. I still have my own doubts. And she has two sons in the Army. In Israel there is always a feeling that children are given us on loan.

In Tel Aviv it is hot and humid. In Jerusalem, where I live, the mountain air is fresh and clean, but the light, as so often in June, is dazzling, with a steady brilliant glare that is almost too harsh to bear. Palestinian terrorists have just put a bomb into an ashcan off the main city square and another under a seat on a bus, wounding three men and two small children. Begin has announced again that Israel will "never, never" permit the establishment of a Palestinian state on the West Bank and in Gaza. As though to ensure his words, activists of the Greater Israel movement are demonstrating on the green hillside across from the Prime Minister's office, calling for immediate annexation and massive settlement of the occupied West Bank even at the cost of abrogating the peace treaty. The surrounding mountaintops, luminous and bare, are ablaze in the glare. I don't know another city where the light is so strong, or so cruel, with such contrasts between brights and shades. "The people that walked in darkness have seen a great light," it says in Isaiah, but I think of Balzac's cry. "Too much light! Call the doctor, quick!" There is a surfeit of light here, and in its glare the nuances are blurred.

Ariel Sharon, Begin's Minister of Agriculture, is quoted in the newspaper as saying that nothing, nothing will stop Israel from building new settlements on requisitioned territory on the occupied West Bank. When Sharon was still a young bravado in the Israeli Army, the late Prime Minister Sharett wrote about him in his diary: "Which of the two souls that battle between the pages of the Bible will gain the upper hand here, the dark and barbaric, or the noble?"

In Jerusalem I finally meet Dr. Sasson Somekh, the Israeli scholar so dear to the Egyptian novelists I encountered. I had heard so much about him in Cairo that I was curious to meet him. According to Mahfouz and Idris, he is the only literary critic who truly understands their work. Sasson is a slim man in his early forties. His eyes, under a high forehead, are dark and unusually intense. He is consumed by two great passions: love of Egyptian literature, and the search for bridges between the two cultures. We talk about Mahfouz and Idris, whom he has never met but has followed from afar with many a paper and review. He questions me intensively. How are they? What are they working on at this moment? He recently received an extremely warm letter from Mahfouz and shows it to me.

> Let us pray together that the efforts being made at this very time will be crowned with success, [writes the novelist, who spoke about peace with Israel well before Sadat] and that our two peoples will live together in mutual benefit as we did in the past. Because it is true that our peoples enjoyed long years of fruitful cooperation in ancient, in medieval, and in modern times, whereas periods of conflict were short and few. Unfortunately we have recorded our moments of conflict a hundred times more than we have documented long generations of friendship and cooperation. I dream of the time that this part of the world will become—as a result of mutual cooperation—a bright temple of science, blessed by divine principles. See you soon, dear Professor. Wishing you and our countries all the best.
>
> Sincerely,
> Naguib Mahfouz.

Sasson lends me his book on Mahfouz, *The Changing Rhythm,** which I now read for the first time. I chastise myself for not having done so before. Somekh's careful analysis of Mahfouz's complicated plots and colorful characters is full of suggestive insights into the spirit of place which I was eager to explore. His great appreciation of Mahfouz's art shines through every page.

"Mahfouz has given modern Arabic literature its first fully-

---

* Sasson Somekh, *The Changing Rhythm* (Leiden: E. J. Brill, 1975).

fledged novelist," he writes in the concluding chapter. "In him Egypt contributes a fresh new voice to world literature." Somekh is not the only Israeli scholar who has translated and written extensively about modern Egyptian literature. I suddenly understood why Mahfouz and Idris thought so highly of him. Almost alone, it seems, among other Israeli students of their work, Somekh consistently pays Mahfouz and Idris the supreme compliment of treating them first and foremost as artists, as fascinating humans rather than as convenient mediums to explore the innermost soul of an enemy. This by itself makes his exertions as generous a contribution to reconciliation as were those of Mahfouz.

It is always easier to make peace between those who would know what to do with it.

INDEX